Comparative Politics Today

A Theoretical Framework

Comparative Politics Today

A Theoretical Framework

Sixth Edition

G. BINGHAM POWELL, JR.

University of Rochester

RUSSEL J. DALTON

University of California, Irvine

KAARE STRØM

University of California, San Diego

Longman

Boston   Columbus   Indianapolis   New York   San Francisco   Upper Saddle River
Amsterdam   Cape Town   Dubai   London   Madrid   Milan   Munich   Paris   Montreal   Toronto
Delhi   Mexico City   São Paulo   Sydney   Hong Kong   Seoul   Singapore   Taipei   Tokyo

Senior Acquisitions Editor: Vikram Mukhija
Assistant Editor: Corey Kahn
Editorial Assistant: Beverly Fong
Senior Marketing Manager: Lindsey Prudhomme
Production Manager: S. Kulig
Project Coordination, Text Design, and Electronic Page Makeup: PreMediaGlobal
Senior Cover Designer/Manager: Nancy Danahy
Cover Image: © Radius Images/Corbis
Photo Researcher: Poyee Oster
Senior Manufacturing Buyer: Dennis J. Para

Library of Congress Cataloging-in-Publication Data

Control number is on record at the Library of Congress.

Library of Congress Control Number: xxxxxxxxxx

Longman
is an imprint of

www.pearsonhighered.com

ISBN-13: 978-0-205-08286-5
ISBN-10:   0-205-08286-6

BRIEF CONTENTS

DETAILED CONTENTS

PREFACE

Comparative Politics Today: A Theoretical Framework, Sixth Edition, presents in the form of a separate book Parts One and Two of Comparative Politics Today: A World View, Tenth Edition (2011). As a text, Comparative Politics Today: A Theoretical Framework is ideally suited for courses that seek to provide a broad and comprehensive thematic overview of comparative politics, which instructors may then combine with their own selection of reading materials from the literature of country and analytic studies.

For the past three decades, Comparative Politics Today: A Theoretical Framework and its "cousins" have been among the most influential textbooks in comparative politics. Our book traces back to the original Almond and Powell, Comparative Politics: A Developmental Approach (Little, Brown 1966), as revised and expanded in Comparative Politics: System, Process and Policy (Little, Brown 1978), by the same authors. The framework these books developed was incorporated into the Comparative Politics Today texts and supplemented with analyses of specific countries by leading specialists. Earlier editions of this book in the 1970s pioneered the teaching of systematic comparison of the political cultures, structures, processes, and policy performances of the world's political systems. Later editions have explored the impact of enormous changes—such as democratization, the breakup of the Soviet empire, globalization, and intensified threats from ethnic and religious conflict—that have shaped politics in many nations. Throughout, these editions reflect Gabriel Almond's creativity and the applicability of his framework to the changing concerns of students of political science.

NEW TO THIS EDITION

This Sixth Edition of Comparative Politics Today: A Theoretical Framework contains a substantially revised set of chapters that include review questions as well as a guide to the key themes in each chapter. The chapters have been revised for greater readability, and we have expanded the number of illustrative example boxes. The new edition also incorporates more thorough discussion of globalization and its components and consequences. In its analysis of public policy, Chapter 7 introduces its concept of "political goods" with reference to the United Nations Millennium Goals and more systematically treats policy goals and consequences, including welfare, fairness, liberty, and security outcomes.

FEATURES

This Sixth Edition, like the previous one, begins by explaining why governments exist, what functions they serve, and how they create political problems as well as solutions. Chapter 1 also introduces the three great challenges facing most states in the world today: building a common identity and sense of community; fostering economic and social development; and securing democracy, human rights, and civil liberties. Chapter 2 sketches the concepts needed to compare politics in very different societies: political systems and their environments, structures and functions, policy performance and its consequences. Jointly, these two chapters constitute Part One, which spells out the unique framework that our book employs.

Part Two elaborates on important components of the system, process, and policy framework, discussing the causes and consequences of political cultures, interest groups, parties and other aggregation structures, constitutions, key structures of policymaking. The continuing and unprecedented spread of democracy in recent decades is not only a development to be celebrated, but also a reason that the issues of democratic representation, as discussed in Chapters 4 through 6, are becoming increasingly relevant to an ever larger share of the world's population. Growing prosperity in many parts of the world means that the challenges of development and public policy (Chapters 1 and 7) are changing. While the global incidence and human costs of war have declined in recent years, conflicts still devastate or threaten communities in areas such as Afghanistan, the Middle East, South Asia, Sudan, and other parts of Africa. Moreover, the world faces enormous challenges, new as well as old, in such areas as climate change, migration, globalization, epidemic disease, international terrorism, and nuclear proliferation. All of these developments make it more important than ever to understand how political decisions are made, and what their consequences might be, in the very different political systems that make up our political world.

The tables, figures, and boxes in *Comparative Politics Today: A Theoretical Framework* provide examples, compare systems, and discuss important trends, such as globalization, democratization and backsliding, the rise of fundamentalism, the challenges to the rule of law, and the recruitment of women into leadership roles in politics. These comparative tables, figures, and examples draw systematically from the same set of countries: Britain, France, Germany, Japan, Russia, China, Mexico, Brazil, Iran, India, Nigeria, and the United States. Our book can therefore be conveniently supplemented with case studies on any or all of these twelve countries. The tenth edition of *Comparative Politics Today: A World View* contains a separate chapter on each of these countries.

SUPPLEMENTS

Longman is pleased to offer several resources to qualified adopters of *Comparative Politics Today* and their students that will make teaching and learning from this book even more effective and enjoyable.

PASSPORT FOR COMPARATIVE POLITICS   With Passport, choose the resources you want from MyPoliSciKit and put links to them into your course management system. If there is assessment associated with those resources, it also can be uploaded, allowing the results to feed directly into your course management system's gradebook. With over 150 MyPoliSciKit assets like video case studies, mapping exercises, comparative exercises, simulations, podcasts, *Financial Times* newsfeeds, current events quizzes, politics blog, and much more, Passport is available for any Pearson introductory or upper-level political science book. Use ISBN 0-205-09515-1 to order Passport with this book. To learn more, please contact your Pearson representative.

MYSEARCHLAB   Need help with a paper? MySearchLab saves time and improves results by offering start-to-finish guidance on the research/writing process and full-text access to academic journals and periodicals. Use ISBN 0-205-11217-X to order MySearchLab with this book. To learn more, please visit www.mysearchlab.com or contact your Pearson representative.

THE ECONOMIST   Every week, *The Economist* analyzes the important happenings around the globe. From business to politics, to the arts and science, its coverage connects seemingly unrelated events in unexpected ways. Use ISBN 0-205-11004-5 to order a 15-week subscription with this book for a small additional charge. To learn more, please contact your Pearson representative.

THE FINANCIAL TIMES   Featuring international news and analysis from journalists in more than 50 countries, *The Financial Times* provides insights and perspectives on political and economic a developments around the world. Use ISBN 0-205-11042-8 to order a 15-week subscription with this book for a small additional charge. To learn more, please contact your Pearson representative.

LONGMAN ATLAS OF WORLD ISSUES (0-205-78020-2)   From population and political systems to energy use and women's rights, the *Longman Atlas of World Issues* features full-color thematic maps that examine the forces shaping the world. Featuring maps from the latest edition of *The Penguin State of the World Atlas*, this excerpt includes critical thinking exercises to promote a deeper understanding of how geography affects many global issues. Available at no additional charge when packaged with this book.

GOODE'S WORLD ATLAS (0-321-65200-2)   First published by Rand McNally in 1923, *Goode's World Atlas* has set the standard for college reference atlases. It features hundreds of physical, political, and thematic maps as well as graphs, tables, and a pronouncing index. Available at a discount when packaged with this book.

ACKNOWLEDGMENTS

The Acknowledgments in the tenth edition of *Comparative Politics Today: A World View* express our debts and appreciation to those who helped us prepare that edition, which is the basis of this volume also. We reiterate our gratitude to the authors of the twelve country studies in that volume—Richard Rose (Britain); Martin A. Schain (France); Russell J. Dalton (Germany);

Frances Rosenbluth and Michael F. Thies (Japan); Thomas F. Remington (Russia); Melanie Manion (China); Wayne A. Cornelius and Jeffery A. Weldon (Mexico); Frances Hagopian and Timothy J. Power (Brazil); Subrata K. Mitra (India); A. Carl Levan, Robert J. Mundt, and Oladimeji Aborisade (Nigeria); Houchang E. Chehabi and Arang Keshavarzian (Iran); and Thad Kousser and Austin Ranney (United States)—who added once more, as they and their predecessors have many times over the years, essential contents and interpretative insights to our basic theoretical framework. We are also grateful to Frances A. Rubio for research assistance and to Michael McKeen for assistance in developing the index for this edition. Finally, we wish to thank the reviewers of both volumes—Jennifer Horan, University of North Carolina-Wilmington; David Myers, Penn State University; Sanghamitra Padhy, Davidson College; Ani Sarkissian, Michigan State University—and the team at Longman and PreMediaGlobal.

Gabriel Almond, from whose innovative work this book derives, had enormous influence on the study and teaching of comparative politics. He wrote at length about many important political topics, including political culture, interest groups, fundamentalism, and the history of political science. One of his greatest achievements was his continuing commitment to finding ways to understand, compare, and explain the most diverse aspects of political life. This text is deeply shaped by that commitment, both through Gabriel Almond's own involvement in writing it and through his influence upon each of us. And one of his greatest legacies is the generations of students who have learned about comparative politics and our world through the insights he provided.

G. BINGHAM POWELL, JR.
RUSSELL J. DALTON
KAARE STRØM

Issues in Comparative Politics

WHAT IS POLITICS?

Some people love politics. They relish the excitement of political events, such as a presidential election, as they would an exciting athletic contest (the World Series of baseball or the World Cup of soccer, perhaps). Others are fascinated with politics because they care about the issues and their consequences for people in their own communities and around the world. Still others hate politics, either because it sets groups and individuals against each other, or because it involves abuse of power, deceit, manipulation, and violence. Finally, some people are indifferent to politics because it has little to do with the things that matter most to them, such as family, friends, faith, hobbies, or favorite activities. All of these reactions involve kernels of truth about politics. Indeed, most of us react to politics with a mixture of these sentiments. Politics has many faces and can be a force for good as well as evil. The core of politics, however, is about human beings making important decisions for their communities and for others.

This book is about the comparative study of politics. In order to make political comparisons, we need to understand what politics is and what it means to study politics comparatively. Comparative politics thus is both a subject of study—comparing the nature of politics and the political process across different political systems, and a method of study—involving how and why we make such comparisons. We address the first point in this chapter; Chapter 2 discusses the second.

Politics deals with human decisions, and political science is the study of such decisions. Yet not all decisions are political, and many of the social sciences study decisions that are of little interest to political scientists. For example, consider when you go with a friend to an event, such as a concert or a soccer match. You can spend your money on the tickets (to get the best seats possible) or on food and drink, or you can save your money for the future. Economists study the spending decisions people make and perhaps how they reach them. Psychologists, on the other hand, might study why you went to the event with this friend and not another, or who suggested going in the first place.

Political scientists seldom examine such private and personal decisions, unless they have political consequences. Instead, political decisions are those that are *public* and *authoritative*. Political decisions take place within some society or community that we call a *political system*, which we describe below. Yet not all social decisions are public. Most of what happens within families, among friends, or in social groups belongs to the *private sphere*. Actions within this sphere do not bind anyone outside that group and are not controlled by the government. In most societies, your choices of concert partners and food are private decisions.

The *public sphere* of politics deals with collective decisions that extend beyond the individual and private life, typically involving government action. Yet political decisions constantly touch our lives. Our jobs are structured by government regulations, our homes are built to conform to government housing codes, public schools are funded and managed by the government, and we travel on roads maintained by the government and monitored by the police. Politics thus affects us in many important ways. Therefore, it is important to study how political decisions are made and what their consequences are.

In totalitarian societies, like Hitler's Third Reich and some communist states, the public sphere is very large and the private sphere is very limited. The state tries to dominate the life of its people, even intruding into family life. On the other hand, in some less developed nations, the private domain may almost crowd out the public one. Many people in various African nations, for instance, may be unaware of what happens in the capital city and untouched by the decisions made there. Western democracies have a more balanced mix of private and public spheres. However, the boundaries between the two spheres are redrawn all the time. A few decades ago, the sex lives of U.S. presidents or members of the British royal family were considered private matters, not to be discussed in public. These norms have changed in Britain and the United States, but the traditional standards remain in other countries. Similarly, in Britain, certain religious beliefs were considered treasonous in the 1500s and 1600s. Today, religious beliefs are considered private matters in most modern democracies, though not in many other parts of the world. Even though politics may be influenced by what happens in the private domain, it deals directly with only those decisions that are public.

Politics is also *authoritative*. Authority means that formal power rests in individuals or groups whose decisions are expected to be carried out and respected. Thus, political decisions are binding for members of that political system. Governments and other authorities may use persuasion, inducements, or brute force to ensure compliance. For instance, a religious authority, such as the Pope, has few coercive powers. He can persuade, but rarely compel, the Catholic Church's followers. In contrast, tax authorities, such as the U.S. Internal Revenue Service, can both exhort and compel people to follow their rules.

Thus, *politics* refers to activities associated with the control of public decisions among a given people and in a given territory, where this control may be backed up by authoritative means. Politics involves the crafting of these authoritative decisions—who gets to make them and for what purposes.

We live in one of the most exciting times to study politics. The end of the Cold War created a new international order, although its shape is still uncertain. Democratic transitions in Latin America, Eastern Europe, East Asia, and parts of Africa have transformed the world, although it is unclear how many of these new democracies will endure and what forms they might take. Throughout the world, globalization has brought the citizens of different countries closer together and made them more dependent on one another, for better or worse. Some of the issues people in many societies confront—such as confronting climate change and achieving international peace—are transnational and indeed global. Part of their solutions, we hope, lies in the political choices that people in different communities make about their collective future. Our goal in this book is to give you a sense of how governments and politics can either address or exacerbate these challenges.

GOVERNMENTS AND THE STATE OF NATURE

Governments are organizations of individuals who have the power to make binding decisions on behalf of a particular community. Governments thus have authoritative and coercive powers and do many things. They can wage war or encourage peace; encourage or restrict international trade; open or close their borders to the exchange of ideas; tax their populations heavily or lightly and through different means; and allocate resources for education, health, and welfare or leave such matters to others. People who are affected by such decisions may welcome them or disapprove, and there is often heated disagreement about the proper role of government.

Debates over the nature and appropriate role of government are far from new. They reflect a classic polemic in political philosophy. For centuries, philosophers have debated whether governments are a force for good or evil. In the seventeenth and eighteenth centuries—the time of the English, French, and American revolutions—much of this debate was couched in arguments concerning the **state of nature**.

Political philosophers thought about the state of nature as the condition of humankind if no government existed. In some cases, they thought that such a situation had existed before the first governments were formed. These philosophers used their ideas about the state of nature to identify an ideal social contract (agreement) on which to build a political system. Even today, many philosophers and political thinkers find it useful to make such a mental experiment to consider the consequences of having governments.

These debates have shaped our images of government, even to the present. The contrast between Thomas Hobbes's and Jean-Jacques Rousseau's ideas about the state of nature is most striking. Hobbes was the ultimate pessimist. He thought of the state of nature as mercilessly inhospitable, a situation of eternal conflict of all against all, and a source of barbarism and continuous fear. He pessimistically argued that "[i]n such condition, there is no place for Industry; because the fruit thereof is uncertain: and consequently no Culture of the Earth; no Navigation, nor use of the commodities that may be imported by Sea; no commodious Building, . . . no Arts; no Letters; no Society; and which is worst of all, continuall feare, and danger of violent death; And the life of man, solitary, poor, nasty, brutish, and short."[1]

Rousseau, in contrast, was more optimistic about the state of nature. For him, it represented humanity before its fall from grace, without all the corruptions that governments have introduced. "Man is born free," Rousseau observed in *The Social Contract*, "and yet everywhere he is in chains." Rousseau saw governments as the source of power and inequality, and these conditions in turn as the causes of human alienation and corruption. "The extreme inequality in our way of life," he argued, "excess of idleness in some, excess of labor in others; . . . late nights, excesses of all kinds, immoderate ecstasies of all the passions; fatigues and exhaustion of mind, numberless sorrows and afflictions . . . that most of our ills are our own work; that we would have avoided almost all of them by preserving the simple, uniform, and solitary way of life prescribed to us by nature."[2]

John Locke's ideas have been particularly important for the development of Western democracies. He took a position between those of Hobbes and Rousseau. Compared with Hobbes, Locke thought of human beings as more businesslike and less war-prone. Yet like Hobbes he proposed a social contract to replace the state of nature with a system of government. While Hobbes thought the main task for government is to quell disorder and protect against violence and war, Locke saw the state's main role as protecting property and commerce and promoting economic growth. He believed government would do this by establishing and enforcing property rights and rules of economic exchange. Whereas Hobbes thought government needed to be a Leviathan—a benevolent dictator to whom the citizens would yield all their power—Locke favored a limited government.

Although these debates began centuries ago, they still underlie current discussions on the appropriate role of government. To some, government is the solution to many human needs and problems—a theme that former U.S. president Bill Clinton often advocated. To others, the government is often part of the problem—a theme that former U.S. president Ronald Reagan articulately argued. To some, government exists to create the social order that protects its citizens; to others, government limits our freedoms. This tension is part of the political discourse in many contemporary nations, including the United States. We explore these contrasting views and different examples of government structures in this book.

WHY GOVERNMENTS?

A recent libertarian science-fiction book begins with the scenario of a group of travelers landing at an airport after a long overseas flight. As they disembark from the plane, they notice that there are no police checking passports, no

BOX 1.1   U.S. GOVERNMENT'S TOP TEN LIST

Paul Light surveyed 450 historians and political scientists to assess the U.S. government's greatest achievements in the past half century. Their top ten list is as follows:

- Help rebuild Europe after World War II
- Expand the right to vote for minorities
- Promote equal access to public accommodations
- Reduce disease
- Reduce workplace discrimination
- Ensure safe food and drinking water
- Strengthen the nation's highway system
- Increase older Americans' access to health care
- Reduce the federal deficit
- Promote financial security in retirement

Several of these policy areas will be discussed in Chapter 7, but note that the first of these accomplishments had to do with the country's external environment: rebuilding Europe after World War II. Other achievements include important public goods (safe water, highways), as well as promoting fairness and building a social safety net.

Source: Paul Light, *Government's Greatest Achievements of the Past Half-Century* (Washington, D.C.: Brookings Institution, 2000) (www.brookings.edu/comm/reformwatch/rw02.pdf).

customs officers scanning baggage, and no officials applying immigration rules.[3] They had landed in a society without government, and the puzzle was what having no government would mean for the citizenry. The answer is a great deal (see Box 1.1). As philosophers have pointed out, there are many reasons why people create governments and prefer to live under such a social order. We shall discuss some of these, beginning with activities that help generate a stable community in the first place and then those that help this community prosper.

Community- and Nation-Building

One of the first purposes of governments is to create and maintain a community in which people can feel safe and comfortable. While humans may be social beings, it is not always easy to build a community in which large numbers of people can communicate, feel at home, and interact constructively. Governments can help generate such communities in many different ways— for example, by teaching a common language, instilling common norms and values, creating common myths and symbols, and supporting a national identity. However, sometimes such actions create controversy because there is disagreement about these norms and values.

Nation-building activities help instill common world views, values, and expectations. Using a concept discussed more in Chapter 3, governments can help create a national **political culture**. The political culture defines the public's expectations toward the political process and its role within the process. The more the political culture is shared, the easier it is to live in peaceful coexistence and engage in activities for mutual gain, such as commerce.

Security and Order

Hobbes believed that only strong governments can make society safe for their inhabitants, and providing security and law and order is among the most essential tasks that governments perform. Externally, security means protecting against attacks from other political systems. Armies, navies, and air forces typically perform this function. Internally, security means protecting against theft, aggression, and violence from members of one's own society. In most societies, providing this is the function of the police.

Providing security and order is a critical role of modern governments. While governments worldwide have privatized many of the services they once performed—for example, those involving post offices, railroads, and telecommunications—few if any governments have privatized their police or defense forces. This shows that security is one of the most essential roles of government. The international terrorist attacks in New York City and Washington, D.C., on September 11, 2001, and subsequent attacks and attempted violence in London, Madrid, and elsewhere underscore the importance of security.

Protecting Rights

John Locke considered property rights to be particularly critical to the development of prosperous communities. Without effective protection of property rights, people will not invest their goods or energies in productive processes. Also, unless property rights exist and contracts can be negotiated and enforced, people will not trust their neighbors enough to trade and invest. Anything beyond a subsistence economy requires effective property rights and contracts. Therefore, Locke believed that the primary role of government is to establish and protect such rights. Similarly, contemporary authors argue that social order is a prerequisite for development and democratization.[4]

Effective property rights establish ownership and provide security against trespass and violations. Such rights must also make the buying and selling of property relatively inexpensive and painless. Finally, people must have faith that their property rights can be defended. Thus, many analysts argue that one of the most restrictive limitations on development in the Third World is the government's inability (or unwillingness) to guarantee such rights. Peasant families in many societies have lived for generations on a plot of land but cannot claim ownership, which erodes their incentive and opportunity to invest in the future.

Although Locke was most concerned with economic property rights, governments also protect many other social and political rights. Among them are freedoms of speech and association, and protection against various forms of discrimination and harassment. Indeed, the protection of these rights and liberties is one of the prime goals of government—with other factors such as nation-building, security, and property rights providing a means toward this goal. Governments also play a key role in protecting the rights of religious, racial, and other social groups. Human development stresses the expansion of these rights and liberties, and governments play a key role in this process.

Promoting Economic Efficiency and Growth

Economists have long debated the government's potential role in promoting economic development. Neoclassical economics shows that markets are efficient when property rights are defined and protected, when competition is rigorous, and when information is freely available. When these conditions do not hold, however, markets may fail and the economy may suffer.[5] At least in some circumstances, governments can ameliorate the results of market failure.

Governments may be especially important in providing **public goods**, such as clean air, a national defense, or disease prevention. Public goods have two things in common. One is that if one person enjoys them, they cannot be withheld from anyone else in that community. The second is that one person's enjoyment or consumption of the goods does not detract from anyone else's. Consider clean air. For most practical purposes, it is impossible to provide one person with clean air without also giving it to his or her neighbors. Moreover, my enjoyment of clean air does not mean that my neighbors have any less of it. Economists argue that people in a market economy therefore will not pay enough for public goods because they can "free-ride" on the goods that others provide. At the very least, people will not pay for public goods until they know that others will also contribute. Analysts therefore often claim that only government can provide the right quantity of such public goods.

Governments can also benefit society by controlling the **externalities** that occur when an activity incurs costs that are not borne by the producer or the user. For instance, many forms of environmental degradation occur when those who produce or consume goods do not pay all of the environmental costs. Polluting factories, waste dumps, prisons, and major highways can impose large costs on those who live near them. NIMBY ("not in my backyard") groups arise when citizens complain about these costs. Governments can help protect people from unfair externalities or ensure that burdens are fairly shared.

Governments can also promote fair competition in economic markets. For example, governments can ensure that all businesses follow minimum standards of worker protection and product liability. In other cases, the government may control potentially monopolistic enterprises to ensure that they do not abuse their market power. This happened in the nineteenth century with railroad monopolies, and more currently with technology monopolies, such as Microsoft, or telecommunications companies. In these cases, the government acts as the policeman to prevent the economically powerful from exploiting their power. Sometimes, the government itself may become the monopolist. In some markets, very large start-up or coordination costs mean that there should be only one producer. If that producer may also easily abuse its power, the government may set itself up as that monopolist, or impose tight controls. Telecommunications have commonly been a government monopoly in many societies, as have mail services and strategic defense industries.

Social Justice

Governments can also play a role in dividing the fruits of economic growth in equitable ways. Many people argue that governments are needed to promote social justice by redistributing wealth and other resources among citizens. In many countries, the distribution of income and property is highly uneven, and this is particularly troubling when there is little upward mobility or when inequalities tend to grow over time. Brazil, for example, has one of the most severe income inequalities in the world, an inequality that grew in every decade from the 1930s to the 1990s but has recently receded a little.

Under such circumstances, social justice may require a "new deal," especially if inequalities deprive many individuals of education, adequate health care, or other basic needs. Government can intervene to redistribute resources from the better-off to the poor. Many private individuals, religious and charitable organizations, and foundations also do much to help the poor, but they generally do not have the capacity to tax the wealthy. Governments do, at least under some circumstances. Many tax and welfare policies redistribute income, although the degree of redistribution is often hotly disputed (see Chapter 7).

Some theorists argue that such transfers should attempt to equalize the conditions of all citizens. Others prefer governments to redistribute enough to equalize opportunities, and then let individuals be responsible for their own fortunes. Yet most individuals agree that governments should provide a social safety net and give their citizens opportunities to reach certain minimum standards of living.

Protecting the Weak

We commonly rely on the government to protect individuals and groups that are not able to speak for themselves. Groups such as the disabled, the very young, or future generations cannot effectively protect their own interests. Governments, however, can protect the interests of the unborn and prevent them from being saddled with economic debts or environmental degradation. In recent decades, governments have become much more involved in protecting groups that are politically weak or disenfranchised, such as children, the old, and the infirm or disabled, as well as nonhumans—from whales and birds to trees and other parts of our natural environment. Thus, governments in many countries have increasingly intervened to protect children from abuse or exploitation in their families, in schools, or in the workplace.

WHEN DOES GOVERNMENT BECOME THE PROBLEM?

Governments can thus serve many political functions, yet their intervention is not always welcomed or beneficial. When and how government intervention is necessary and desirable are among the most disputed issues in modern politics. During the twentieth century, the role of governments expanded enormously in most nations. At the same time, criticisms of many government policies have persisted and sometimes intensified. Such skepticism is directed at virtually all government activities, especially the economic role of government. **Anarchism** and **libertarianism** are two political and philosophical traditions that are critical of the role of modern governments. But they differ in their main concerns. Libertarians see the greatest problem of government as its encroachment on individual freedoms, whereas anarchists are concerned primarily with the threats that governments pose to social communities.

Destruction of Community

Whereas some see governments as a way to build community, others argue that governments destroy natural communities. Government, they hold, implies power and inequality among human beings. While those who have power are corrupted, those without it are degraded and alienated. According to Rousseau, only human beings unfettered by government can form bonds that allow them to develop their full human potential. By imposing an order based on coercion, hierarchy, and the threat of force, governments destroy natural communities. The stronger government becomes, the greater the inequalities of power. Such arguments stimulated criticism of communism as limiting the potential and freedom of its citizens. Others argue that strong governments create a "client society," in which people learn to be subservient to authorities and to rely on governments to meet their needs. In such societies, governments patronize and pacify their citizens, as seen in many developing nations today.

Violations of Basic Rights

Just as governments can help establish many essential rights, they can also use their powers to violate these rights in the most serious manner. The twentieth century witnessed enormous progress in the extension of political, economic, and social rights in societies worldwide. At the same time, however, some governments violated basic **human rights** on an unprecedented scale. The millions of lives lost to political persecution is the most serious example of this. Such horrors happened not only in Nazi extermination camps and during Stalin's Great Terror in the Soviet Union, but also on a huge scale in China, Cambodia, and Rwanda, and on a somewhat smaller scale in Saddam Hussein's Iraq, as well as in the Sudan and in Afghanistan under the Taliban.

These extreme abuses of government power illustrate a dilemma that troubled James Madison and other Founders of the American Revolution: the challenge of creating a government strong enough to govern effectively but not so strong that it could destroy the rights of its citizens. They understood the irony that to protect individuals from each other, societies can create a government that has even more power to coerce the individual. Libertarians are especially concerned about the abuses and violations of basic freedoms that large governments may thus entail.

Economic Inefficiency

Governments can help economies flourish, but they also can distort and restrict a state's economic potential. President Robert Mugabe, for instance, has destroyed the economy of Zimbabwe, which was once Africa's most prosperous state, and similar examples exist in many struggling economies. Economic problems might arise even if government officials do not actively abuse their power. Government regulation of the economy may distort the terms of trade and lower people's incentives to produce. Further inefficiencies may arise when governments actually own or manage important economic enterprises. This is particularly likely if the government holds a monopoly on an important good, since monopolies generally cause goods to be undersupplied and overpriced. Moreover, government industries may be especially prone to inefficiency and complacency because management and workers often have better job protection than those in the private sector. Therefore, they may worry less about the economic performance of the firm. Such experiences have caused citizens in both developing and advanced industrial economies to worry about the performance of government monopolies and stimulated calls to restrict the economic role of governments.

Government for Private Gain

Society also may suffer if government officials make decisions to benefit themselves personally, or select policies to get themselves reelected regardless of whether those policies would be the best for the society. A politician or political group may use the government to reap benefits unfairly at the public's expense—what is called **rent-seeking**. *Rents* are benefits created through government intervention in the economy—for example, tax revenue or profits created because the government has restricted competition. Rent-seeking refers to efforts by individuals, politicians, groups, firms, or organizations to reap such benefits. The idea is really quite simple. For instance, a local mayor plans an economic development project that will benefit his friends or supporters who own suitable land or who will supply contracts for the project. Rent-seeking can impose large costs on society because policies are chosen for the private benefits they produce rather than for their social efficiency and because groups may expend great resources to control these spoils of government. Rent-seeking may turn into outright corruption when influence is traded for money or other advantage (see Box 1.2).

This kind of political exploitation is a particularly serious problem in poor societies. Holding political office is often an effective way to enrich oneself

BOX 1.2 RENT-SEEKING AND THE CASE OF MOBUTU SESE SEKO

What happens if politicians use their power in their own self-interest or to benefit individuals or groups that support them? President Mobutu Sese Seko (1930–1997) of Zaire offers a tragic example of the costs that rent-seeking politicians can impose on their societies. After seizing power in a 1965 coup, Mobutu ruled the large African state of Congo (which he renamed Zaire) for more than thirty years. During his long rule, President Mobutu used government funds, including aid from Western states such as the United States, to amass a huge personal fortune, which he invested abroad. In addition to large sums of money, he is reported to have owned about thirty luxury residences abroad, including a number of palatial estates on the French Riviera. Meanwhile, living standards in Zaire, a poor country despite significant natural resources, plummeted, and the country was racked with epidemic disease and civil war. Mobutu was finally overthrown and died of natural causes shortly after his ouster.

when political watchdogs such as courts and mass media are too weak to constrain government officials. Besides, many developing societies do not have strong social norms against using government for private gain. On the contrary, people often expect those in government to use their power to benefit themselves, their families, and their neighbors. Even in many advanced democratic societies, public officeholders are expected to appoint their supporters to ambassadorships and other public posts, although civil-service rules designed to reward merit may in part constrain such appointments. The temptations of officeholding are great. Despite legal rules, press scrutiny, and citizen concerns, few governments anywhere finish their terms of office untainted by some corruption scandal. In Lord Acton's famous words, "Power corrupts, and absolute power corrupts absolutely."

Vested Interests and Inertia

Government-created private gains are difficult to change or abolish once they have been established because some people enjoy government jobs, contracts, or other favors that they otherwise might not have had. The larger the government and the more attractive the benefits it provides, the more likely it is that such **vested interests** will resist change (unless change means even larger benefits). Therefore, any government will foster officeholders and beneficiaries with a vested interest in maintaining or enlarging the government itself. Such groups may become a powerful force in favor of the status quo.

Vested interests make it difficult to change government policies or make them more efficient. Once established, agencies and policies often live on far beyond their usefulness. For example, when the Spanish Armada threatened to invade England in 1588, the government established a military observation post at Land's End in southwest England. This observation post remained in place for four centuries! In the United States, the Rural Electrification Administration was created in 1935 to bring electricity to rural America. Although the country had long been electrified by then, the agency persisted for almost sixty years until it was finally merged into the Rural Utilities Service in 1994.

Vested interests are particularly likely in political systems that contain many safeguards against rapid political change. While the checks and balances in political systems such as in the United States are designed to safeguard individual rights, they may also protect the privileges of vested interests. Yet even political systems that contain far fewer such checks may exhibit an excess of political inertia. Britain is an excellent example. Until recently, the House of Lords represented the social groups that dominated British society before the Industrial Revolution more than two hundred years ago (noblemen, bishops, and judges). Only in the last few years has Britain begun reforming the House of Lords to eliminate features that reflect Britain's feudal and preindustrial past.

POLITICAL SYSTEMS AND STATES

We began by discussing governments, but governments are only one part of a larger political system. Since the term **political system** is a main organizing concept of this book, it deserves a full explanation. A system by definition has two properties: (1) a set of interdependent parts, and (2) boundaries toward its environment.

A political system is a particular type of social system that is involved in the making of authoritative public decisions. Central elements of a political system are the institutions of government—such as legislatures, bureaucracies, and courts—that formulate and implement the collective goals of a society or of groups within it.

Political systems also include important parts of the society in which governments operate. For example, political organizations, such as political parties or interest groups, are part of the political system. Such organizations do not have coercive authority, except insofar as they control the government. Likewise, the mass media only indirectly affect elections, legislation, and law enforcement. A whole host of institutions—beginning with the family and including communities, churches, schools, corporations, foundations, and think tanks—influence political attitudes and public policy. The term *political system* refers to the whole collection of related, interacting institutions and agencies.

The political systems that we compare in this book are all independent states (we also more casually refer to them as *countries*). They represent some of the most politically important countries in the contemporary world. At the same time, they reflect the diversity of political systems that exist today. A **state** is a particular type of political system. It has **sovereignty**—independent legal authority over a population in a particular territory, based on the recognized right to self-determination. Sovereignty rests with those who have the ultimate right to make political decisions.

External sovereignty is the right to make binding agreements (treaties) with other states. For instance, France's external sovereignty means that it can enter into treaties with other states. The city of Bordeaux, however, does not have this right (nor do other subnational units of government in France). Internal sovereignty is the right to make political decisions having to do with one's own citizens. For example, the French government has internal sovereignty so that it can impose taxes on French citizens.

Yet states mold and are molded by a domestic environment and an international environment. The system receives inputs from these environments and shapes them through its outputs. The boundaries of political systems are defined in terms of persons, territory, and property. Most people have citizenship rights in only one country, and such citizenship implies a bundle of rights and obligations related to that state. Similarly, territory is divided between states. A given piece of land is supposed to belong to only one country. Of course, disputes over citizenship, territory, and property are by no means uncommon and are among the most frequent causes of international conflict.

Every state faces some constraints on its external and internal sovereignty. For example, with the increasing integration of France into the **European Union (EU)**, the French government has given up parts of its sovereignty to the EU, for example by adopting the common currency of the euro, and this loss of sovereignty is a major topic of political debate. In the United States, we confuse things a bit by calling the fifty constituent units "states," even though they share their power and authority with the federal government in Washington, D.C., and enjoy much less sovereignty than France.

We often think of the world as a patchwork of states with sizable and contiguous territories, and a common identity shared by their citizens. A nation is a group of people, often living in a common territory, who have such a common identity. In **nation-states**, national identifications and sovereign political authority largely coincide—the state consists of individuals who share a common national identity. We have come to think of nation-states as the natural way to organize political systems, and often as an ideal. The national right to self-determination—the idea that every nation has a right to form its own state if it wants to do so—was enshrined in the Treaty of Versailles at the end of World War I.

Nation-states are often a desirable way to organize a political system. The national right to self-determination, however, is a relatively modern invention born in late medieval Europe. Until the end of the Middle Ages, Europe consisted of many very small political systems and a few very large ones, whose territorial possessions were not always very stable or contiguous. Nor did states always consist of people with the same national identity. But gradually, a set of European nation-states evolved, and the 1648 Treaty of Westphalia established that principle for the political organization of Europe. The nation-state thus emerged as the dominant political system during the eighteenth and nineteenth centuries in Europe.

Europe did not transform itself into distinct nation-states accidentally—indeed, the governments of the emerging nation-states had a great deal to do with it. They sought to instill a common national identity among the peoples they controlled. They did so, often heavy-handedly, by promoting a common language, a common educational system, and often a common religion. While this process of nation-building was often harsh, it produced a Europe in which the inhabitants of most states have a strong sense of community.

Many societies in the developing world today face similar challenges. Especially in Africa, the newly independent states that emerged in the 1950s and 1960s had very weak national identities. In many parts of Africa, large-scale national communities simply had not existed before these areas were colonized by Europeans and others. Even where such national identities did exist, they were rarely reflected in the boundaries that the colonial powers (such as Britain, France, and Portugal) drew between their possessions. After independence, many new states therefore faced huge nation-building tasks.

There are additional challenges to contemporary nation-states. After World War II, the states of the world have experienced an increasingly rapid process of **globalization,** in which they have become more open to and dependent on one another. Globalization has many faces (see Chapter 7). One is increasing trade in goods and services, which means that many of the products we buy are made in China and many of the telephone calls we make are answered in India. Outsourcing and loss of local jobs have been among the negative consequences of this aspect of globalization. Globalization also means migration across state boundaries, which has increased greatly in recent decades and caused controversy and conflict in many societies. Finally, globalization means that citizens of all (or most) countries increasingly have to share in cultures that have developed elsewhere (see Chapter 3). Globalization has lowered the prices of many products and increased the richness of life, but it has also created serious challenges for many states. Some, such as North Korea and Myanmar, have sought to isolate themselves from its effects. Others have responded in a more accepting manner. Most of the industrialized countries of Europe have thus gradually created a common market economy and a set of supranational political institutions, such as a common parliament and a common court of justice. The EU originally consisted of six countries—France, Germany, Italy, Belgium, the Netherlands, and Luxembourg—but has expanded to twenty-seven members, with several additional states currently applying for membership.

The **United Nations (UN),** formed at the end of World War II in 1945, has also acquired new responsibilities with globalization and especially since the collapse of the Soviet Union in 1991. As of early 2010, UN forces were peacekeepers in sixteen countries. These operations—involving more than 120,000 peacekeepers—seek to separate combatants in domestic and international conflicts, settle disputes, and form effective governing institutions. The UN has increased authority over world security, constraining, supporting, and sometimes replacing the unilateral actions of individual states. Yet while the sovereignty of states may be diminishing, they are still the most important political systems. That, of course, is the main reason that they are the subject of our study.

THE DIVERSITY OF STATES

Today, just about the entire surface of the world is covered by independent states. There were 192 UN "member-states" in 2010.[6] A few countries are not members of the UN (for example, Taiwan and the Vatican), and ongoing independence movements could create even more states. When the United States declared its independence in 1776, most independent states were European (see Figure 1.1). Much of the rest of the world existed as colonies to one of the European empires.

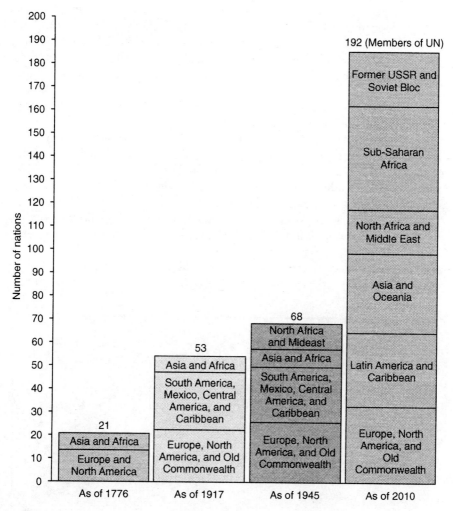

FIGURE 1.1

Formation of States Since 1776

Most states emerged during the 20th Century.

Source: For Contemporary Members, Information Office, United Nations. Data to 1945 from Charles Taylor and Michael Hudson, *World Handbook of Political and Social Indicators* (New Haven, CT: Yale University Press, 1972), 26ff.

In the nineteenth and early twentieth centuries, the number of states increased, principally in Latin America, where the Spanish and Portuguese empires broke up into twenty independent states. In Europe, newly independent countries emerged in the Balkans, Scandinavia, and the Low Countries.

Between the two world wars, new states came into being in North Africa and the Middle East, and Europe continued to fragment as the Russian and Austro-Hungarian empires broke up. After World War II, the development of new states took off, especially with the independence of India and Pakistan in 1947. By 2010, 126 new countries had joined the 68 states that existed in 1945. The largest group of new states is in Sub-Saharan Africa. More than twenty new countries formed in the 1990s—mostly the successor states of the Soviet Union, Yugoslavia, and Czechoslovakia. Four states have joined the UN since 2000— most notably Switzerland, which until 2002 had stayed out because of its strict neutrality policy—but there have been few newly independent countries over the past decade.

All these countries—new as well as old—share certain characteristics. They have legal authority over their territories and people; most have armies, air forces, and in some cases navies; they collect taxes and spend money; and they regulate their economies and maintain public order. Countries send and receive ambassadors; most belong to international organizations. But they also vary, often profoundly, in physical size, histories, institutions, cultures, religions, economies, and social structures—factors that shape their politics.

States come in all sizes. The smallest legally independent political entity in territory as well as population is Vatican City, the headquarters of the Catholic Church, with less than half a square kilometer of turf and fewer than a thousand residents. The contrasts between geographic size and population size can be graphically seen in the following two maps. In Map 1.1, the countries of the

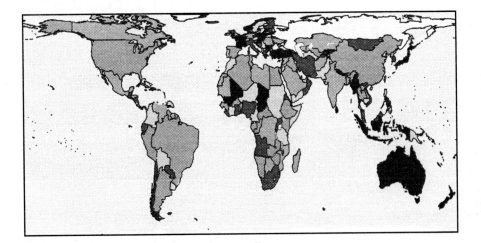

MAP 1.1

Map of the World Based on Geographic Size

Source: Copyright © *The Real World Atlas,* Thames & Hudson, Ltd., London, 2008.

world are displayed, as we often see them, according to their size. Russia, with its landmass extending over eleven contiguous time zones, is the world's largest state, with more than 17 million square kilometers. The United States, Canada, and China are among the next set of countries, with around 9 million square kilometers each. Many of the established democracies in Europe are relatively small (Britain has 242,000 square kilometers and Germany 349,000).

Map 1.2 instead displays the world's states by their population size. Instantly, China and India balloon in size because of their large populations. China alone accounts for about a fifth of the world's population (with 1.3 billion people), and India is not far behind (with 1.2 billion). Important European democracies such as Britain, France, and Germany look much smaller because their populations only number between 60 and 80 million. Even more dramatically, Australia shrinks from a continent in the first map to a small dot in the second because of its small population (21 million). And although the United States has roughly the same territory as China and is larger than India, it is much smaller than these Asian giants in population (310 million and a distant third in the world). And while Russia has almost twice as much land as any other country, its population (142 million) is less than half that of the United States and shrinking.

The political implications of these striking contrasts in population size and geographic area are not always obvious. Size matters in politics, and big states are often more powerful than small ones. Yet big countries do not always prevail over small ones: the United States broke away from Britain when the latter was the most powerful country in the world; both Britain and the Soviet Union tried to conquer Afghanistan and failed; Cuba has challenged the

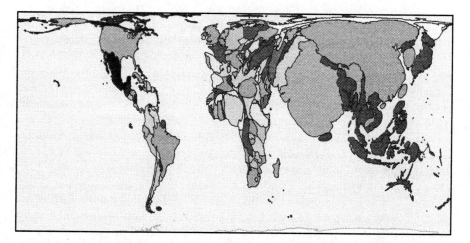

MAP 1.2
Map of the World Based on Population Size

Source: Copyright © *The Real World Atlas,* Thames & Hudson, Ltd., London, 2008.

United States for almost fifty years; Israel stands off the much larger Arab world; and tiny Vatican City has great power and influence in spiritual and moral affairs. Nor do area and population size determine a country's political system. Both little Luxembourg and large India are democracies. Autocratic (nondemocratic) regimes are similarly found in small, medium, and large countries. These enormous contrasts in size show only that the states now making up the world differ greatly in their physical and human resources.

A state's geographic location can also have important strategic implications. In the sixteenth through nineteenth centuries, European states typically required a large land army to protect themselves from the threats of their neighbors. These countries had difficulties developing free political institutions, since they needed a strong government to extract resources on a large scale and keep the population under control. Britain was protected by the English Channel and could defend itself through its navy, a smaller army, lower taxation, and less centralization of power—which aided political liberalization. Most peoples of Asia, Africa, and Latin America were colonized by the more powerful Western nations. Those that had the richest natural resources, the most convenient locations, and the most benign climates tended to attract the largest numbers of settlers. Areas that were landlocked or more geographically inhospitable were less likely to be colonized but have also often remained poor and isolated from world markets.

CHALLENGES: BUILDING COMMUNITY

Whether they are old or new, large or small, most of the world's states face a number of common challenges. The first is building community. Most states do not have a homogeneous population, and instilling a sense of shared identity can be a serious challenge. Second, even the wealthiest states face the challenge of fostering continued economic and social development. Finally, most states face significant challenges in advancing democracy and civil liberties. These challenges should be familiar from our discussion of the purposes and dangers of governments. In the remainder of this chapter, we discuss these challenges successively.

One of the most important challenges facing political systems worldwide is to build a common identity and a sense of community among their citizens. The absence of a common identity can have severe political consequences. Conflicts over national, ethnic, or religious identities are among the most explosive causes of political turmoil, as we have witnessed in Northern Ireland, the former Yugoslavia, Rwanda, and elsewhere. But while building community is a pervasive challenge, some countries are in a much better situation than others. Japan, for example, has an ethnically homogeneous population, a common language, and a long national political history. A large majority of the Japanese share in the religions of Buddhism and Shintoism, and the country is separated by miles of ocean from its most important neighbors. Nigeria, in contrast, is an accidental and artificial creation of British colonial rule and has no common precolonial history. The population is sharply divided between Muslims and Christians; the Christians are divided equally into Catholics and Protestants. There are some 250 different ethnic groups, speaking a variety of local languages, in addition to English. Obviously, the challenges of building community are much greater in Nigeria than they are in Japan. Although few countries face problems as complicated as those of the Nigerians, the community-building challenge is one of the most serious issues facing many states today.

States and Nations

The word *nation* is sometimes used to mean almost the same as the word *state*, as in the *United Nations*. Strictly speaking, however, we wish to use the term **nation** to refer to a group of people with a common identity. When we speak of a "nation," we thus refer to the self-identification of a people. That common identity may be built upon a common language, history, race, or culture, or simply upon the fact that this group has occupied the same territory. Nations may or may not have their own state or independent government. In some cases—such as Japan, France, or Sweden—there is a close correspondence between the memberships of the state and the nation. Most people who identify themselves as Japanese do in fact live in the state of Japan, and most people who live in Japan identify themselves as Japanese.

In many instances, the correspondence between the nation and the state is not so neat. Nor is it obvious that it should be. In some cases, states are *multinational*—consisting of a multitude of different nations. The Soviet Union, Yugoslavia, and Czechoslovakia were multinational states that broke apart. In other cases, some nations are much larger than the corresponding states, such as Germany for most of its history or China. Some nations have split into two or more states for political reasons, such as Korea today and Germany between 1949 and 1990. Some groups with claims to be nations have no state at all, such as the Kurds, the Basques, and the Tamils. When states and nations do not coincide, it can cause explosive political conflict, as discussed later. At the same time, the presence of several nations within the same state can also be a source of diversity and cultural enrichment.

Nationality and Ethnicity

There is a fine line between nations and *ethnic groups*, which may have common physical traits, languages, cultures, or history. Like nationality, **ethnicity** need not have any objective basis in genetics, culture, or history. German sociologist Max Weber defined ethnic groups as "those human groups that entertain a subjective belief in their common descent because of similarities of physical type or of customs or both, or because of memories of colonization and migration. . . . [I]t does not matter whether or not an objective blood relationship exists."[7] Similarly, groups that are physically quite similar, but differ by language, religion, customs, marriage patterns, and historical memories (for example, the Serbs, Croats, and Muslim Bosnians) may believe they are descended from different ancestors and hence are physically different as well. Over centuries, originally homogeneous populations may intermix with other populations, even though the culture may continue. This is true, for example, of the Jewish population of Israel, which has come together after more than two millennia of global dispersion.

Ethnic differences can be a source of political conflict.[8] Since the end of the Cold War, many states of the former Soviet Bloc have come apart at their ethnic and religious seams. In the former Yugoslavia, secession by a number of provinces triggered several wars. The most brutal of these was in Bosnia-Herzegovina, where a Muslim regime faced rebellion and murderous "ethnic cleansing" by the large Serbian minority. Intervention by the UN, the North Atlantic Treaty Organization (NATO), and the United States contained Serbian aggression and led to an uneasy settlement, but considerable tension remains. Similar tensions and violent aggression occurred in Kosovo as well.

In many developing countries, boundaries established by former colonial powers cut across ethnic lines. In 1947, the British withdrew from India and divided the subcontinent into a northern Muslim area—Pakistan—and a southern Hindu area—India. The most immediate consequence was a terrible civil conflict and "ethno-religious" cleansing. There still are almost 100 million Muslims in India and serious religious tension. Similarly, forty years ago, the Ibo ethnic group in Nigeria fought an unsuccessful separatist war against the rest of the country, resulting in the deaths of roughly a million people. The Tutsi and Hutu peoples of the small African state of Rwanda engaged in a civil war of extermination in the 1990s, with hundreds of thousands of people slaughtered, and millions fleeing the country in fear of their lives.

The migration of labor, forced or voluntary, across state boundaries is another source of ethnic differentiation. The American descendants of Africans forcefully enslaved between the seventeenth and the nineteenth centuries are witnesses of the largest coercive labor migration in world history. In contrast, voluntary migration takes the form of Indians, Bangladeshi, Egyptians, and Palestinians seeking better lives in the oil sheikhdoms around the Persian Gulf; Mexican and Caribbean migrant workers moving to the United States; and Turkish and North African migrants relocating to Europe. Some migration is politically motivated, triggered by civil war and repression. Two scholars refer to the contemporary world as living through an "Age of Migration,"[9] comparable in scale to that of the late nineteenth and early twentieth centuries.

Table 1.1 provides examples of politically significant "ethnicity," broadly defined, in our selected twelve countries. Five sets of traits are included, beginning with physical differences, then language, norms against intermarriage, religion, and negative historical memories. The table illustrates the importance of each distinction to ethnic identity. The most important bases of distinction lie in intermarriage, religion, and historical memories. Language differences are of great importance in four cases and of some importance in six; and finally, and perhaps surprisingly, physical differences are of great importance in only two cases. Recent migration has made such previously homogeneous states as France, Japan, and Germany more multiethnic. Other countries, such as the United States and Canada, have long been multiethnic and have become even more so. Indeed, globalization and migration seem destined to increase the diversity of many societies worldwide.

TABLE 1.1

The Many Faces of Ethnicity: Identity is sometimes based on physical differences, sometimes on language, sometimes on neither.*

	Physical Differences	Language	Norms Against Intermarriage	Religion	Negative Historical Memories
Brazil: Blacks	XX	0	XX	X	X
Britain: South Asians	X	0	X	XX	X
China: Tibetans	X	XX	XX	XX	XX
France: Algerians	X	X	XX	XX	XX
Germany: Turks	X	XX	XX	XX	0
India: Muslims	0	X	XX	XX	XX
Iran: Kurds	X	XX	XX	XX	XX
Japan: Buraku-min	0	0	XX	0	XX
Mexico: Mayan	X	X	XX	X	XX
Nigeria: Ibo	0	X	XX	XX	XX
Russia: Chechens	X	XX	XX	XX	XX
United States: African-Americans	XX	X	XX	0	XX
United States: Hispanics:	X	X	X	0	X

*Salience is estimated at the following levels of importance in affecting differences: 0 = none or almost none; X = some; XX = much.

Language

Language can be a source of social division that may overlap with ethnicity. There are approximately five thousand different languages in use in the world today, and a much smaller number of language families. Most of these languages are spoken by relatively small tribal groups in North and South America, Asia, Africa, or Oceania. Only 200 languages have a million or more speakers, and only 8 may be classified as world languages.

English is the most truly international language. Close to one-third of the world's population lives in countries in which English is one of the official languages. Other international languages include Spanish, Arabic, Russian, Portuguese, French, and German. The language with the largest number of speakers, though in several varieties, is Chinese (with well over a billion speakers). The major languages with the greatest international spread are those of the former colonial powers—Great Britain, France, Spain, and Portugal.[10]

Linguistic divisions can create particularly thorny political problems. Political systems can choose to ignore racial, ethnic, or religious differences among their citizens, but they cannot avoid committing themselves to one or several languages. Linguistic conflicts typically show up in controversies over educational policies, or over language use in the government. Occasionally, language regulation is more intrusive, as in Quebec, where English-only street signs are prohibited and large corporations are required to conduct their business in French.

Religious Differences and Fundamentalism

States also vary in their religious characteristics. In some—such as Israel, the Irish Republic, and Pakistan—religion is a basis of national identity for a majority of the population. Iran is a theocratic regime, in which religious authorities govern and religious law is part of the country's legal code. In other societies, such as Poland under communism, religion can be a rallying point for political movements. In many Latin American countries, the clergy have embraced a liberation theology that fosters advocacy of the poor and criticism of government brutality.

Table 1.2 indicates that Christianity is the largest and most widely spread religion. Roughly one-third of the world's population belongs to the Christian church, which is divided into three major groups—Roman Catholics, Protestants (of many denominations), and Orthodox (e.g., Greek and Russian). The Catholics are dominant in Europe and Latin America; there is a more equal distribution of Catholics and Protestants elsewhere. While the traditional Protestant denominations have declined in North America in the last decades, three forms of Protestantism—Fundamentalist, Pentecostal, and Evangelical—have increased there and especially in Latin America and Asia.

The Muslims are the second largest religious group and the most rapidly growing religion. Between one-fourth and one-fifth of the world's population is Muslim, and it is primarily concentrated in Asia and Africa, with growing numbers in Europe also. Islam has become revitalized in Central Asia, and Muslims have been particularly successful in missionary activities in Sub-Saharan Africa.

Religion can be a source of intense disagreement, since beliefs may take the form of deep personal convictions that are difficult to compromise. Religious groups often battle over such issues as the rules of marriage and divorce, childrearing, sexual morality, abortion, euthanasia, the roles of women, and the regulation of religious observances. Religious communities often take a special interest in educational policies in order to transmit their ideas and ethics. On such issues, religious groups may clash with one another as well as with more secular groups. Although religious groups can coexist peacefully, and are often the source of exemplary acts of compassion and reconciliation, some may also commit acts of violence, cruelty, and terrorism.

TABLE 1.2

Faiths of the World: Adherents of All Religions by Six Continents (mid-2009, in millions)

Religion	Africa	Asia	Europe	Latin America	North America	Oceania	Total	Percentage
Christians	483.4	345.2	585.4	542.3	280.7	27.6	2,264.4	33.2
Muslims	408.0	1,066.3	40.8	1.8	5.6	0.6	1,523.2	22.3
Nonreligious and Atheists	6.7	608.7	97.0	19.8	41.7	4.9	778.7	11.4
Hindus	2.8	928.5	1.0	0.8	1.8	0.5	935.5	13.7
Buddhists	0.3	456.7	1.8	0.8	3.6	0.6	463.8	6.8
Jews	0.1	5.9	1.8	0.9	5.7	0.1	14.5	0.2
Other	108.1	709.6	3.3	20.2	6.2	0.8	848.2	12.4
Total	1,009.4	4,120.9	731.3	586.6	345.3	35.1	6,826.6	100%

Source: Adherents as defined in Encyclopedia Britannica 2009.

BOX 1.3 THE ORIGINS OF "FUNDAMENTALISM"

Fundamentalism is today often associated with militancy and even violence in the clash between religious groups, but its original meaning was less dramatic. Fundamentalism got its name in the decades before World War I when some Protestant clergymen in the United States banded together to defend the "fundamentals" of religious belief against the secularizing influences of a modernizing society. This was a reaction to new biblical scholarship at the time that questioned the divine inspiration and authorship of the Bible, and to the expansion of science and Darwinist theories of evolution. These church leaders were also distressed by the apparent erosion of morality and tradition in the United States. In 1920, a journalist and Baptist layman named Curtis Lee Laws appropriated the term "fundamentalist" as a designation for those who were ready "to do battle royal for the Fundamentals." The fundamentalists affirmed the inerrancy (the absolute truth) of the Bible and formed enclaves to protect themselves from error and sin. Religious fundamentalism has recently emerged in some form in all major faiths in reaction to social modernization.

Even societies in which most people supposedly belong to the same community of faith may be split by conflicts between "fundamentalists" and those who are more moderate in their beliefs. **Religious fundamentalism** has emerged in some form in all major faiths in reaction to social modernization (see Box 1.3). Judaism, Christianity, and Islam are all "religions of the book," although not exactly the same book. The Jews believe only in the Old Testament; the Christians add on the New Testament; and the Muslims add the Koran to these two. While each religion disagrees over the interpretation of these texts, Jewish, Christian, and Muslim fundamentalists all believe in the truth of their respective sacred books. Some want political life to be organized according to these sacred texts and doctrines. There are also Hindu and Buddhist fundamentalists. The rise of fundamentalism has affected the entire world. Israel, for example, struggles with militancy among Jews as well as among the Muslim and Palestinian population. India has frequent confrontations between Hindus and Muslims, and Nigeria between Muslims and Christians.

Religious symbols can often become a rallying point for groups with other grievances, such as poverty or ethnic discrimination. Religious and other extremists employ violence in many forms, from threats and property destruction to assassination and destructive suicide. These acts of terrorism are intended to stagger the imagination, frighten, and weaken the will. From this point of view, the September 11, 2001, attacks on the World Trade Center and the Pentagon involved not only suicide pilot-hijackers but also aircraft filled with volatile fuel and innocent passengers converted into immense projectiles.

These attacks were followed by terrorist assaults in Bali, Madrid, London, Riyadh, and other cities. Dealing with international terrorism by religious and other extremists is now a challenge that faces many nations worldwide.

FOSTERING ECONOMIC DEVELOPMENT

Two major forces are transforming political systems and nations, and the lives of their citizens; they provide major sources of comparison across the nations in this book. The first is the process of economic development, and the second is political democratization.

A political system cannot generally satisfy its citizens unless it can foster social and economic development. Thus, as significant as nation-building may be, economic and social development are exceptionally important. Economic development implies that citizens can enjoy new resources and opportunities, and that parents can expect their children to do at least as well as themselves. Many people expect government to improve their living conditions through economic growth, providing jobs, and raising income standards. However, development can also create social strains and damage nature. Yet the success of governments—both democratic and autocratic—is often measured in economic terms.

In affluent, advanced industrial societies, contemporary living standards provide for basic social needs (and much more) for most of the public. Indeed, the current political challenges in these nations often focus on problems resulting from the economic successes of the past, such as protecting environmental quality or managing the consequences of growth. New challenges to social-welfare policies are emerging from the medical and social-security costs of aging populations. For most of the world, however, substantial basic economic needs still exist, and governments focus on improving the socioeconomic conditions of the nation.

Over the past two to three decades, globalization, democratization, and marketization have transformed living conditions in many nations more than in any similar period in the past. The United Nations Development Program (UNDP) combines measures of economic well-being, life expectancy, and educational achievement into its Human Development Index (HDI).[11] The HDI shows dramatic improvements in life conditions in many regions of the world over the past three decades (see Figure 1.2 and Table 1.3). East Asia and South Asia have made substantial improvements since 1975. For instance, in 1975, South Korea and Taiwan had a standard of living close to many poor African nations, and they are now affluent societies. Even more striking is the change in the two largest nations in the world. China improved from an HDI of 0.52 in 1975 (the same as Botswana or Swaziland) to 0.77 in 2007 (close to Russia or Brazil); India improved from an HDI of 0.41 to 0.61. These statistics represent improved living conditions for billions of people. At the same time, however, living conditions have changed less in Sub-Saharan Africa over this period. Though Nigeria's score rose from 0.32 to

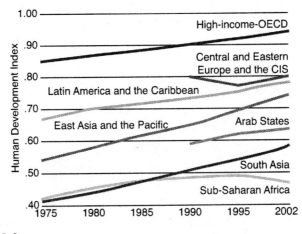

FIGURE 1.2

Changes in Human Development Index by Region

Source: United Nations Development Program, *Human Development Report 2004* (New York: United Nations, 2004), 134.

0.51, much of it due to improving oil revenues, it remains among the poorest countries in the world. And the HDI for Russia stagnated in the 1990s, though it has since improved.

The process of economic development typically follows a similar course. One element is a transformation of the structure of the labor force. The five advanced industrial countries in our comparisons all have agricultural employment of less than 10 percent of the labor force. Poor countries, in contrast, often have more than two-thirds of their labor forces employed in agriculture. In addition, economic development is typically linked to urbanization as peasants leave their farms and move to the cities. In nations undergoing rapid economic development, such as China, urban migration creates new opportunities for the workers but also new economic and social policy challenges for the governments.

The UNDP's Human Development Index provides a means to compare the differences in current life conditions across the twelve comparison nations in this chapter (Table 1.3). Perhaps the most striking feature of this table is the wide gap in living standards that still exists across nations worldwide. For instance, the **gross domestic product (GDP)** per capita, which is a measure of national economic development, is about twenty times higher in the Western advanced industrial democracies than in Nigeria.[12] Similarly, there are notable gaps in life expectancy and educational opportunities between the affluent Northern societies and the developing nations in Africa and Asia. In highly industrialized countries, education is virtually universal and practically everyone over age fifteen can read and write. In India and Nigeria, less than two-thirds of the adult population has this minimal level of education. Moreover, the countries with the fewest literate citizens also have the fewest radios and television sets—even though these devices do not require literacy.

TABLE 1.3

The Race for Social Progress: Human Development Indicators show improvements in many countries.

Nation	Life Expectancy	Percent Enrolled in School	GDP/capita (USD, ppp)	1975 HDI	2007 HDI	2007 World Rank
United States	79.1	92.4	45,592	0.867	0.956	13
Japan	82.7	86.6	33,632	0.857	0.960	10
United Kingdom	79.3	89.2	35,130	0.845	0.947	21
France	81.0	95.4	33,674	0.853	0.961	8
Germany	79.8	88.1	34,401	—	0.947	22
Mexico	76.0	80.2	14,104	0.689	0.854	53
Russia	66.2	81.9	14,690	—	0.817	71
Brazil	72.2	87.2	9,567	0.645	0.813	75
China	72.9	68.7	5,383	0.525	0.772	92
Iran	71.2	73.2	10,955	0.566	0.782	88
India	63.4	61.0	2,753	0.412	0.612	134
Nigeria	47.7	53.0	1,969	0.318	0.511	158

Source: United Nations Development Program, *World Development Report 2009* (New York: United Nations, 2009) (www.undp.org).

Economic development is also associated with better nutrition and medical care. In the economically advanced countries, fewer children die in infancy, and the average citizen has a life expectancy at birth of around eighty years (almost eighty-three in Japan). Improvements in living conditions have substantially increased life expectancy in many low-income nations, such as Mexico and China. However, the average life expectancy for an Indian is sixty-three years, and for a Nigerian less than fifty years. Material productivity, education, exposure to communications media, and longer and healthier lives are closely interconnected.

In order to become more productive, a country needs to develop a skilled and healthy labor force and to build the infrastructure that material welfare requires. Preindustrial nations face most urgently the issues of economic development: how to improve the immediate welfare of their citizens yet also invest for the future. Typically, these are newer nations that also face the challenges of building community and effective political institutions. Political leaders and celebrities, such as Bono and Angelina Jolie have mobilized public awareness that these differences in living conditions are a global concern—for those living in the developing world, for the affluent nations and their citizens, and for international organizations such as the United Nations and the World Bank.

Problems of Economic Development

Wealth, income, and opportunity are rarely evenly distributed within nations, and the unequal distribution of resources and opportunities is among the most serious causes of political conflict. A large GDP may conceal significant poverty and lack of opportunities. A high rate of national growth may benefit only particular regions or social groups, leaving large parts of the population even less well-off than before. Parts of the "inner cities" of the United States, the older parts of such Indian cities as Delhi and Calcutta, remote and land-locked parts of many African states, many rural areas in China, and the arid northeast of Brazil all suffer from poverty and hopelessness, while other parts of these countries experience growth and improved welfare. Moreover, there is some evidence that rapid economic development tends to increase such inequalities.

A country's politics may be sharply affected by internal divisions of income, wealth, and other resources. Table 1.4 displays income distributions for our twelve comparison countries. Generally speaking, economic develop-ment improves the **equality of income**, at least past a certain stage of economic growth. Wealthy nations like Japan, Germany, and France have relatively more egalitarian income distributions than middle- or low-income countries. Still, the wealthiest 10 percent in Japan receive about the same total income as the poorest 40 percent receive. This is a large gap in life conditions between rich and poor, but the gap is even wider in less affluent nations. In Mexico, a middle-income country, the ratio is closer to three to one; in Brazil it is more than five to one. The United States is at a middling level of inequality, higher

TABLE 1.4

Income Distribution: Middle-income countries have the greatest inequalities; wealthy ones tend to be more equal.

Country	Year	Wealthiest 10%	Poorest 40%	Wealthy/Poor Gap
Germany	2000	22.1	22.2	−0.1
Russia	2002	23.8	20.9	2.9
Japan	1993	21.7	24.8	3.1
France	1995	25.1	19.8	5.3
Britain	1999	28.5	17.5	11.0
India	2004–05	31.1	19.4	11.7
United States	2000	29.9	16.2	13.7
Iran	1998	33.7	19.5	14.2
Nigeria	2003	33.2	14.6	18.6
China	2004	34.9	12.8	22.1
Mexico	2004	39.4	12.6	26.8
Brazil	2004	44.8	9.2	35.6

Source: World Bank, *World Development Indicators 2007,* Table 2-7 (www.worldbank.org); distribution of income or consumption.

than Japan and the countries of Western Europe but lower than most of the rest. The table also suggests that a nation's political characteristics make a difference. India has consciously worked to narrow inequality, which places it higher in the table, while inequality in China has steadily increased.

Although industrialization and high productivity may eventually encourage a more equal distribution of income, the first stages of industrialization may actually increase income inequality. As economies modernize, they create a dual economy—a rural sector and an urban industrial and commercial sector, both with inequalities of their own. These inequalities increase as education and communication spread more rapidly in the modern sector, which may contribute to the political instability of developing countries. Moreover, there is no guarantee that inequality will diminish in later stages of development. In Brazil, for instance, income inequality increased for decades, even as the economy developed. In the United States and Britain, income inequality has increased substantially since the 1970s. In Russia and other postcommunist societies, the development of new capitalist markets was accompanied by new income inequalities. Inequality is an issue that many nations face.

Various policy solutions can mitigate the hardships economic inequality causes in developing societies. If there is equality of opportunity and high social mobility, inequality may decline over time and may not seem so oppressive to younger generations. Investments in education can therefore lessen these problems. Also, Taiwan and South Korea show how early land reforms equalized opportunity early in the developmental process. Investment in primary and secondary education, in agricultural inputs and rural infrastructure (principally roads and water), and in labor-intensive industries produced remarkable results for several decades. A comparative advantage in cheap and skilled labor enabled Taiwan and South Korea to compete effectively in international markets. Thus, some growth policies mitigate inequalities, but it can be very difficult to put them into practice, especially where substantial inequalities already exist.

Another correlate of development is population growth. As health care improves, living standards increase, life expectancies lengthen, and populations grow. This is a positive development because it represents improved living conditions for these people, but rapid population growth also can pose policy challenges for many developing nations.

Table 1.5 puts this issue in sharp relief. The table divides the world population into three strata: low-income economies, middle-income economies, and high-income economies. In 1990, the low-income countries had a population total of almost 2 billion, or about a third of the total world population. In contrast, the high-income nations had about a sixth of the world's population.

Some projections estimate that world population will increase by 2015 to 7 billion and that the poorer countries will see a more rapid rate of growth. In 2005, Hania Zlotnik of the UN population division estimated that "out of every 100 persons added to the [world's] population in the coming decade, 97 will live in developing countries."[13] Rapid economic growth in the developing world can create significant burdens for these nations.

TABLE 1.5

Population by Economic Development Level in 1990 and Projected to 2015 (in millions): The ranks of the poor are growing.

Economic Development Level	In 1990		Projected to 2015	
	Number	Percentage	Number	Percentage
Low-income economies	1,777	33.9	2,794	39.4
Middle-income economies	2,588	49.3	3,299	46.5
High-income economies	887	16.8	1,007	14.1
Total	5,252	100.0	7,100	100.0

Source: World Bank, *World Development Report Indicators 2005*, Table 2-1 (www.worldbank.org), population dynamics.

These prospects have produced a development literature that mixes both light and heat. Economist Amartya Sen warns of a "danger that in the confrontation between apocalyptic pessimism on one hand, and a dismissive smugness, on the other, a genuine understanding of the nature of the population problem may be lost."[14] He points out that the first impact of "modernization" on population is to increase it rapidly as new sanitation measures and modern pharmaceuticals reduce the death rate. As an economy develops, however, changing conditions tend to reduce fertility. With improved education (particularly of women), health, and welfare, the advantages of lower fertility become clear, and population growth declines.

Fertility decreased in Europe and North America as they underwent industrialization. Today, the native populations are decreasing in many European nations because fertility rates are below levels necessary to sustain a constant population size. This pattern also appears to be occurring in parts of the developing world. Thus, annual population growth in the world has declined over the last two decades. The rate of population growth in India, for example, rose to 2.2 percent in the 1970s and has since declined. Latin America peaked at a higher rate and then came down sharply. The major problem area is Sub-Saharan Africa, which continues to experience very high birth rates.[15] Yet, even the fertility rate in Africa has recently dropped dramatically because of the tragically rising death rate from the AIDS epidemic.

While population growth rates appear to be slowing, governments are addressing this issue in different ways. China adopted a coercive policy of limiting families to a single child, which in urban areas produced dramatic results at great costs. India followed a collaborative approach involving governmental intervention and education to affect family choices.[16] Kerala in southern India shows what can be accomplished by the collaborative approach, where expanding education (particularly among women) and otherwise improving living conditions has reduced fertility more than in China.

Economic growth can have other social costs. For instance, advanced industrial societies are dealing with the environmental costs of their industrial development. Despoiled forests, depleted soils and fisheries, polluted air and water, nuclear waste, endangered species, and a threatened ozone layer now burden their legislative dockets. With increasing industrialization and urbanization in the developing world, many of these environmental problems could worsen. Thus, economic development can impose serious environmental costs as well as benefits. At the same time, some environmental problems are even more acute in less developed countries, where rapid increases in population and urbanization create shortages of clean air, clean water, and adequate sanitation.[17] Thus, economic development generally improves the living conditions of the public, but in the process it produces new policy problems that governments must address.

FOSTERING DEMOCRACY, HUMAN RIGHTS, AND CIVIL LIBERTIES

The second major force transforming contemporary political systems is the process of democratization, which includes the enhancement of human rights and the expansion of freedom. Democracy is the form of government to which most contemporary countries, more or less sincerely and successfully, aspire. A **democracy**, briefly defined, is a political system in which citizens enjoy a number of basic civil and political rights, and in which their most important political leaders are elected in free and fair elections and are accountable under a rule of law. Democracy literally means "government by the people."

In small political systems, such as local communities, it may be possible for "the people" to share directly in debating, deciding, and implementing public policy. In large political systems, such as contemporary states, democracy must be achieved largely through indirect participation in policymaking. Elections, competitive political parties, free mass media, and representative assemblies make some degree of democracy—some degree of "government by the people"—possible. This indirect, or representative, democracy is not complete or ideal. But the more citizens are involved and the more influential their choices, the more democratic the system.

The most important general distinction in classifying political systems is between democratic systems and **authoritarian** (also known as **autocratic**) systems. Autocracies lack one or several defining features of democracy. In democracies, competitive elections give citizens the chance to shape the policymaking process through their selection of key policymakers. In authoritarian systems, the policymakers are chosen by military councils, hereditary families, dominant political parties, and the like. Citizens are either ignored or pressed into symbolic assent to the government's choices.

Authoritarian states can take several forms (see Chapter 6). In **oligarchies**, literally "rule by the few," important political rights are withheld from the majority of the population. South Africa until the abolition of apartheid in the early 1990s is a good example. Other authoritarian states, such as Egypt, are **party, military, or personal dictatorships. Totalitarian systems**—such as Nazi Germany, or the Soviet Union under Stalin, or North Korea today—are systems in which the government constricts the rights and privacy of its citizens in a particularly severe and intrusive manner.

As societies become more complex, richer, and more technologically advanced, the probability of citizen involvement and democratization increases. In the first half of the twentieth century, most Western states were transformed from autocracies or oligarchies to democracies. After World War II, a second democratic wave—which lasted from 1943 until the early 1960s—saw both newly independent states (such as India and Nigeria) and defeated authoritarian powers (such as Germany and Japan) set up the formal institutions of democracy.[18]

Another round of democratic transitions began in 1974, involving Southern Europe, East Asia, Latin America, and a number of African states. Samuel P. Huntington speaks of this latest move toward democracy as a "Third Wave" of worldwide **democratization**.[19] The most dramatic changes came in Central and Eastern Europe, where in a few short years the Soviet empire collapsed, the nations of Eastern Europe rapidly converted to democracy, and many of these nations have now joined the European Union. A few years earlier, much of Latin America had shifted from dictatorships (often military) to democracy. The People Power Revolution in the Philippines and the end of the apartheid regime in South Africa were equally dramatic.

As a result of these three democratization waves, democracy has become a common goal of the global community (see Figure 1.3). As late as 1978, only a

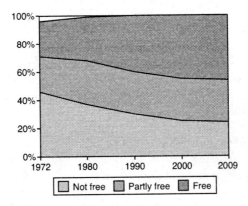

FIGURE 1.3

Growth in Free Governments over Time (as percentages of all states)

The Free World has been growing.

Source: Freedom House, *Freedom in the World 2010* (www.freedomhouse.org).

third of the world's independent countries had competitive party and electoral systems. Communist governments, other single-party governments, and other authoritarian regimes dominated the landscape. By 2004, almost two-thirds of states had a system of electoral democracy, and human rights and liberties were similarly spreading to more of the world's population.[20] However, this democratization trend has come to a halt over the past few years, so we should not be overconfident about further progress in democratization around the world.

This democratization process results from a combination of factors. Economic development transforms societies in ways that typically encourage democratization by creating autonomous political groups that demand political influence, by expanding the political skills of the citizenry, and by creating economic complexity that encourages systems of self-governance. Social modernization transforms the political values and political culture of the public, which increases demands for a more participatory system (see Chapter 3). New democracies are also much more likely to endure when founded in economically developed societies.[21]

Democracy is not an all-or-nothing proposition, however. No democracy is perfect, and we can speak of shades or gradations of democracy. Democracy typically does not come about overnight. It often takes time to establish democratic institutions and to have citizens recognize them and comply with the rules of the democratic process.

It can be especially difficult to consolidate democracy in less economically developed societies. Not all of the newly democratizing countries are succeeding beyond the first few years. In some, democratic processes fail to produce stable institutions and effective public policies and give way to some form of authoritarianism. In Nigeria, military coups overthrew democratically elected (but badly flawed) governments in 1966 and again in 1983, and redemocratization did not happen until 1999. Nigeria is by no means unique. Transition can move in either direction, toward or away from democracy. The recent wave of democratization is supported by the more favorable environments of more modernized societies and because there are now more democracies in the world to support new democracies. However, democracy is difficult to sustain when severe economic or political problems face a nation, or where the public remains uncertain about democracy.

Even when states democratize, there is no guarantee that they will grant human rights and civil liberties to all their people. In some countries, majority rule turns into a "tyranny of the majority" against ethnic or religious minorities. Therefore, democracies have to balance between respecting the will of the majority and protecting the rights of the minority. Even when political rulers sincerely try to promote human rights and civil liberties (which is by no means always the case), they do not always agree on the nature of those rights.

A good example of the spread of rights and liberties—and cultural differences in the definition of rights—involves gender issues. Governments in Western industrial societies favor gender policies that guarantee equal access for women in society, the workplace, and politics. The UN and other international organizations have become advocates of women's rights. But gender norms

BOX 1.4 WOMEN AND POLITICAL DEVELOPMENT

If a poor nation could do one thing to stimulate its development, what should it do? Opening the fiftieth session of the United Nations Commission on the Status of Women in 2006, UN Deputy-Secretary General Louise Fréchette said the international community finally comprehends that empowering women and girls around the globe is the most effective tool for a country's development. She stated that studies have repeatedly shown that by giving women equal education and work opportunities, and access to a society's decision-making processes, a country can boost its economic productivity, reduce infant and maternal mortality rates, and improve the general population's nutrition and health. These results are achieved because women's education and participation in the labor force increase family output, increase the likelihood that children will be better educated and benefit from health care, improve nutrition in the family, and better the quality of life for women and their families.

Source: UN News Center, February 27, 2006.

often vary across cultural zones. The UN's statistics indicate that many developing nations hesitate to grant equal rights to women, restricting their education and involvement in the economy and politics.[22] Restrictions on women's rights are even starker in many Arab states, where they often clash with social norms and religious beliefs. Ironically, improving the status of women is one of the most productive ways to develop a nation politically and economically (see Box 1.4), for example by improving educational and health standards and stabilizing birth rates. In short, expanding human rights is an ongoing process in the world today, and there is much room for further progress.

LOOKING FORWARD

The last several decades have been a period of tremendous social, economic, and political change in the world. Economic development, improved living standards, the spread of human rights, and democratization improved the life chances and life conditions of billions of individuals. In most of the world, the average child born today can look forward to a longer, better, and freer life than his or her parents—especially if she is a girl.

At the same time, continuing social, economic, and political problems remain. Progress in one area can create new opportunities, but also new problems in another. Economic development, for example, can sometimes stimulate ethnic strife and destabilize political institutions. Economic development can also disrupt social life. And the process of development has been uneven across and within nations. Many basic human needs still remain in too short supply.[23]

Even in the affluent democracies, as one set of policy issues is addressed, new issues come to the fore. Western democracies struggle to address issues of environmental quality, changing lifestyles, and the challenges of globalization. A more affluent and better informed citizenry may also be less inclined to trust political parties, interest groups, parliaments, and political executives. Success in meeting these old and new challenges can improve the living conditions for the world's populations, decrease international conflict, and come closer to meeting the ideals of humankind.

Governments and politics have played a large role in human societies of the past. Some of their policies have greatly improved the quality of life of their citizens, while others have been disasters. Yet one way or another, governments and their activities are central to our political futures. Our goal in this book is to examine the ways in which citizens, policymakers, and governments address the policy challenges that face them today.

REVIEW QUESTIONS

1. What is politics?
2. What are the contrasting images of the "state of nature" of humankind?
3. What are the potential positive and negative outcomes of government activity?
4. What are the main challenges that countries face in building a political community?
5. What are the causes and consequences of economic development?
6. What are the causes and consequences of democratization?

KEY TERMS

anarchism
authoritarian
autocratic
democracy
democratization
equality of income
ethnicity
European Union
   (EU)
externalities
globalization

governments
gross domestic product
   (GDP)
human rights
libertarianism
military dictatorships
nation
nation-states
oligarchy
party dictatorships
personal dictatorships

political culture
political system
public goods
religious fundamentalism
rent-seeking
sovereignty
state
state of nature
totalitarian systems
United Nations (UN)
vested interests

SUGGESTED READINGS

Cornelius, Wayne, et al., eds. *Controlling Immigration: A Global Perspective.* Stanford, CA: Stanford University Press, 1995.

Dalton, Russell, and Doh Chull Shin, eds. *Citizens, Democracy, and Markets Around the Pacific Rim.* Oxford: Oxford University Press, 2006.

Diamond, Larry, ed. *Developing Democracy: Towards Consolidation.* Baltimore: Johns Hopkins University Press, 1999.

Horowitz, Donald. *Ethnic Groups in Conflict.* Berkeley: University of California Press, 1985.

Huntington, Samuel. *The Third Wave: Democratization in the Late Twentieth Century.* Norman: University of Oklahoma Press, 1991.

———. *The Clash of Civilizations and the Remaking of World Order.* New York: Simon & Schuster, 1996.

Lijphart, Arend. *Patterns of Democracy.* New Haven, CT: Yale University Press, 1999.

Linz, Juan, and Alfred Stepan, eds. *Problems of Democratic Transitions and Consolidation.* Baltimore: Johns Hopkins University Press, 1996.

Przeworski, Adam, et al. *Democracy and Development: Political Institutions and Well-Being in the World, 1950–1990.* New York: Cambridge University Press, 2000.

Putnam, Robert. *Making Democracy Work: Civic Traditions in Modern Italy.* Princeton, NJ: Princeton University Press, 1993.

Sachs, Jeffrey. *The End of Poverty: Economic Possibilities for Our Time.* New York: Penguin, 2005.

United Nations. *World Development Report.* New York: Oxford University Press, annual editions.

Weiner, Myron. *The Global Migration Crisis: Challenge to States and to Human Rights.* New York: HarperCollins, 1995.

Zakaria, Fareed. *The Future of Freedom: Illiberal Democracy at Home and Abroad.* New York: Norton, 2003.

ENDNOTES

1. Thomas Hobbes, *Leviathan,* ed. C. B. Macpherson (New York: Penguin, 1968), 186.
2. J. J. Rousseau, *Second Discourse on Inequality, The First and Second Discourses* (New York: St. Martin's Press, 1964), 109–10.
3. Martin Greenberg and Mark Tier, *Visions of Liberty* (New York: Baen Publishers, 2004).
4. See, for example, Fareed Zakaria, *The Future of Freedom: Illiberal Democracy at Home and Abroad* (New York: Norton, 2003).
5. See, for example, Douglas North, *Institutions, Institutional Change, and Economic Performance* (Cambridge: Cambridge University Press, 1990); Mancur Olson, "The New Institutional Economics: The Collective Choice Approach to Economic Development," in *Institutions and Economic Development,* ed. C. Clague (Baltimore: Johns Hopkins University Press, 1997); S. Knack and P. Keefer, "Institutions and Economic Performance," *Economics and Politics* 7 (1995): 207–29.
6. The Vatican is not a member of the UN but maintains a permanent observer mission at the UN headquarters. Taiwan was expelled from the UN in 1971 to accommodate mainland China (the People's Republic).
7. Max Weber, *Economy and Society,* ed. Guenther Roth and Claus Wittich (Berkeley: University of California Press, 1978), 389.
8. Even before the end of the Cold War, ethnic autonomy movements in parts of old countries—such as the United Kingdom (the Scots and Welsh) and Canada (the Quebecois)—sought to break free or achieve greater autonomy.
9. Stephen Castles and Mark J. Miller, *The Age of Migration: International Population Movements in the Modern World* (New York: Guilford, 1994).
10. Erik V. Gunnemark, *Countries, Peoples, and Their Languages: The Geolinguistic Handbook* (Gothenburg: Lanstryckeriet, 1991).
11. United Nations Development Program, *Human Development Report 2005* (New York: United Nations, 2005). See also www.undp.org for additional data and interactive presentations.

12. The per capita *gross national product (GDP)* is the total economic output per person, corrected for exports and imports. Rather than the traditional measures computed according to the exchange rates of the national currencies, the *purchasing power parity (ppp)* index takes into account differences in price levels from one country to another. Most analyses assume that the GDP/ppp statistics are more comparable measures of living conditions. The income gap increases, however, if one uses the traditional exchange-rate measure of GDP.

13. Hania Zlotnik, "Statement to the Thirty-Eighth Session of the Commission on Population and Development," April 4, 2005 (www.un.org/esa/population/cpd/Statement_HZ_open.pdf).

14. Amartya Sen, "Population: Delusion and Reality," *New York Review of Books,* 22 September 1994, 62ff.

15. World Bank, *World Development Report, 1998–1999* (New York: Oxford University Press, 1999).

16. Sen, "Population: Delusion and Reality."

17. Regina Axelrod, David Downie, and Norman Vig, eds., *The Global Environment: Institutions, Law, and Policy* (Washington, D.C.: CQ Press, 2004); Yale Center for Environmental Law and Policy and Center for International Earth Science Information Network, *2005 Environmental Sustainability Index: Benchmarking National Environmental Stewardship* (New Haven, CT: Yale University, 2005) (www.yale.edu/esi/).

18. While many countries became formally democratic in these years, most of them quickly lapsed into authoritarianism. Many of these would-be democracies failed in their first decade; another "reverse wave" in the 1960s and early 1970s swept away some older democracies (Chile, Greece, and Uruguay, for example) as well.

19. Samuel Huntington, *The Third Wave: Democratization in the Late Twentieth Century* (Norman: University of Oklahoma Press, 1991).

20. Freedom House, *Freedom in the World 2004* (Washington, D.C.: Freedom House, 2005) (www.freedomhouse.org).

21. Seymour Martin Lipset, "Some Social Requisites of Democracy," *American Political Science Review 53* (September 1959): 69–105; Larry Diamond, "Economic Development and Democracy Reconsidered," in *Reexamining Democracy,* ed. G. Marks and L. Diamond (Newbury Park, CA: Sage, 1992); Tatu Vanhanen, *Prospects of Democracy* (New York: Routledge, 1997); Adam Przeworski et al., *Democracy and Development: Political Institutions and Well-Being in the World, 1950–1990* (New York: Cambridge University Press, 2000).

22. See United Nations Development Program, *Human Development Report 2005* (New York: United Nations, 2005) (http://hdr.undp.org/reports/global/2005/), Tables 25–30, and associated discussion.

23. Many of these issues are addressed by the United Nations' Millennium Development Goals. Visit the UN Web site (www.un.org/millenniumgoals/) or see United Nations, *Millennium Development Goals Report 2005* (New York: United Nations, 2005) (http://unstats.un.org/unsd/mi/pdf/MDGBook.pdf).

Comparing Political Systems

WHY WE COMPARE

The great French interpreter of American democracy, Alexis de Tocqueville, while traveling in America in the 1830s, wrote to a friend explaining how his own ideas about French institutions and culture entered into his writing of *Democracy in America*. Tocqueville wrote: "Although I very rarely spoke of France in my book, I did not write one page of it without having her, so to speak, before my eyes."[1] Tocqueville taught us that the only way we can fully understand our own political system is by comparing it to others. Comparing our experience with that of other countries deepens our understanding of our own politics and permits us to see a wider range of alternatives. It illuminates the virtues and shortcomings of our own political life. By taking us beyond our familiar arrangements and assumptions, comparative analysis helps expand our awareness of the potentials, for better or worse, of politics.

On the comparative method, Tocqueville offered this comment: "Without comparisons to make, the mind does not know how to proceed."[2] Tocqueville was telling us that comparison is fundamental to all human thought. It is the methodological core of the humanistic and scientific methods, including the scientific study of politics. Comparative analysis helps us develop and test explanations and theories of how political processes work or when political change occurs. The goals of the comparative methods used by political scientists are similar to those used in more exact sciences such as physics. But political scientists often cannot design experiments, a major path to knowledge in many natural sciences. We cannot always control and manipulate political arrangements and observe the consequences. We are especially limited when dealing with large-scale events that drastically affect many people. For example, researchers cannot and would not want to start a war or a social revolution to study its effects.

BOX 2.1 ARISTOTLE'S LIBRARY

There is historical evidence that Aristotle had accumulated a library of more than 150 studies of the political systems of the Mediterranean world of 400 to 300 BC. Many of these had probably been researched and written by his disciples.

While only the Athenian constitution survives of this library of Aristotelian polities, it is evident from the references to such studies that do survive that Aristotle was concerned with sampling the variety of political systems then in existence, including the "barbarian" (Third World?) countries, such as Libya, Etruria, and Rome: "[T]he references in ancient authorities give us the names of some 70 or more of the states described in the compilation of 'polities.' They range from Sinope, on the Black Sea, to Cyrene in North Africa; they extend from Marseilles in the Western Mediterranean to Crete, Rhodes, and Cyprus in the East. Aristotle thus included colonial constitutions as well as those of metropolitan states. His descriptions embraced states on the Aegean, Ionian, and Tyrrhenian Seas, and the three continents of Europe, Asia, and Africa."

Source: Ernest Barker, ed., *The Politics of Aristotle* (London: Oxford University Press, 1977), 386.

We can, however, use the comparative method to describe the political events and institutions found in different societies and to identify their causes and consequences. More than two thousand years ago, Aristotle in his *Politics* contrasted the economies and social structures of Greek city-states in an effort to determine how social and economic environments affected political institutions and policies (see Box 2.1). More contemporary political scientists also try to explain differences between the processes and performance of political systems. They compare two-party democracies with multiparty democracies, parliamentary with presidential regimes, poor countries with rich countries, and elections in new party systems with those in established democracies. These and many other comparisons have greatly enriched our understanding of politics.

HOW WE COMPARE

We study politics in several different ways: we describe it, we seek to explain it, and sometimes we try to predict it. These are all parts of the scientific process, though as we move from description to explanation and prediction, our task gets progressively harder. Each of these tasks may use the comparative method. The first stage in the study of politics is description. If we cannot describe a political process or event, we cannot really hope to understand or explain it, much less predict what might happen next or in similar situations.

Description may sound easy and straightforward enough, but often it is not. In order to describe a political event or institution well, we need to use words and phrases that our audience can understand clearly and in the same way, and which they can apply broadly. In order to describe politics, we thus need a set of concepts, a **conceptual framework**, which is clearly defined and well-understood. In other words, we want our concepts to be **intersubjective** (understood and used in the same way by different subjects) and **general**. The easier our set of concepts is to understand, and the more broadly it can be applied, the more helpful it is to the study of politics. Conceptual frameworks are not generally right or wrong, but they may be more or less useful to the task at hand.

HOW WE EXPLAIN AND PREDICT

Once we are able to describe politics with the help of the conceptual framework that we choose, the next task is to explain it. Explanation typically means answering "why?" questions. More precisely, explaining political phenomena means identifying causal relationships among them, pointing out one phenomenon as the cause or consequence of another.[3] It is often important to be able to go beyond description to explanation. For example, we might be interested in the relationship between democracy and international peace (see Box 2.2). Description can tell us that in the contemporary world, peace and democracy tend to go together. Democratic states are mostly (though not always) peaceful, and many peaceful states are democracies. But we do not fully understand why this is so. Are democratic states more peaceful because they are democratic, are they democratic because they are peaceful, or are they perhaps both peaceful and democratic because they are more prosperous than other states, or because they have market economies, or because their citizens have values (a political culture) that support both democracy and peace? A good explanation helps us find the right answer to such questions. Ideally, we want to put many political relationships in causal terms, so we can say that one political feature is the cause of another, and the latter is an effect of the former.

Theories are precisely formulated and well-supported statements about causal relationships among general classes of political events—for example, about the causes of democracy, war, election victories, or welfare policies. Theories need to be testable, and a good theory is one that holds up after continued tests, preferably after a series of concerted efforts to prove it wrong. **Hypotheses** are causal explanations that have not yet been proven. In other words, they are candidate theories that have not yet been adequately tested or confirmed. Yet scientific theories are always tentative; they are subject to modification or falsification at any time as our knowledge improves. Theories are often modified and made more precise as we test them again and again with better and better data. A well-tested theory allows us to explain confidently what happens in specific cases or sets of cases—for example, that two countries have a peaceful relationship because they are democracies, or perhaps the other way around (see again Box 2.2).

Political scientists often develop theories as they seek to understand a puzzling case or an interesting difference between two or three political

> ## BOX 2.2 STATISTICAL METHODS

A popular contemporary research program known as *democratic peace research* illustrates the pros and cons of statistical and case-study research. It has been of primary interest to international relations scholars, who took the diplomatic history of the Cold War period and asked whether democratic countries are more peaceful in their foreign policy than authoritarian and nondemocratic ones. Many scholars in the democratic peace research group took the statistical route. They counted each year of interaction between two states as one case. With roughly half a century of diplomatic history involving a state system of 100 countries or more, they had a very large number of cases, even after eliminating the many irrelevant cases of countries that never, or rarely, had any relations with one another. Political scientists Andrew Bennett and Alexander George drew these conclusions after surveying the statistical research:

> Statistical methods achieved important advances on the issue of whether a non-spurious interdemocratic peace exists. A fairly strong though not unanimous consensus emerged that: (1) democracies are not less war-prone in general; (2) they have very rarely if ever fought one another; (3) this pattern of an interdemocratic peace applies to both war and conflicts short of war; (4) states in transition to democracy are more war-prone than established democracies; and (5) these correlations were not spuriously brought about by the most obvious alternative explanations.

Although much was learned from the statistical studies, they were not as successful at answering "why" questions. Case studies make clinical depth possible, revealing causal interconnections in individual cases. Careful repetition of these causal tracings from case to case strengthens confidence in these relationships. Thus, Bennett and George concluded that the best research strategy uses statistical and case study methods together, with each method having its own strengths.

Source: Andrew Bennett and Alexander George, "An Alliance of Statistical and Case Study Methods: Research on the Interdemocratic Peace," APSA-CP: *Newsletter of the APSA Organized Section in Comparative Politics* 9 no. 1 (1998): 6.

systems. For example, Tocqueville was intrigued by the fact that democracy was so widely supported in the United States, while it was fiercely contested in his native France. Researchers also often generate hypotheses about the causes and consequences of political change by comparing countries at different historical periods. In his other famous study, Tocqueville contributed to a general theory of revolution by comparing prerevolutionary and postrevolutionary France.[4] Theda Skocpol, on the other hand, based her explanation of the causes of revolution on a comparison of the "old regimes" of France, Russia, and China with their revolutionary and postrevolutionary regimes.[5]

But for an explanatory hypothesis to become a useful theory, we generally want it to explain not only the case(s) on which it was based, but also other cases (revolutions, wars, elections, etc.) that fall into the same set. Hypotheses are therefore tested against many different kinds of political **data**. Researchers in political science distinguish between studies based on large numbers (large *n*) and small numbers (small *n*) of cases or observations. In large-*n* studies, particularly when the number of cases is beyond twenty or thirty, it is often possible and helpful to use statistical analysis. Such studies are usually referred to as *statistical studies*; small-*n* studies are usually called *case studies*. Many small-*n* studies examine only a single case, whereas others compare two or three or four (or occasionally more).

Statistical analysis enables us to consider possible alternative causes at the same time, accepting some and rejecting others. Large-*n* studies often have a sufficient number and variety of cases to enable the researcher to examine the relation among the variables associated with each case. **Variables** are the features on which our cases differ—for example, "religious heritage: Christian, Muslim, or Buddhist" or "rank in the UN Quality of Life index," or "income per capita." Large-*n* statistical studies thus allow us to be more certain and precise in our explanations. On the other hand, we need the depth that case studies provide. Small-*n* studies permit investigators to go deeply into a case, identify the particularities of it, get the clinical details, and examine each link in the causal process. They encourage us to formulate insightful hypotheses for statistical testing in the first place. They allow us to trace the nature of the cause-and-effect relations (sometimes called "causal mechanisms") better than large-*n* studies. In this manner, political scientists may come to know not only whether democracies are more peaceful than dictatorships, but more precisely why democratic leaders behave in the way that they do. Most researchers recognize that these methods are complementary (see again Box 2.2).

The final and most challenging task in the scientific process is prediction. Prediction is testing hypotheses against data that were not known by the researchers who developed these explanations, often because the events had not yet happened. It is generally far more difficult to formulate predictions about events that have not yet happened than to explain events whose outcome we already know. This is both because we never know whether we have captured all the relevant factors that might affect the future and because the world itself may change as we try to understand it. Often political actors learn from the mistakes of the past, so that the same patterns do not necessarily repeat themselves. Yet political scientists have made improvements in the act of prediction as well as in description and explanation. Many researchers have, for example, observed the close relationship between economic conditions and the results of U.S. presidential elections. When economic conditions are good (low inflation and unemployment, high growth), the candidate of the incumbent party tends to win; when times are bad, the opposition party tends to prevail. This theory is sufficiently strong that it allows researchers to make fairly precise and reliable predictions about the electoral result after observing economic conditions a few months before the election. Yet sometimes the predictions get it wrong, as they did in the 2000 presidential election, when most researchers predicted that Democratic candidate Al Gore would win handily. Such failed predictions imply the need to revise the theory to take additional factors into account. Successful predictions greatly increase our confidence in a theory, as well as being interesting for their own sake or to guide policy.

An example may suggest how you might go about theorizing in comparative politics, going beyond "just mastering the facts." It is well known that rich countries are more likely to be democracies than are poor countries; democracy and economic development are strongly associated. But there are many possible reasons for this association. Some persons have suggested that this relationship comes about because democracy encourages education and economic development. Others have argued that as countries develop economically, their new middle classes or their emerging working class are more likely to demand democratization. Yet others have seen that both democracy and economic development are commonly found in some regions of the world, such as Western Europe, while both tend to be scarce in the Middle East and Africa. This fact suggests that certain cultures may encourage or discourage both of them.

Yet the causal nature of this association is important, for reasons of both science and policy. Fostering economic development and securing democracy are two of the significant political challenges that we discussed in Chapter 1. Let us therefore consider how Adam Przeworski and his associates examined the full experience of democracies, nondemocracies, and transitions between them in the world between 1950 and 1990.[6] Their statistical analysis led them to conclude that the explanation for the association between democracy and prosperity did not lie in regional effects or in superior economic growth under democracy. Moreover, countries at any level of development seemed able to introduce democracy, although economically developed countries were somewhat more likely to do so. Instead, Przeworski and his associates argue that the key to the relationship lies in the greater fragility of democracies in economically poor societies. Democracy can easily be introduced in poor societies with less educated populations, but it is often replaced by some kind of dictatorship. In rich countries, on the other hand, democracy tends to survive once it has been introduced. These democratic failures in poor countries produce a strong association between development and democracy. We still need to understand exactly why democracy is more precarious in less developed societies, but we are making progress in understanding the causal relationship between development and democracy, as well as the failures of democratization in poor countries.

Comparative analysis is a powerful and versatile tool. It enhances our ability to describe and understand political processes and political change in any country. The comparative approach also stimulates us to form general theories of political relationships. It encourages and enables us to test our political theories by confronting them with the experience of many institutions and settings.

POLITICAL SYSTEMS: ENVIRONMENT AND INTERDEPENDENCE

In this text we compare political processes with a systems framework. Specifically, we do that with the help of a structural-functional framework. To do so, we need to discuss three general concepts that we use throughout this book: (1) system, (2) structure, and (3) function. A **system**, as we defined it in Chapter 1, is an object with interdependent parts, acting within a setting or an **environment**. The **political system** is a set of institutions and agencies concerned with formulating and implementing the collective goals of a society or of groups within it. **Governments** are the policymaking parts of political systems. The decisions of governments are normally backed up by legitimate coercion, and governments can thus typically compel their citizens to comply with their decisions. (We discuss legitimacy at greater length in Chapter 3.)

Figure 2.1 tells us that a political system exists in both an international environment and a domestic environment. It is molded by these environments and it tries to mold them. The system receives **inputs** from these environments.

FIGURE 2.1
The Political System and Its Environments
The political system of the United States interacts with domestic and international environments.

Its policymakers attempt to shape them through its **outputs**. In the figure, which is quite schematic and simple, we use the United States as the central actor. We include other countries as our environmental examples—Russia, China, Britain, Germany, Japan, Mexico, and Iran.

Exchanges among countries may vary in many ways. For example, they may be "dense" or "sparse." U.S.–Canadian relations exemplify the dense end of the continuum in that they affect many of the citizens of these countries in significant ways, while U.S.–Nepalese relations are far sparser.

Relationships among political systems may be of many different kinds. The United States has substantial trade relations with some countries and relatively little trade with others. Some countries have an excess of imports over exports, whereas others have an excess of exports over imports. Military exchanges and support with such countries as the NATO nations, Japan, South Korea, Israel, and Saudi Arabia have been of significant importance to the United States.

The interdependence of countries—the volume and value of imports and exports, transfers of capital, international communication, and the extent of foreign travel and immigration—has increased enormously in the last decades. This increase is often called **globalization**. We might represent this process as a thickening of the input and output arrows between the United States and other countries in Figure 2.1. Fluctuations in this flow of international transactions and traffic attributable to depression, inflation, protective tariffs, international terrorism, war, and the like may wreak havoc with the economies of the countries affected.

The interaction of a political system with its domestic environment—the economic and social systems and the political culture of its citizens—is also depicted in Figure 2.1. We can illustrate this interaction in the U.S. case by the rise of the "high-tech information-based economy." The composition of the U.S. labor force, and consequently its citizenry, has changed dramatically in the last century. Agriculture has declined to under 2 percent of the gainfully employed. Employment in heavy extractive and manufacturing industries has decreased substantially. Newer, high-technology occupations, the professions, and the service occupations have increased sharply as proportions of the labor force. The last half century has also witnessed significant improvements in the educational level of the U.S. population. Many more young people complete high school and go on to college. Moreover, people move more easily from one region to another. These and other changes in the U.S. social structure have altered the challenges facing the U.S. system and the resources available to meet these challenges.

These changes in the economy and the citizenry are associated with changes in American **political culture**. (Political culture—the attitudes, beliefs, and values of the people in a country—is discussed at more length in Chapter 3.) People want different things from politics. For example, an educated and culturally sophisticated society is more concerned with quality of life, the beauty and healthfulness of the environment, and similar issues.

At the same time, the globalization of the economy leads to demands from firms and workers in some industries for protection of their jobs. Natural disasters, such as the hurricane that devastated New Orleans in 2005, spur calls for the national government to lead reconstruction. Man-made disasters, such as the huge oil spill that contaminated the beaches of the Gulf of Mexico in 2010, also stimulate calls for government action to limit the environmental and economic damages and prevent future disasters. Local issues are seen as the responsibility of the entire country. People live longer. An aging population demands that governments do more to help with medical benefits. In input/output terms, socioeconomic changes transform the political demands of the electorate and the kinds of policies that it supports.

Thus, a new pattern of society results in different policy outputs, different kinds and levels of taxation, changes in regulatory patterns, and changes in welfare expenditures. The advantage of the system-environment approach is that it directs our attention to the **interdependence** of what happens between and within countries. It provides us with a vocabulary to describe, compare, and explain these interacting events.

If we are to make sound judgments in politics, we need to be able to place political systems in their domestic and international environments. We need to recognize how these environments both set limits on and provide opportunities for political choices. This approach keeps us from reaching quick and biased political judgments. If a country is poor in natural resources and lacks the capabilities necessary to exploit what it has, we cannot fault it for having a low industrial output or poor educational and social services. Each country chapter in the second half of this book begins by discussing the current policy challenges facing the country and its social and economic environment.

POLITICAL SYSTEMS: STRUCTURES AND FUNCTIONS

Governments do many things, from establishing and operating school systems, to maintaining public order, to fighting wars. In order to carry on these disparate activities, governments have specialized **structures** (which we may also refer to as *institutions* or *agencies*), such as parliaments, bureaucracies, administrative agencies, and courts. These structures perform **functions**, which in turn enable the government to formulate, implement, and enforce its policies. The policies reflect the goals; the agencies provide the means to achieve them.

Figure 2.2 locates six types of political structures—political parties, interest groups, legislatures, executives, bureaucracies, and courts—within the political system. These are formal organizations engaged in political activities. They exist in most contemporary political systems. This list is not exhaustive. Some structures, such as ruling military councils or governing royal families, are found in only a few countries. Some, such as Iran's Council of Guardians, are unique to one country's political system.

We might think that if we understand how such structures work in one political system, we can apply this insight to any other system. Unfortunately, that is not always the case. The sixfold classification in Figure 2.2 will not carry us very far in comparing political systems with each other. The problem is that similar structures may have very different functions across political

FIGURE 2.2
The Political System and Its Structures
Six types of political structures perform functions in the Japanese political system.

systems. For example, Britain and China have all six types of political structures. However, these institutions are organized differently in the two countries. More important, they function in dramatically different ways.

The political executive in Britain consists of the prime minister and the Cabinet, which includes the heads of major departments and agencies. These officials are usually selected from among the members of Parliament. There is a similar structure in China, called the State Council, headed by a premier and consisting of the various ministers and ministerial commissions. But while the British prime minister and Cabinet have substantial policymaking power, the State Council in China is closely supervised by the general secretary of the Communist Party, the Politburo, and the Central Committee of the party, and has far less influence over public policy.

Both Britain and China have legislative bodies—the House of Commons in Britain and the National People's Congress in China. Their members debate and vote on prospective public policies. But while the House of Commons is a key institution in the British policymaking process, the Chinese Congress meets for only brief periods, ratifying decisions made mainly by the Communist Party authorities. Usually, the Chinese delegates do not even consider alternative policies.

There are even larger differences between political parties in the two countries. Britain has a competitive party system. The majority members in the House of Commons and the Cabinet are constantly confronted by an opposition party or parties, competing for public support. They look forward to the next election when they may unseat the incumbent majority, as happened in 1997, when the Labour Party replaced the Conservatives in government, and in 2010 when the Labour Party was in turn replaced by a coalition of Conservatives and Liberal Democrats. In China, the Communist Party controls the whole political process. There are no other political parties. The principal decisions are made within the Communist Party. The governmental agencies simply implement these policies.

Thus, an institution-by-institution comparison of British and Chinese politics that did not spell out the functions that the various agencies perform would not bring us far toward understanding the important differences in the politics of these two countries. Each country study in this book therefore includes a figure that shows how some of the major structures select and control each other. Another figure illustrates how they fit into the policymaking process.

Figure 2.3 shows the functions of the political process that we can use to compare all political systems. The center of Figure 2.3 under the heading

FIGURE 2.3
The Political System and Its Functions
System, process and policy functions convert inputs into outputs.

"process functions" lists the distinctive activities necessary for policy to be made and implemented in any kind of political system. (We discuss each concept in greater detail in Chapters 4, 5, and 6.) We call these *process functions* because they play a direct and necessary role in the process of making policy.

- **Interest articulation** involves individuals and groups expressing their needs and demands.
- **Interest aggregation** combines different demands into policy proposals backed by significant political resources.
- **Policymaking** is deciding which policy proposals become authoritative rules.
- **Policy implementation** is carrying out and enforcing public policies; **policy adjudication** is settling disputes about their application.

Before policy can be decided, some individuals and groups in the government or the society must decide what they want and hope to get from politics. The political process begins as these interests are expressed or articulated. The many arrows on the left of the figure show these initial expressions. To be effective, however, these demands must be combined (aggregated) into policy alternatives—such as lower taxes or more social security benefits—for which substantial political support can be mobilized. Thus, the arrows on the left are consolidated as the process moves from interest articulation to interest aggregation. Governments then consider alternative policies and choose between them. Their policy decisions must then be enforced and implemented, and if they are challenged, there must be some process of adjudication. Any policy may affect several different aspects of society, as reflected in the three arrows for the implementation phase.

These process functions are performed by such political structures as parties, legislatures, political executives, bureaucracies, and courts. The **structural-functional approach** stresses two points. One is that in *different countries, the same structure may perform different functions*. A second is that while a particular institution, such as a legislature, may specialize in a particular function, such as policymaking, *institutions often do not have a monopoly on any one function*. Presidents and governors may share in the policymaking function (and in the extreme case, each may be a veto power), as may the higher courts (especially in states that feature judicial review of statutes for their constitutionality).

The three functions listed at the top of Figure 2.3—socialization, recruitment, and communication—do not directly concern the making and implementation of public policy but are of fundamental importance to the political system. We refer to them as **system functions**. In the long run, they help determine whether the system will be maintained or changed. For example, will the military be able to maintain its dominance of policymaking, or will it be replaced by competitive parties and a legislature? Will a sense of national community persist, or will it be eroded by new experiences?

The arrows leading from these three functions to all parts of the political process suggest their crucial role in underpinning and permeating the political process.

- **Political socialization** involves families, schools, communications media, churches, and all the various political structures that develop, reinforce, and transform the political culture, the attitudes of political significance in the society (see Chapter 3).
- **Political recruitment** refers to the selection of people for political activity and government offices. In a democracy, competitive elections play a major role in political recruitment. In authoritarian systems, recruitment may be dominated by a single party, as in China, or by unelected religious leaders, as in Iran.
- **Political communication** refers to the flow of information through the society and the various structures that make up the political system. Gaining control over information is a key goal of most authoritarian rulers, as shown in the elaborate efforts of Chinese leaders to control content on the Internet.

Understanding the performance of the system functions is essential to understanding how political systems respond to the great contemporary challenges of building community, fostering economic development, and securing democracy that we discussed in Chapter 1.

The right side of Figure 2.3 illustrates the consequences of the policy process. The outputs are the ways in which policy decisions affect the society, the economy, and the culture. They include various forms of **extraction** of resources in the form of taxes and the like, **regulation** of behavior, and **distribution** of benefits and services to various groups in the population. The **outcomes** of all these political activities reflect the way the policies interact with the domestic and international environments. Sometimes, these outcomes are the desired results of public policies. But the complexities of policy and society sometimes result in unintended consequences. Among these may be new demands for legislation or administrative action, or increases or decreases in the support given to the political system and incumbent officeholders. We shall return to the policy level after providing an example of a structural-functional comparison. The functional concepts shown in Figure 2.3 describe the activities carried on in any society regardless of how its political system is organized or what kinds of policies it produces. Using these functional categories, we can determine how institutions in different countries combine in making and implementing public policy.

AN ILLUSTRATIVE COMPARISON: REGIME CHANGE IN RUSSIA

Figures 2.4 and 2.5[7] offer a simplified graphic comparison of structures and functions in Russia before and after the breakdown of communist rule in the Soviet Union. They use our comparative method to illustrate the way a

	Social institutions	Organized interest groups	Independent parties	Communist Party	Parliament	Mass media	Bureaucracy	General Secretary/ President
Socialization								
Recruitment								
Communication								
Interest articulation								
Interest aggregation								
Policymaking								
Policy implementation								
Policy adjudication								

Heavily engaged in performing this function

Involved in performing this function somewhat

Involved in performing this function only a little or not at all

FIGURE 2.4
The Soviet Political System in 1985
The Communist Party and the state bureaucracy dominated all functions in the Soviet Union.

political regime changed significantly in a short period of time. The point here is to illustrate how we can use the tools of political analysis, rather than provide the details of the Russian case.

The figures depict the changes in the functioning of the major structures of the political system brought about by the collapse of communism. These include two revolutionary changes. One is the end of the single-party political system dominated by the Communist Party of the Soviet Union, which held together the vast, multinational Soviet state. The other is the dissolution of the Soviet Union itself into its fifteen member republics. As a result of these two remarkable events, Russia, the republic that was the core republic of the old union, became an independent noncommunist state.

Figure 2.4 therefore shows how the basic functions of the political system were performed in 1985, when the Soviet Union was a communist state. The Communist Party was the dominant political institution, overseeing schools and media, the arts and public organizations, the economy, and the courts through a massive state bureaucracy. For this reason, all the cells of the chart in the column marked "Communist Party" are shaded dark, as are the cells under the column marked "Bureaucracy." Although social institutions—such

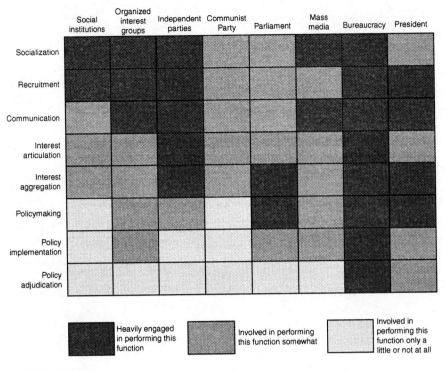

	Social institutions	Organized interest groups	Independent parties	Communist Party	Parliament	Mass media	Bureaucracy	President
Socialization								
Recruitment								
Communication								
Interest articulation								
Interest aggregation								
Policymaking								
Policy implementation								
Policy adjudication								

Heavily engaged in performing this function

Involved in performing this function somewhat

Involved in performing this function only a little or not at all

FIGURE 2.5
The Russian Political System in 2000
Many more structures played important roles in policymaking in Russia in 2000.

as the family, workplace, arts, and hobby groups—exercised some influence over such system-level functions as socialization, recruitment, and communication, it was the Communist Party and the state bureaucracy that dominated process-level functions. Under their tutelage, the mass media in 1985 were a key agent of communist political socialization and communication. Parliament was a compliant instrument for ratifying decisions made by the party and bureaucracy. No other parties were allowed by law in addition to the Communist Party. The only organized interest groups were those authorized by the party. The party's general secretary was the most powerful official in the country.

By 2000, the political system had undergone fundamental changes, as shown in Figure 2.5. Many more structures played a role in the political process, as is immediately evident by the larger number of cells that are heavily shaded. In particular, Parliament, independent political parties, and regional governments had all acquired important new policymaking powers. The freedom enjoyed by ordinary citizens to articulate their interests and to organize to advance them had expanded enormously. The Communist Party, no longer an official or monopolistic party, had declined substantially in power and was reduced to the role of an opposition party in the parliamentary game. The lighter shading for the Communist Party in Figure 2.5 shows its diminished influence. The state bureaucracy remained an important element in the political system, although adapting itself to the new trend of movement toward a market economy by adopting quasi-commercial forms.

The presidency has been a dominant policymaking institution in the new Russia, as shown in Figure 2.5. The Parliament, although fairly representative of the diversity of opinion in the country, was frustrated in its policymaking and oversight roles by the inertia of the vast state bureaucracy, by its inability to compel compliance with its laws, by its weak links with the voters, and by the president's political power. Nevertheless, Parliament played a much greater role than before in aggregating interests and policymaking, as demonstrated by a comparison of Figures 2.4 and 2.5.

An updating of Figure 2.5 would show the eclipse of parties, Parliament, and the mass media by the president and the bureaucracy after 2000. This movement in a more authoritarian direction, although not back to communism, would be shown by fewer dark-shaded columns in the middle of the figure.

The brief comparisons presented here illustrate the use of the structural-functional approach. This approach enables us to examine how the same functions are performed in different countries, or in the same country at two different points in time. Similarly, we may examine changes in the functions performed by the same structures over time or across different political systems. In a country undergoing as rapid and dramatic a transition as Russia in the 1990s, this framework demonstrates substantial changes in the distribution of power.

Neither the analysis of structures nor that of functions is complete without the other. A structural analysis tells us the number of political parties, or the organization of the legislature. It describes how the executive branch, the courts, the bureaucracy, the mass media, interest groups, and other structures of a political system are set up and by what rules or standards they operate. A functional analysis tells us how these institutions and organizations interact to produce and implement policies. This kind of analysis is especially essential when we are comparing very different kinds of political systems.

The country chapters of this book do not present formal structural-functional sketches like Figures 2.4 and 2.5. But at the core of each chapter is a set of discussions of these functions and the structures that perform them. We can see these in the section headings of the country studies and in the analytic guide at the beginning of this book. These tools make it possible to compare the workings of the very different political systems in this book.

THE POLICY LEVEL: PERFORMANCE, OUTCOME, AND EVALUATION

Now, what differences do these variations in political structures and functions make for the citizens of the different states that we analyze? This question directs our attention to the **policy level** of the political system. We call the outputs of a political system—its extractions, distributions, regulations, and symbolic acts—its *policy performance*. We have to distinguish among these efforts, the things a government does, and the actual outcome of these efforts. Governments may spend equal amounts on education and health, or defense, but with different consequences. Government efficiency or corruption plays a role in the effectiveness of politics. But so do the underlying cultural, economic, and technological conditions.

Americans spend more per capita on education than any other people in the world. But their children perform worse in some subjects, such as mathematics, than do children in some other countries that spend substantially less. The United States spent enormous sums and many lives on the war in Vietnam in the 1960s and 1970s, as did the Soviet Union on its war in Afghanistan in the 1980s. Yet both countries were held at bay by far less well-equipped armed forces or guerrilla groups resolved to resist at all costs. Because of these costly failures, the United States and the Soviet Union were weakened internally. In the latter case, the costs of the war in Afghanistan contributed directly to the downfall of the communist regime. The outcome of public policy is thus never wholly in the hands of the people and their leaders. Legislatures may vote to wage a military conflict, but neither their votes nor the promises of political leaders can guarantee success. Conditions in the internal environment, conditions and events in the larger external world, and simple chance may frustrate the most thoughtfully crafted programs and plans. Each country study in this book concludes with a discussion of the country's performance, describing both policies and their outcomes.

Finally, we must step even further back to evaluate the politics of different systems. Evaluation is complex because people value different things and put different emphases on what they value. We will refer to the different conditions, outputs, and outcomes that people may value as political "goods." In Chapter 7, we outline a typology of various kinds of political goals and political goods. These include goods associated with the system level, such as the stability or adaptability of political institutions, and goods associated with the process level, such as citizen participation in politics. Finally, we consider and describe goods associated with the policy level, such as welfare, security, fairness, and liberty. To evaluate what a political system is doing, we assess performance and outcomes in each of these areas. We must also be aware of how these broad outcomes affect specific individuals and groups in the society, which may often be overlooked if we simply consider national averages.

A particularly important problem of evaluation concerns building for the future as well as living today. The people of poor countries wish to survive and alleviate the suffering of today but also to improve their children's lot for tomorrow. The people of all countries, but especially rich ones, must deal with the costs to their children of polluted and depleted natural resources as the result of the thoughtless environmental policies of the past.

REVIEW QUESTIONS

1. How do the main elements in the environment of a political system affect the way it performs?
2. Why are we unable to compare political systems simply by describing the different structures we find in them?
3. What are the functions performed in all political systems as policies are made?
4. What is the difference between outputs and outcomes of policy?
5. How do we use theories to explain political events?

KEY TERMS

conceptual framework
data
distribution
environment
extraction
functions
general
globalization
governments
hypotheses
inputs
interdependence

interest aggregation
interest articulation
intersubjective
outcomes
outputs
policy adjudication
policy implementation
policy level
policymaking
political communication
political culture
political recruitment

political socialization
political system
process functions
regulation
structural-functional
 approach
structures
system
system functions
theories
variables

SUGGESTED READINGS

Brady, Henry E., and David Collier. *Rethinking Social Inquiry: Diverse Tools, Shared Standards*. Lanham, MD: Rowman and Littlefield, 2004.

Collier, David. "The Comparative Method," in *Political Science: The State of the Discipline II*, ed. Ada W. Finifter. Washington, D.C.: American Political Science Association, 1993.

Dogan, Mattei, and Dominique Pelassy. *How to Compare Nations: Strategies in Comparative Politics*. Chatham, NJ: Chatham House, 1990.

Goodin, Robert E., and Hans-Dieter Klingemann. *A New Handbook of Political Science*. New York: Oxford University Press, 1996 (Chapters 2 and 3, and Part 4).

King, Gary, Robert O. Keohane, and Sidney Verba. *Scientific Inference in Qualitative Research*. New York: Cambridge University Press, 1993.

Lichbach, Mark, and Alan Zuckerman. *Comparing Nations: Rationality, Culture, and Structure*. New York: Cambridge University Press, 1997.

Little, Daniel. *Varieties of Social Explanation: An Introduction to the Philosophy of Social Science*. Boulder, CO: Westview, 1991.

Przeworski, Adam, and Henry Teune. *The Logic of Comparative Social Inquiry*. New York: Wiley, 1970.

ENDNOTES

1. Alexis de Tocqueville to Louis de Kergolay, 18 October 1847, in *Alexis de Tocqueville: Selected Letters on Politics and Society*, ed. Roger Boesche (Berkeley: University of California Press, 1985), 191.

2. Alexis de Tocqueville to Ernest de Chabrol, 7 October 1831, in *Selected Letters*, 59.
3. For some related and alternative concepts of explanation, see Daniel Little, *Varieties of Social Explanation* (Boulder, CO: Westview, 1991).
4. Alexis de Tocqueville, *The Old Regime and the French Revolution*, trans. Stuart Gilbert (New York: Doubleday, 1955).
5. Theda Skocpol, *States and Social Revolutions* (New York: Cambridge University Press, 1979).
6. Adam Przeworski et al., *Democracy and Development: Political Institutions and Well-Being in the World, 1950–1990* (New York: Cambridge University Press, 2000).
7. Figures 2.4 and 2.5 and the text of this section were contributed by Thomas Remington.

Political Culture
and Political
Socialization

I f you have ever traveled to a foreign country, you were probably surprised
by how many of the normal things in your life were different there. The
food was different, people wore different clothes, houses were constructed
and furnished differently, and the pattern of social relations differed (for
instance, whether people talked to strangers or stood in queues). You were
observing how social norms shape what people eat, how they dress, how they
live, and maybe even on which side of the road they drive.

Similarly, each nation has its own political norms that influence how people
think about and react to politics. To understand the political tendencies in a
nation, we must begin with public attitudes toward politics and their role within
the political system—what we call a nation's *political culture*. Americans' strong
feelings of patriotism, the Japanese deference to political elites, and the French
proclivity for protest all illustrate how cultural norms shape politics. The way
political institutions function at least partially reflects the public's attitudes,
norms, and expectations. Thus, the English use their constitutional arrangements to sustain their liberty, while the same institutions were once used as a
means of repression in South Africa and Northern Ireland.

When a new regime forms, a supportive public can help develop the new
system, while the absence of public support may weaken the new system. The
content of the political culture has been a very important aspect of the transitions to democracy in the past two decades, as new democracies needed to
develop democratic orientations and behaviors among their citizens. It is hard
to sustain democracy without a nation of democrats.

Chapter 1 stated that one main goal of any government, and a special
challenge for a new government, is to create and maintain a political community. In part, this involves developing common structures and systems (such
as a single economy), common political institutions, and common political
processes. For the public, this involves developing common worldviews,

57

values, and expectations among the public that together comprise the nation's political culture. Thus, studying political culture partially explains how a political community is created and sustained.

In this chapter, we map the important parts of political culture. We then discuss political socialization: how individuals form their political attitudes and thus, collectively, how citizens form their political culture. We conclude by describing the major trends in political culture in world politics today.

MAPPING THE THREE LEVELS OF POLITICAL CULTURE

A nation's **political culture** includes its citizens' orientations at three levels: the political system, the political and policymaking process, and policy outputs and outcomes (Table 3.1). The *system* level involves how people view the values and organizations that comprise the political system. Do citizens identify with the nation and accept the general system of government? The *process* level includes expectations of the political rules and decision-making methods, and individuals' relationship to the government. The *policy* level deals with the public's policy expectations for the government. What should the policy goals of government be, and how are they to be achieved?

The System Level

Orientations toward the political system are important because they tap basic commitments to the polity and the nation. It is difficult for any political system to endure if it lacks the support of its citizens.

Feelings of national pride are considered an affective, emotional tie to a political system. National pride seems strongest in nations with long histories that have emphasized feelings of patriotism—the United States is a prime example (see Figure 3.1). Such a common sense of identity and national

---

TABLE 3.1

Political Culture

There are three levels of political culture, which tap different orientations toward politics.

Aspects of Political Culture	Examples
System	Pride in nation
	National identity
	Legitimacy of government
Process	Role of citizens
	Perceptions of political rights
Policy	Role of government
	Government policy priorities

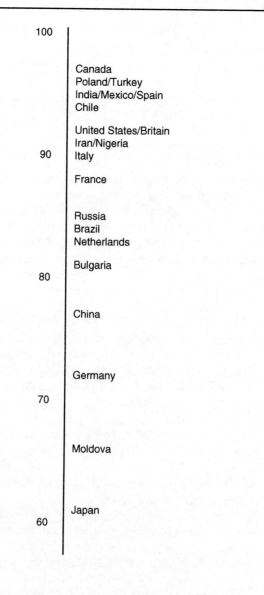

FIGURE 3.1
Be Proud
Feelings of National Pride Vary across Nations

Source: Selected nations from the 2005–2008 *World Values Survey* and the 2000–2002 *World Values Survey* for Nigeria. Figure entries are the percent "proud" and "very proud"; missing data are excluded from the calculation of percentages.

history often binds a people together in times of political strain. The figure indicates that high levels of pride exist in nations with very different political and economic systems, such as Vietnam, Canada, Poland, and Turkey. Large majorities in most countries are proud of their nations. In contrast, national pride is low in Japan and Germany, two nations that have avoided nationalist sentiments in reaction to World War II regimes and their excesses. And Russia's resurgence in the past decade has substantially improved levels of national pride from earlier surveys in the late 1990s and early 2000s, while Moldova's continuing struggles since independence are signaled by the weak sense of national pride among its citizens.

Feelings of popular **legitimacy** are another basis for a stable political system. Citizens may grant legitimacy to a government for different reasons.[1] In a traditional society, legitimacy may depend on the ruler's inheriting the throne or on the ruler's commitment to religious customs. In a modern democracy, the legitimacy of the authorities depends on their selection by voters in competitive elections and on the government's following constitutional procedures. Theocratic regimes, such as Iran, base their legitimacy on adherence to religious principles. In other political cultures, the leaders may base their claim to legitimacy on their special wisdom or ideology, which is typical for communist regimes or countries that emerged from recent national independence movements. Thus, legitimacy presumes an agreement on the broad form of government that defines the political system and thus the standards of legitimacy: monarchical rule, a tribal system, a communist order, or a democratic system. Based on these different principles, people in widely differing political systems can still express support for their political systems because they are using different standards of legitimacy.[2]

Whether legitimacy is based on tradition, religion, elections, or ideology, feelings of legitimacy reflect a basic understanding between citizens and political authorities. People obey the laws; in return, the government meets the obligations set by the terms of its legitimacy. As long as the government meets its obligations, the public is supposed to be supportive and act appropriately. If legitimacy is violated—the line of succession is broken, the constitution is subverted, or the ruling ideology is ignored—the government may expect resistance and perhaps rebellion. A political system and a government with high legitimacy are typically more effective in carrying out policies and are more likely to overcome hardships and reversals.

In systems with low legitimacy, people often resort to violence or extragovernmental actions to solve political disagreements. Legitimacy is lacking where the public disputes the boundaries of the political system (as in Northern Ireland or Kashmir), rejects the current arrangements for recruiting leaders and making policies (as when Ukrainians took to the streets in 2004 to 2005, demanding new democratic elections), or loses confidence that the leaders are fulfilling their part of the political bargain (as when the Thai opposition battled the government in 2010).

The Soviet Union disintegrated in the early 1990s because all three legitimacy problems appeared. After the communist ideology failed as a legitimizing force, there was little basis for a national political community without a common language or ethnicity. Similarly, the loss of confidence in the Communist Party as a political organization led many people to call for institutional reform. Finally, shortages of food and consumer goods caused people to lose faith in the government's short-term economic and political policies. Soviet President Mikhail Gorbachev failed in his efforts to deal with all three problems at the same time.

The Process Level

The second level of the political culture involves what the public expects of the political process. Whether you are English or Nigerian, what do you think about the institutions of your political system and what is expected of you as a citizen?

One of the great advances in comparative politics research is the relatively recent expansion of our knowledge of the political culture in developing societies, and this has transformed our understanding of political culture on a global scale. Until then, researchers worried that the cultural bases of democracy were essentially limited to those nations that were already democratic, and thus the prospects for further democratization were limited.[3] Researchers reached this conclusion by assuming that economic development and affluence were prerequisites for democracy, and that autocratic states persisted because the public tolerated or even supported autocratic government.

However, as public opinion surveys have become more common in developing nations, our images have changed. Cross-national studies of political culture document broad support for democratic principles and norms even in many autocratic nations.[4] Democratic norms emphasize the importance of a participatory process, majority rule and minority rights, and the values of political tolerance. Moreover, as more nations democratize (refer back to Figure 1.3) and alternative regime forms lose their legitimacy, democratic norms have diffused to even more societies. Many of the nondemocratic forms of governance are no longer widely accepted. Communism still has strongholds in China and Cuba, but it has lost its image as a progressive force for global change.

Consequently, current research finds that support for democratic norms is widespread in many developing nations in Africa, East Asia, and Latin America.[5] The World Values Survey asked respondents in more than 60 nations to state their approval of democracy and two nondemocratic regimes (military rule or rule by a strong leader). Figure 3.2 displays respondents (from the nations covered in this book) who prefer democracy, prefer either nondemocratic regime, or have mixed opinions.[6] In the established democracies, citizens express overwhelming support for democracy, but even here there are some citizens who are ambivalent about the regime form and about a tenth who actually prefer some autocratic form of government. In the developing nations in this book, the picture is more mixed. Only small percentages favor an autocracy over democracy, with the most autocrats in Russia (23 percent). However, a fair number in these developing nations give equal ratings to democracy and autocracy. Among the seven developing nations, only in Nigeria and China do a majority clearly prefer democracy. It is not a positive sign for democracy in Brazil and Mexico, for example, if less than half of the public prefers democracy over autocracy. Democracy often receives plurality support in these developing nations, but there is clearly a need to increase public support for democracy.

Furthermore, we should be cautious about taking support for democracy at full face value in less democratic nations. Even if most of the people in the world today seem to favor a democratic political process, they differ in their understanding of how the democratic process actually functions. Expressions

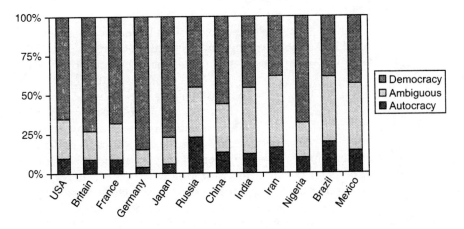

FIGURE 3.2

Democratic Aspirations

Support for Democracy versus Autocracy Is Widespread across Regions

Source: 2000–2002 *World Values Survey* and 2005–2008 *World Values Survey.* Respondents were asked their support for either democracy or autocracy (either a nondemocratic leader or military regime); the ambiguous category is those who express equal approval for both.

of support for liberty and tolerance are easier than actually supporting these values when applied to your political opponents. Cultures also differ in how those principles should be applied. In some nations, the public expresses support for equal rights for women, but then imposes Shari'a restrictions on women. Still, the breadth of democratic aspirations is strikingly different than our images of developing nations in the past. These patterns seem to reaffirm Amartya Sen's claim that democracy is a basic human striving—something many scholars doubted a few short years ago.[7]

Another aspect of political culture is the role of the individual in the political system. At one time, social scientists considered the population in developing nations as largely disinterested or even unaware of politics because they were concerned with sustenance and lacked access to political information.[8] Again, this image has softened in recent years as research has documented considerable political interest even in unexpected places (see Box 3.1). The spreading norms of democratization and the development of a global marketplace connect an increasingly larger share of the world to domestic and international politics.

Still, actual participation often involves resources, skills, and norms of active citizenship that are in short supply in many developing nations. Consequently, research shows that industrialization, urbanization, and improved living standards develop the cultural bases of active citizenship.[9] Exposure to modernity through work, education, and the media shapes an individual's personal experiences and sends messages about norms in other societies. It encourages citizen participation, a sense of individual equality, the desire for improved living standards and increased life expectancy, and government legitimacy based on policy performance. It also frequently disrupts familiar ways

> ### BOX 3.1 A SMALL WORLD
>
> With a radio deep in a rural village, a person is abreast with a bomb blast in Bombay, and can follow a political crisis in Moscow.... People will take sides on issues far beyond their national borders. Whether the wife of dictator Ferdinand Marcos should be prosecuted or should be pardoned; whether the genocide in Rwanda could have been averted are issues which are enlivening beer-drinking discussions on a scale unprecedented in African history.... This knowledge revolution is making it difficult for African leaders to keep people ignorant of what they are entitled to or to stop them from demanding change and working for it. Hence there are shivers of change all over the continent.
>
> *Source:* A Ugandan government official cited in Bruce Gilley, *The Right to Rule: How States Win and Lose Legitimacy* (New York: Columbia University Press, 2009), 78.

of life, traditional bases of legitimacy, and political arrangements that limit political engagement. In addition, the secularizing influences of science can alter economic and social systems, which then reshape the political culture. This **modernization** trend has powerful effects as it penetrates societies (or parts of societies).

This modernization process is spread unevenly across the globe. The recent economic growth in East Asia is transforming the political culture and political behavior in these nations. In contrast, modernization has proceeded more slowly and uncertainly in Africa and Arab nations. Some political leaders in these nations even reject the principles of modernization as incongruent with their national values. However, there is persuasive evidence that where social and economic modernization occurs, it transforms the political culture to emphasize self-expression, participatory values, and autonomy.

The Policy Level

What is the appropriate role of government? If you ask political theorists, you get a wide range of answers—from the minimal state to the all-encompassing polity (see Chapter 1). And if you travel to other nations, you quickly realize that there is wide variation in how people answer this question.

Public images of what constitutes the good of society and the government's role in achieving these goals influence the policy activities of a country. Should government manage the economy, or should private property rights and market forces guide economic activity? Should the state intervene in addressing social and moral issues, or should it follow a minimalist strategy? The ongoing debates over "big government" versus "small government" in democratic states, and between socialist and market-based economies, reflect these different images of the scope of government.

We can illustrate differences in policy expectations with an opinion survey question that asks whether the government is responsible for providing for everyone versus individuals being responsible for providing for themselves (see Figure 3.3). The range in opinions is considerable; more than three-quarters of Russians believe government is responsible, compared with only two-fifths among Americans, Canadians, Britons, or the French. In general, people in

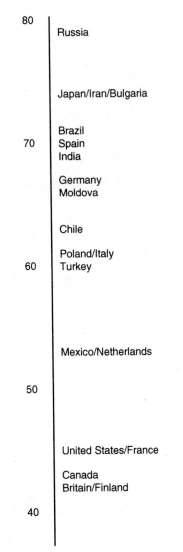

FIGURE 3.3
Who Is Responsible?

The Belief That Government Is Responsible for Individuals' Well-Being

Source: Selected nations from the 2005–2008 *World Values Survey;* missing data are excluded from the calculation of percentages.

developing nations and in the formerly communist nations of Eastern Europe are more supportive of a large government role—reflecting both their social condition and their past political ideologies. In some Western nations, traditions include a large role for the government. In general, however, support for government action generally decreases as national affluence increases.[10]

Policy expectations also involve specific issue demands.[11] Indeed, each country study in this book begins with a discussion of the policy challenges facing the nation and the public's issue concerns. This sets the agenda of politics that responsive governments should address.

Some policy goals, such as economic well-being, are valued by nearly everyone. Concern about other policy goals may vary widely across nations because of the nation's circumstances and because of cultural traditions. People in developing countries are more likely to focus on the government's provision of basic services to ensure public welfare. In advanced industrial societies, people are often more concerned with quality-of-life goals, such as preservation of nature and even government support for the arts.[12] One basic measure of a government's performance is its ability to meet the policy expectations of its citizens.

Another set of expectations involves the functioning of government. Some societies put more weight on the policy outputs of government, such as providing welfare and security. Other societies also emphasize how the process functions, which involves values such as the rule of law and procedural justice. Among Germans, for example, the rule of law is given great importance; in many developing nations, political relations are personally based, and there is less willingness to rely on legalistic frameworks.

Consensual or Conflictual Political Cultures

Although political culture is a common characteristic of a nation, values and beliefs can vary within it. Political cultures may be consensual or conflictual on issues of public policy and, more fundamentally, on views of legitimate governmental and political arrangements. In some societies, citizens generally agree on the norms of political decision-making and their policy expectations. In other societies—because of differences in histories, conditions, or identities—the citizens are sharply divided, often on both the legitimacy of the regime and solutions to major problems.[13]

When a country is deeply divided in its political values and these differences persist over time, distinctive **political subcultures** may develop. The citizens in these subcultures may have sharply different points of view on some critical political matters, such as the boundaries of the nation, the nature of the regime, or the correct ideology. They may affiliate with different political parties and interest groups, read different newspapers, and even have separate social clubs and sporting groups.

In some instances, historical or social factors generate different cultural trajectories. For instance, *ethnic, religious,* or *linguistic* identities in many parts of the world shape citizen values.[14] Moreover, as such groups increase their political skills and self-confidence, they may express their identities and demand equal treatment. In fact, the processes of globalization might actually heighten these cultural contrasts.[15] Where political subcultures coincide with ethnic, linguistic, or religious differences—as in Northern Ireland, Bosnia, and Lebanon—the divisions can be enduring and threatening. The breakup of Yugoslavia and the impulses toward autonomy and secession among ethnically distinct regions (such as in Scotland or separatist movements in Africa) all reflect the lasting power of language, culture, and historical memory to create and sustain the sense of ethnic and national identity. The exposure to values from other cultures also may intensify one's own self-image, which may increase cultural tensions. Although such exposure may eventually lead to greater tolerance, that outcome is not guaranteed.

WHY CULTURE MATTERS

Political culture does not explain everything about politics. Even people with similar values and skills might behave differently from each other when they face different situations. Nor is political culture unchangeable. However, cultural norms typically change slowly and reflect stable values. Thus, political culture is important first because it encapsulates the history, traditions, and values of a society. To understand how most people in a nation think and act politically, we can begin by understanding their political culture. Political culture can create the common political community that is one goal of government.

In addition, the distribution of cultural patterns is typically related to the type of political process that citizens expect and support. This is the principle of *congruence theory*. For instance, support for a democratic system is typically higher in societies that have a more participatory political culture. Authoritarian states are more likely to endure where people lack the skills or motivations to participate and the state discourages their participation. These cultural norms represent the "rules of the game" for the political system, and the system works better when citizens accept these rules. Where political structures and political cultures are mutually reinforcing, a stable political system is likely to emerge.

We can illustrate the logic of congruence theory in terms of the relationship between political culture and the democratic development of a nation (Figure 3.4). The horizontal axis of the figure displays the public's adherence to self-expressive values, reflecting the participatory norms we discussed earlier. The vertical axis represents the democratic development of the nation based on a variety of expert evaluations. You can see that participatory norms and democratic development are interrelated. The nations in this book that are in these analyses differ between the established Western democracies, democratizing nations (such as Mexico and Eastern European nations), and nondemocracies (such as China and several Middle East nations). Structure and culture do overlap in these nations.[16]

Do democracies create a participatory democratic public or does such a political culture lead to a democratic political system? It works both ways. For

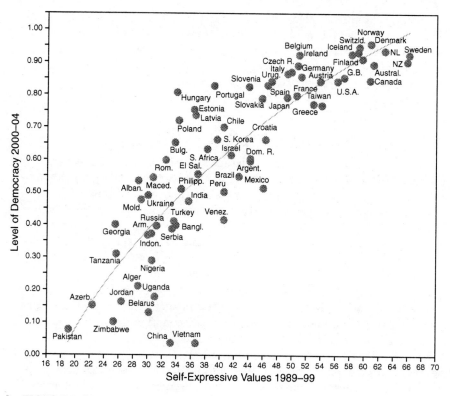

FIGURE 3.4

Culture Matters

The Congruence of Self-Expressive Values and the Level of Democracy

Source: The self-expressive values measure is from the *World Values Survey;* higher scores represent more citizen emphasis on self-expression. The level of democracy measure is a composite of the ranking of democracy by the Freedom House and other national rankings. Higher scores indicate a higher level of democratic development. For additional discussion of these measures, see Ronald Inglehart and Christian Welzel, *Modernization, Cultural Change, and Democracy* (New York: Cambridge University Press, 2005).

example, immediately after World War II, Germans were less supportive of democracy, but political institutions and political experiences transformed their culture over the next generation.[17] At the same time, democracy endured in Britain during the strains of the Great Depression and World War II, at least in part because the British public supported the democratic process. The important conclusion is that there is normally a relationship between political culture and political structures.

Beyond shaping the structure of the political system, a nation's political culture also influences the style of politics and the content of policymaking. We have stressed how the policy elements of a political culture can influence the content of policy. In addition, research suggests that cultural factors, such as social trust and engagement, influence the efficiency and effectiveness of government.[18]

Finally, culture can also divide nations and regions of the world. Samuel Huntington divided the world into different civilizations defined by their religious and cultural traditions.[19] He then predicted that these cultural differences will be a major source of international conflict in this century. While culture may have the power to divide, it also has the potential to build a common political community as people interact and learn which values they share.

POLITICAL SOCIALIZATION

Political cultures are sustained or changed as people acquire their attitudes and values. **Political socialization** refers to the way in which political values are formed and political culture is transmitted from one generation to the next. Most children acquire their basic political values and behavior patterns by adolescence.[20] Some of these attitudes will evolve and change throughout their lives, while other attitudes will remain part of their political selves throughout life.

At any specific time, a person's political beliefs are a combination of various feelings and attitudes. At the deepest level, there are general identifications, such as nationalism, ethnic or class self-images, religious and ideological commitments, and a fundamental sense of rights and duties in the society. At the middle level, people develop attitudes toward politics and governmental institutions. Finally, there are more immediate views of current events, policies, issues, and personalities. All these attitudes can change, but those in the first level usually were acquired earliest, have been most frequently reinforced, and tend to be the most durable.

Three points about political socialization deserve mention. First, the socialization process can occur in different ways. **Direct socialization** involves an actor explicitly communicating information, values, or feelings toward politics. Examples of direct socialization include civics courses in the schools, public education programs of the government, and the political information campaigns of interest groups. Communist political systems also heavily use direct indoctrination programs (see Box 3.2). **Indirect socialization** occurs when political views are inadvertently molded by our experiences. For example, children normally learn important political values by observing the behavior of their parents, teachers, and friends. Or, people may learn by observing the political and social context that surrounds them, watching what governments do and how other citizens react.

Second, socialization is a lifelong process. Early family influences can create an individual's initial values, but subsequent life experiences—becoming involved in new social groups, moving from one part of the country to another, shifting up or down the social ladder, becoming a parent, finding or losing a job—may change one's political perspectives. More dramatic experiences—such as relocating to a new country or suffering through an economic depression or a war—can alter even basic political attitudes. Such events seem to have their greatest impact on young people, but people at any age are affected to some degree.

▶ BOX 3.2 SOCIALIZING VALUES

Communist East Germany had a special ceremony for eighth-graders to mark their passage to adulthood. The heart of the ceremony was the endorsement of the following four pledges:

- As young citizens of our German Democratic Republic, are you prepared to work and fight loyally for the great and honorable goals of socialism, and to honor the revolutionary inheritance of the people?
- As sons and daughters of the worker-and-peasant state, are you prepared to pursue higher education, to cultivate your mind, to become a master of your trade, to learn permanently, and to use your knowledge to pursue our great humanist ideals?
- As honorable members of the socialist community, are you ready to cooperate as comrades, to respect and support each other, and to always merge the pursuit of your personal happiness with the happiness of all the people?
- As true patriots, are you ready to deepen the friendship with the Soviet Union, to strengthen our brotherhood with socialist countries, to struggle in the spirit of proletarian internationalism, to protect peace and to defend socialism against every imperialist aggression?

Third, patterns of socialization can unify or divide. Governments design public education systems, for instance, to create a single national political culture. Some events, such as international conflict or the death of a popular public figure, can affect nearly the entire nation similarly. In contrast, subcultures in a society can have their own distinctive patterns of socialization. Social groups that provide their members with their own newspapers, their own neighborhood groups, and perhaps their own schools can create distinctive subcultural attitudes. Divisive patterns of socialization can lead to a political gap among members of a nation.

AGENTS OF POLITICAL SOCIALIZATION

How do we learn our political attitudes? Individuals in all societies are affected by **agents of political socialization**: individuals, organizations, and institutions that influence political attitudes. Some, like civics courses in schools, are direct and deliberate sources of political learning. Others, like playgroups and work groups, affect political socialization indirectly.

The Family

Most of us first learn about politics through our families. The family has distinctive influences on attitudes toward authority. Participation in family decision-making can increase a child's sense of political competence, providing skills for political interaction and encouraging active participation in the political system as an adult. Similarly, unquestioning obedience to parental decisions may lead a child toward a more passive political role. The family also shapes future political attitudes by defining a social position for the child: establishing ethnic, linguistic, class, and religious ties; affirming cultural values; and influencing job aspirations.

The nature of the family is changing in many societies. Family sizes are generally decreasing, which changes the pattern of family life. In addition, there has been a marked rise of single-parent families, especially in the advanced industrial democracies. The political impact of these structural changes on family socialization patterns is still unclear.

Social Groups and Identities

Our social characteristics also shape political orientations because these reflect different social needs, experiences, and social networks. For instance, social divisions based on class or occupation affect our life changes and political orientations. For instance, industrialization in Britain created a working class that lived in particular neighborhoods, worked at the same factories, and visited the same pubs. This working class developed its own forms of speech, dress, recreation, and entertainment, as well as its own social organizations (such as social clubs, trade unions, and political parties). In addition, labor unions provide an organizational base for informing their members on the politics of the day. Similarly, the life experience of the rural peasantry in many less developed nations is radically different from that of urban dwellers. Often, these social divisions are politically relevant; identifying yourself as a member of the working class or the peasantry leads to ties to groups representing these interests and distinct political views about what issues are important and which political parties best represent your interests.

The religions of the world are also carriers of cultural and moral values, which often have political implications. The great religious leaders have seen themselves as teachers, and their followers have usually attempted to shape the socialization of children through schooling, preaching, and religious services. In most nations, there are formal ties between the dominant religion and the government. In these instances, religious values and public policy often overlap. Catholic nations, for instance, are less likely to have liberal abortion policies, just as Islamic governments enforce strict moral codes.

Religious institutions of many kinds offer valuable moral and ethical guidance that individuals often need to make choices in complex societies. Religious affiliations are often important sources of partisan preferences and can guide people in making other political choices. Where churches teach values that may be at odds with the controlling political system, the struggle over socialization can be intense. These tensions can take a wide variety of forms: the clash between secular and religious roles in the French educational system, the efforts of American fundamentalists to bridge the separation of church and state, or the conflict between Islamic fundamentalists and secular governments in Algeria and Egypt. In such cases, religious groups may oppose the policies of the state, or even the state itself.[21]

In addition, gender shapes social experiences and life chances, and in many nations provides cues about issue interests and political roles. Gender differences in politics have narrowed in many industrial nations, although they persist in many less developed nations.[22] The modern women's movement encourages women to become politically active and change social cues about how women should relate to politics. The lessening of gender differences in self-images, in parental roles, and in relation to the economy and the political system is affecting patterns of political recruitment, political participation, and public policy. Especially in the developing world, the changing role of women may have profound influences in modernizing the society and changing political values.[23]

Social identities are also often linked to membership in a racial or ethnic group. Whether it is an African-American in the United States, an ethnic Pakistani living in London, or an Asian businessperson in South Africa, their distinctiveness partially defines their social and political identity. Ethnic and racially oriented groups provide social cues and information for members of these communities. In many instances, their identity creates a social network of interactions and life experiences that shape their values, while specific groups represent their interests in the political process and provide a network for political socialization and education.

Schools

Schools are often an important agent of political socialization. They educate children about politics and their role in the process, and provide them with information on political institutions and relationships. Schools can shape attitudes about the political system, the rules of the political game, the appropriate role of the citizen, and expectations about the government. Schools typically reinforce attachments to the political system and reinforce common symbols, such as the flag and Pledge of Allegiance, that encourage emotional attachments to the system.

When a new nation comes into being, or a revolutionary regime comes to power in an old nation, it usually turns to the schools as a means to supplant "outdated" values and symbols with ones more congruent with the new ideology.

In some nations, educational systems do not provide unifying political socialization but send starkly different messages to different groups. For instance, some Muslim nations segregate girls and boys within the school system. Even if educational experiences are intended to be equal, segregation creates different experiences and expectations. Moreover, the content of education often differs between boys and girls. Perhaps the worst example occurred under the Taliban in Afghanistan, where for several years young girls were prohibited from attending school. Such treatment of young girls severely limits their life chances, and ensures that they will have restricted roles in society and the economy—which was the intent of the Taliban system. The current Afghanistan government reversed this policy and included girls in the education system, but this is still resisted in parts of the nation.

Education also affects people's political skills and resources. Educated people are more aware of the impact of government on their lives and pay more attention to politics.[24] The better educated have mental skills that improve their ability to manage the world of politics. They also have more information about political processes and participate in a wider range of political activities.

Peer Groups

Peer groups include childhood playgroups, friendship cliques, school and college fraternities, small work groups, and other groups in which members share close personal ties. They can be as varied as a group of Russian mothers who meet regularly at the park, to a street gang in Brazil, to a group of Wall Street executives who are members of a health club.

A peer group socializes its members by encouraging them to share the attitudes or behavior common to the group. Individuals often adopt their peers' views because they like or respect them or because they want to be like them. Similarly, a person may become engaged in politics because close friends do so. One example of peer networks is the international youth culture symbolized by rock music, T-shirts, and blue jeans (and often more liberal political values). Some observers claim that it played a major role in the failure of communist officials to mold Soviet and Eastern European youth to the "socialist personality" that was the Marxist–Leninist ideal. Likewise, the "skinhead" groups that have sprouted up among lower-class youth in many Western countries have adopted political views that are based on peer interactions.

Interest Groups

Interest groups, economic groups, and similar organizations also shape political attitudes. In most industrial countries, the rise of trade unions transformed the political culture and politics, created new political parties, and ushered in new social benefit programs. Today, unions are active participants in the political process and try to persuade their members on political matters. Other professional associations—such as groups of peasants and farmers, manufacturers, wholesalers and retailers, medical societies, and lawyers—also regularly influence political attitudes in modern and modernizing societies. These groups ensure the loyalty of their members by defending their economic and professional interests. They can also provide valuable political cues to nonmembers, who might identify with a group's interests or political ideology. For instance, when a group that you like (or dislike) publicly supports a policy, it gives you information on the likely content of the policy.

The groups that define a civil society are also potential agents of socialization. These groups might include ethnic organizations, fraternal associations, civic associations (such as parent–teacher associations), and policy groups (such as taxpayers' associations, women's groups, and environmental groups). Such groups provide valuable political cues to their members and try to reinforce distinct social and political orientations. They also provide settings to learn about how making political choices in small groups can be extended to politics. For instance, Vietnam has an active network of social groups that socialize individuals into the norms of the communist regime, while civil society groups in the United States are treated as democracy-building organizations. In addition, these groups—using the media and other sources—send out large quantities of information on political, social, and economic issues to the public and elites.

Political Parties

Political parties normally play an important role in political socialization (also see Chapter 5). In democratic systems, political parties try to mold issue preferences, arouse the apathetic, and find new issues to mobilize support. Party representatives provide the public with a steady flow of information on the issues of the day. Party organizations regularly contact voters to advocate their positions. In addition, every few years, an election enables parties to present their accomplishments and discuss the nation's political future. Elections can serve as national civics lessons, and the political parties are the teachers.

Partisan socialization can be also a divisive force. In their efforts to gain support, party leaders may appeal to class, language, religious, and ethnic divisions and make citizens more aware of these differences. The Labour and Conservative parties in Britain, for example, use class cues to attract supporters. Similarly, the Congress Party in India tries to develop a national program and appeal, but other parties emphasize the ethnic and religious divisions. Leaders of preindustrial nations often oppose competitive parties because they fear such divisiveness. Although this is sometimes a sincere concern, it is also self-serving to government leaders, and is increasingly difficult to justify against contemporary demands for multiparty systems.

Authoritarian governments often use a single party to inculcate common attitudes of national unity, support for the government, and ideological agreement. The combination of a single party and controlled mass media is potent: The media present a single point of view, and the party activities reinforce that perspective by directly involving the citizen. In a closed environment, single-party governments can be potent agents of socialization.

Mass Media

The mass media—newspapers, radio, television, and magazines—are important in socializing attitudes and values in nations around the globe. The mass media are typically the prime source of information on the politics of the day. There is virtually no place so remote that people lack the means to be informed about events elsewhere—in affluent nations, the public is wired to the Internet; satellite dishes sprout from houses in Iran; and inexpensive transistor radios are omnipresent even in Third World villages far removed from urban centers.

There is one thing that most people in the world share in common: we sit before our televisions to learn about the world. Television can have a powerful cognitive and emotional impact on large public audiences by enlisting the senses of both sight and sound. Watching events on television—such as the broadcasts of government affairs or the war in Iraq—gives a reality to the news. Seeing the world directly can shape political attitudes.

Today, the Internet provides another powerful source of news for those with access to it.[25] The Web provides unprecedented access to information on a global scale, especially in developing nations with limited traditions of a free press. One can hardly travel to any city in the world and not see Internet cafés or WiFi access. At the same time, the Internet empowers individuals to connect to others and to develop social and political networks. This may be why autocratic governments struggle to restrict unfettered access to the Internet (see Box 3.3).

Access to information thus becomes an important political commodity in the contemporary world. Western democracies put a premium on freedom of the media, even if they frequently complain about what the media reports. In many European nations, the government still manages television and radio stations because it views the media as a public service. Autocratic governments typically seek to control the media and what they can report, as well as the public's access to information. Similarly, the communist regimes of Eastern Europe tried to limit access to news reports from the West because they feared it would undermine their regimes, and the democracy movements were strengthened by the image of another way of life in the West. In the contemporary world of Internet and satellite broadcasting, it is becoming increasingly difficult for governments to control the spread of information.

Direct Contact with the Government

In modern societies, the wide scope of governmental activities brings citizens into frequent contact with various bureaucratic agencies. Surveys of Americans find that about a third have contacted a government official in the preceding

BOX 3.3 THE GREAT FIREWALL OF CHINA

The People's Republic of China has the largest number of Internet users of any nation in the world, and this fact has government officials worried. Chinese "netizens" find themselves surfing in the shadow of the world's most sophisticated censorship machine. A large Internet police force monitors Web sites and e-mails. On a technical level, the gateways that connect China to the global Internet filter traffic coming into and going out of the country. Even the Internet cafés are now highly regulated and state-licensed, and all are equipped with standard surveillance systems. Google was one of the Western companies that initially provided keyword-blocking technology to prevent access to offending sites. Pornography was banned, but also searches for the word "democracy" or "Tiananmen Square." After struggling with censorship requirements, Google removed its search computers from China in early 2010 and relocated them to Hong Kong. But China continues to restrict Internet access through Chinese-based search engines.

year, and online interactions with government are increasing dramatically.[26] Citizens contact a wide range of government offices, from federal officials to state and local governments to school boards and the police. In addition, the government touches our lives in a myriad of other ways, from running the public schools to providing retirement checks to providing social services. The degree of government intervention in daily life, and hence the necessity for contact with government, varies greatly across nations as a function of the political system and the role of government in the society.

These personal experiences are powerful agents of socialization, strengthening or undercutting the images presented by other agents. Does the government send retirement checks on time? Do city officials respond to citizen complaints? Are the schools teaching children effectively? Do unemployment offices help people find jobs? Are the highways well-maintained? These are very direct sources of information on how well the government functions. No matter how positive the view of the political system that people have learned as children, citizens who face a different reality in everyday life are likely to change their early-learned views. Indeed, the contradictions between ideology and reality proved to be one of the weaknesses of the communist systems in Eastern Europe.

In summary, the country-specific chapters in this book all examine the patterns of political socialization for several reasons. The sources of political socialization often determine the content of what is learned about politics. If people learn about new events from their friends at church, they may hear different information than people who rely on the workplace or the television for information. The role of these different socialization agents and the content of their political messages also vary systematically across nations. In addition, the ability of a nation to recreate its political culture in successive generations is an important factor in perpetuating the political system. Finally, cultures change when new elements are added to the process of political learning. Thus, socialization provides the feedback mechanism that enables a political culture to endure or change.

TRENDS SHAPING CONTEMPORARY POLITICAL CULTURES

A political culture exists uniquely in its own time and place. Citizens' attitudes and beliefs are shaped by personal experiences and by the agents of political socialization. Yet in any historical period, there may be trends that change the culture in many nations. The major social trends of our time reflect both general societal developments and specific historic events.

For the past two decades, a major new development is the trend toward democracy in Eastern Europe, East Asia, and other parts of the developing world. This **democratization** trend reflects long-term responses to modernity as well as immediate reactions to current events. Modernization gradually eroded the legitimacy of nondemocratic ideologies, while the development of citizens' skills and political resources made their claim to equal participation in policymaking (at least indirectly) more plausible. Thus, many studies of political culture in Eastern Europe and the former Soviet Union uncovered surprising popular support for democratic norms and processes as the new democratic system formed.[27]

Ironically, as democracy has begun taking root in Eastern Europe, citizens in many Western democracies are increasingly skeptical about politicians and political institutions. In 1964, three-quarters of Americans said they trusted the government; in 2010, less than a fifth of the public say as much—and the malaise is spreading to Western Europe and Japan.[28] At the same time, public support for democratic norms and values has strengthened over time in most Western democracies. Thus, these publics are critical of politicians and political parties when they fall short of these democratic ideals. Although this cynicism is a strain on democratic politicians, it presses democracy to continue to improve and adapt, which is ultimately democracy's greatest strength.

Another recent major trend affecting political cultures is a shift toward **marketization**—that is, an increased public acceptance of free markets and private profit incentives, rather than a government-managed economy. One example of this movement appeared in many Western European nations and the United States beginning in the 1980s, where economies had experienced serious problems of inefficiency and economic stagnation. Margaret Thatcher in Britain and Ronald Reagan in the United States rode to power on waves of public support for reducing the scale of government. Public opinion surveys show that many people in these nations feel that government should not be responsible for individual well-being (see again Figure 3.3).

Just as Western Europeans began to question the government's role in the economy, the political changes in Eastern Europe and the Soviet Union reinforced this trend toward marketization. The command economies of Eastern Europe were almost exclusively controlled by state corporations and government agencies. The government set both wages and prices and directed the economy. The collapse of these systems raised new questions about public support for marketization. Surveys generally find that Eastern Europeans support a capitalist market system and the public policies that would support such an economic system.[29]

Globalization is another trend affecting political cultures of many nations. Increasing international trade and international interactions tend to diffuse the values of the overall international system. Thus, as developing nations become more engaged in the global economy and global international system, the development of certain norms—such as human rights, gender equality, and democratic values—increases.[30] People in developing nations also learn about the broader opportunities existing in other nations, which can spur cultural change as well as economic change. Thus, although globalization has been a deeply divisive political issue for the past decade in many nations, the Pew Global Values Survey found broad support for globalization among citizens worldwide—especially in developing nations where it is seen as improving living standards and life chances.[31]

Clearly, political culture is not a static phenomenon, so our understanding of political culture must be dynamic. It must encompass how the agents of political socialization communicate and interpret historic events and traditional values. It must juxtapose these factors with the exposure of citizens and leaders to new experiences and new ideas. But it is important to understand the political culture of a nation, because these cultural factors influence how citizens act, how the political process functions, and what policy goals the government pursues.

REVIEW QUESTIONS

1. What are the three key elements of a political culture?
2. Why does political culture matter?
3. Why is the process of political socialization important?
4. What are the main agents of political socialization? List the possible agents of socialization, and then compare their relative importance across two different nations included in this book.
5. What are the major trends in cultural change in the contemporary world?

KEY TERMS

agents of political
 socialization
democratization
direct socialization

globalization
indirect socialization
legitimacy
marketization

modernization
political culture
Political socialization
political subcultures

SUGGESTED READINGS

Almond, Gabriel A., and Sidney Verba. *The Civic Culture*. Princeton, NJ: Princeton University Press, 1963.

——, eds. *The Civic Culture Revisited*. Boston: Little Brown, 1980.

Booth, John, and Mitchell A. Seligson, *The Legitimacy Puzzle in Latin America: Political Support and Democracy in Eight Nations*. New York: Cambridge University Press, 2009.

Bratton, Michael, Robert Mattes, and E. Gyimah-Boadi. *Public Opinion, Democracy, and Market Reform in Africa*. Cambridge: Cambridge University Press, 2004.

Dalton, Russell. *Democratic Challenges, Democratic Choices: The Erosion of Political Support in Advanced Industrial Democracies*. Oxford: Oxford University Press, 2004.

Gilley, Bruce. *The Right to Rule: How States Win and Lose Legitimacy*. New York: Columbia University Press, 2009.

Horowitz, Donald. *Ethnic Groups in Conflict*. Berkeley: University of California Press, 2000.

Huntington, Samuel. *The Clash of Civilizations and the Remaking of World Order*. New York: Simon & Schuster, 1996.

Inglehart, Ronald, and Pippa Norris. *Sacred and Secular: Religion and Politics World-wide.* Cambridge: Cambridge University Press, 2004.

Inglehart, Ronald, and Christian Welzel. *Modernization, Cultural Change, and Democracy: The Human Development Sequence.* New York: Cambridge University Press, 2005.

Inkeles, Alex, and David H. Smith. *Becoming Modern.* Cambridge, MA: Harvard University Press, 1974.

Jennings, M. Kent. "Political Socialization," in *Oxford Handbook of Political Behavior,* ed. Russell Dalton and Hans-Dieter Klingemann. Oxford: Oxford University Press, 2007.

Jennings, M. Kent, and Richard Niemi. *Generations and Politics: A Panel Study of Young Adults and Their Parents.* Princeton, NJ: Princeton University Press, 1981.

Klingemann, Hans Dieter, Dieter Fuchs, and Jan Zielonka, eds. *Democracy and Political Culture in Eastern Europe.* London: Routledge, 2006.

Norris, Pippa, ed. *Critical Citizens: Global Support for Democratic Government.* Oxford: Oxford University Press, 1999.

Norris, Pippa, and Ronald Inglehart. *Rising Tide: Gender Equality and Cultural Change around the World.* New York: Cambridge University Press, 2003.

———. *Cosmopolitan Communications: Cultural Diversity in a Globalized World.* New York: Cambridge University Press, 2009.

Pharr, Susan, and Robert Putnam. *Disaffected Democracies: What's Troubling the Trilateral Democracies?* Princeton, NJ: Princeton University Press, 2000.

Putnam, Robert. *The Beliefs of Politicians.* New Haven, CT: Yale University Press, 1973.

———. *Making Democracy Work: Civic Traditions in Modern Italy.* Princeton, NJ: Princeton University Press, 1993.

Rose, Richard, Christian Haerpfer, and William Mishler. *Testing the Churchill Hypothesis: Democracy and Its Alternatives in Post-Communist Societies.* Cambridge, UK: Polity/Baltimore: Johns Hopkins University Press, 2000.

ENDNOTES

1. This concept of legitimacy and its bases in different societies draws on the work of Max Weber. See, for example, Max Weber, *Basic Concepts in Sociology*, trans. H. P. Secher (New York: Citadel Press, 1964), Chapters 5–7.

2. Bruce Gilley, *The Right to Rule: How States Win and Lose Legitimacy* (New York: Columbia University Press, 2009).

3. Lucian Pye and Sidney Verba, eds., *Political Culture and Political Development* (Princeton, NJ: Princeton University Press, 1965); Samuel Huntington, "Will More Countries Become Democratic?" Political Science Quarterly 99 (Summer 1984): 193–218.

4. Ronald Inglehart and Christian Welzel, *Modernization, Cultural Change, and Democracy: The Human Development Sequence* (New York: Cambridge University Press, 2005); Pippa Norris, ed., *Critical Citizens: Global Support for Democratic Government* (Oxford: Oxford University Press, 1999).

5. Inglehart and Welzel, *Modernization, Cultural Change, and Democracy*; Russell Dalton and Doh Chull Shin, eds., *Citizens, Democracy, and Markets around the Pacific Rim* (Oxford: Oxford University Press, 2006); Yun-han Chu, Larry Diamond, Andrew J. Nathan, and Doh Chull Shin, eds., *How East Asians View Democracy* (New York: Columbia University Press, 2008); Michael Bratton, Robert Mattes, and E. Gyimah-Boadi. *Public Opinion, Democracy, and Market Reform in Africa* (Cambridge: Cambridge University Press, 2004).

6. For the list of nations in the World Values Survey, see the project Web site: www. worldvaluessurvey.org.

7. Amartya Sen, *Development as Freedom* (New York: Knopf, 1999).

8. In prior editions, we discussed the differences among parochial, subject, and participatory roles, and the concentration of parochials in less developed nations. Current research leads us to consider this categorization as too stark, as technological and communications changes have spread political information and interest on a broad global scale.

9. Inglehart and Welzel, *Modernization, Cultural Change, and Democracy.*

10. Ronald Inglehart, *Modernization and Postmodernization* (Princeton, NJ: Princeton University Press, 1997), Chapters 6–7.

11. Ole Borre and Elinor Scarbrough, eds., *The Scope of Government* (Oxford: Oxford University Press, 1995).

12. Ronald Inglehart, *Culture Shift in Advanced Industrial Societies* (Princeton, NJ: Princeton University Press, 1990).

13. Even within established Western democracies, there are internal differences in the appropriate role of government, the role of the citizen, and the perceived goals of government. See Max Kaase and Ken Newton, *Beliefs in Government* (Oxford: Oxford University Press, 1995).

14. W. Kymlicka and N. Wayne, eds., *Citizenship in Divided Societies* (Oxford: Oxford University Press, 2000); Donald Horowitz, *Ethnic Groups in Conflict* (Berkeley: University of California Press, 2000).

15. Amy Chua, *World on Fire: How Exporting Free Market Democracy Breeds Ethnic Hatred and Global Instability* (New York: Doubleday, 2003).

16. See also Inglehart and Welzel, *Modernization, Cultural Change, and Democracy.*

17. Kendall Baker, Russell Dalton, and Kai Hildebrandt, *Germany Transformed* (Cambridge, MA: Harvard University Press, 1981).

18. Robert Putnam, *Making Democracy Work: Civic Traditions in Modern Italy* (Princeton, NJ: Princeton University Press, 1993); Robert Putnam, *Bowling Alone: The Collapse and Revival of American Community* (New York: Simon & Schuster, 2000).

19. Samuel P. Huntington, *The Clash of Civilizations and the Remaking of World Order* (New York: Simon & Schuster, 1996); see also Fareed Zakaria, *The Future of Freedom: Illiberal Democracy at Home and Abroad* (New York: Norton, 2003).

20. See Gabriel A. Almond and Sidney Verba, *The Civic Culture* (Princeton, NJ: Princeton University Press, 1963), Chapter 12; M. Kent Jennings, Klaus R. Allerbeck, and Leopold Rosenmayr, "Generations and Families," in Samuel H. Barnes et al., *Political Action* (Beverly Hills, CA: Sage, 1979), Chapters 15–16.

21. Such fundamentalism is often a defensive reaction against the spread of scientific views of nature and human behavior, and the libertarian values and attitudes that accompany these views. The influence of fundamentalism has been most visible in Muslim countries, but also in Christian countries. Broadly speaking, fundamentalism seeks to raise conservative social, moral, and religious issues to the top of the contemporary policy agenda.

22. Pippa Norris and Ronald Inglehart, *Rising Tide: Gender Equality and Cultural Change around the World* (New York: Cambridge University Press, 2003).

23. Martha Nussbaum and Jonathan Glover, eds., *Women, Culture, and Development* (New York: Oxford University Press, 1995).

24. For example, see Sidney Verba, Norman H. Nie, and Jae-on Kim, *Participation and Political Equality* (New York: Cambridge University Press, 1978); Pippa Norris,

Democratic Phoenix: Reinventing Political Activism (New York: Cambridge University Press, 2003).

25. Pippa Norris and Ronald Inglehart, *Cosmopolitan Communications: Cultural Diversity in a Globalized World* (New York: Cambridge University Press, 2009).

26. Aaron Smith et al., "The Internet and Civic Engagement," Pew Internet and American Life Project (September 2009) (www.pewinternet.org).

27. Richard Rose, Christian Haerpfer, and William Mishler, *Testing the Churchill Hypothesis: Democracy and Its Alternatives in Post-Communist Societies* (Cambridge, UK: Polity/Baltimore: Johns Hopkins University Press, 2000).

28. Norris, *Critical Citizens*; Russell Dalton, *Democratic Challenges, Democratic Choices: The Erosion of Political Support in Advanced Industrial Democracies* (Oxford: Oxford University Press, 2004).

29. See William Zimmerman, *The Russian People and Foreign Policy: Russian Elite and Mass Perspectives* (Princeton, NJ: Princeton University Press, 2002), Chapter 2; Raymond Duch, "Tolerating Economic Reform," *American Political Science Review* 87 (1993): 590–608. Russian support for marketization noticeably lags behind that of most Eastern Europeans.

30. Wayne Sandholtz and Mark Gray, "International Integration and National Corruption," *International Organization* 57 (Autumn 2003): 761–800; Mark Gray, Miki Kittilson, and Wayne Sandholtz, "Women and Globalization: A Study of 180 Countries, 1975–2000," *International Organization* 60 (Spring 2006): 293–333.

31. Pew Global Attitudes Project, *Views of a Changing World, June 2003* (Washington, D.C.: Pew Global Attitudes Project, 2003), 71–81 (http://pewglobal.org/reports/display.php?ReportID=185).

Interest Articulation

S uppose an unjust or unfair law was being passed by the government—what could you do to express your dissatisfaction and try to stop the legislation? Or suppose you see a need that the government is not addressing—what could you do to encourage government action? These are the questions that often face us as citizens. What choices do we have for making our interests and needs known to policymakers?

People and social groups have some way to express their needs and demands to their government in almost every political system. This process, known as **interest articulation**, can take many forms. For example, a person might contact a city council member, or in a more traditional system, he or she might meet with the village head or tribal chieftain. Or, a group of people might work together on a common concern. In large, established political systems, formal interest groups are a primary means of promoting political interests.

As societies become internally more complex and the scope of government activity increases, the quantity and variety of ways to articulate public interests grow proportionately. People work together to address local and national needs, ranging from providing clean water in a village to passing national clean-water standards. Social movements involve the public in issues as diverse as protecting the rights of indigenous people in the Amazon to debating nuclear power. Formal, institutionalized interest groups develop to represent labor, farmers, businesses, and other social interests. Large numbers of interest groups work in capitals like London, Washington, D.C., and Tokyo. Today, Internet chatrooms and blogging provide another forum for expression. In countries with powerful local governments, interest groups are active at the provincial or local level as well.

This chapter considers the multiple ways in which people can express their interests in contemporary political systems. First, we discuss the means of interest articulation that are available to individuals. Then, we describe how formal interest groups and associations provide another means of interest

81

articulation. For example, in most countries that allow them, labor unions, manufacturers' associations, farm groups, and associations of doctors, lawyers, engineers, and teachers represent these interests. In the end, most political systems have many different forms of interest articulation to determine what the public and social groups want from their government.

CITIZEN ACTION

One aspect of interest articulation involves what you might do as an individual citizen. People can make requests and demands for policies in various ways (Table 4.1).[1] Each of these forms of citizen action has different characteristics, as described in the table. The most common form of citizen participation is voting in an election. When elections are free and meaningful, they enable people to express their interests and to make a collective choice about the government's past progress and the future policies for the nation. Although elections select political elites, they often are a blunt policy tool because they involve many different issues; between elections, officeholders may stray from the voters' preferences.

People can also work with others in their community to address common needs, as when parents work to better the local schools or residents express their worries about how the community is developing. These activities are typically very policy-focused and exert direct pressure on decision-makers. Such group activity exists in both democratic and authoritarian systems, although

TABLE 4.1

Articulating Interests

The forms of political participation vary in their scope and pressure on elites.

Form	Scope of Interests	Degree of Pressure on Elites
Voting, participation in elections	Broad, collective decision on government leaders and their programs	Modest pressure, but not policy-focused
Informal group	Collective action focused on a common interest	High pressure
Direct contact on personal matter	Normally deals with specific, personal problem	Low pressure
Direct contact on policy issue	Action on a government policy	Modest pressure
Protest activity	Highly expressive support for specific interests	High pressure
Political consumerism	Focused on specific issues, activities	High pressure

BOX 4.1 THE *SHANGFANG* SYSTEM

In 1949, the communist government in China created the *Shangfang* system, which allows individuals to petition the government formally to intervene on their behalf. This system was intended as a safety valve to allow disgruntled individuals to express their grievances, and as a method for the state to mobilize expression of support from the populace. The petitioners typically are concerned about personal problems or local issues, and this system allows them to bypass unresponsive local officials and petition Beijing. Sometimes, they even travel to the capital to present their petition in person. The use of *Shangfang* has ebbed and flowed over time, but it illustrates how even authoritarian governments seek input from their citizens. Experts estimate that the government in Beijing receives more than 10 million petitions, ranging from a complaint over an eviction notice to protests about the effects of the Three Gorges Dam. However, only a minuscule fraction of these petitions receive a government response, and sometimes local officials retaliate against the people who petittioned to a higher authority instead of coming to them.

nondemocracies may limit the methods of expression to those that do not openly confront authorities.

Some interest articulation involves direct contact with government, such as writing a letter to an elected official or to a government bureaucracy (see Box 4.1). Some direct contact involves personal issues, such as when a veteran writes to his legislator for help in getting benefits approved, or when a homeowner asks the council member to ensure her driveway is snowplowed regularly. These forms of personal contact are common across political systems, including the authoritarian ones. Other direct contact involves broader political issues facing the government, such as campaigns to support or block new legislation. Direct contact on policy issues occurs primarily in democratic systems, where citizen input is broadly encouraged. However, even in autocratic nations, the public often finds ways to petition the government on policy matters.[2]

The expression of interests also may involve **protests** or other forms of contentious action. The spontaneous protest of outraged ghetto dwellers, the public protests that overthrew the communist governments of Eastern Europe, and the environmental actions of Greenpeace are all examples of how protest articulates policy interests. Protests and other direct actions tend to be high-pressure activities that can both mobilize the public and directly pressure elites; these activities can also be very focused in their policy content.

Recent participation studies found that political consumerism—buying or boycotting a product for political reasons—is another active form of participation, at least in Western democracies.[3] Such participation allows individuals to protest the activities of a firm that pollutes or has unfair labor practices. For example, organized boycotts against child-labor practices have affected the sales and public images of many clothing manufacturers, and led to new public policies. Such efforts are very focused. If they become politically visible, they can have broader policy effects as well.

In summary, people can take many routes to express their interests, and each of these routes has particular characteristics associated with it.

HOW CITIZENS PARTICIPATE

The amount of citizen political participation varies widely according to the type of activity and the type of political system. Table 4.2 shows examples of the types of citizen participation in several of the nations examined in this book.

The most frequent forms of political participation revolve around elections: turning out to vote, trying to convince others how to vote, or working with political parties. Because elections are the most common form of public involvement in the political process, they are important forms of interest articulation. During elections, citizens speak their minds on current issues, attend meetings, contribute to campaigns, express their opinions to pollsters, and ultimately cast their ballots. At the same time, elections perform many other functions: aggregating political interests, recruiting political elites, and even socializing political values and preferences through the campaign process (see Chapter 2).

Among the democracies, the United States has rather low levels of national voting participation: both Western Europeans (with their long democratic experience) and several new democracies vote more frequently than Americans. However, as the table shows, Americans' low level of election turnout does not simply reflect apathy. Americans are relatively interested in politics and participate in other ways beyond elections.

Public efforts to express political interests and influence public policy extend beyond elections. Grassroots politics—people working together to address a common problem—is a very direct method for articulating political interests and attempting to influence policy. Alexis de Tocqueville considered such grassroots community action to be the foundation of democracy in America. Today, such activities are often identified with middle-class participation in affluent societies—such as parent–teacher association groups, community associations, and public interest groups—but group activity occurs in almost any nation.[4] Indian villagers working together to build a communal latrine or to develop rural electricity and indigenous people protecting their land rights are other examples of community action. Table 4.2 presents membership in an environmental group as one example of public-interest group activity. About a sixth of the public in the United States, Britain, and France belong to an environmental group, but such citizen action is lower in less developed nations and new democracies.

Perhaps the most expressive and visible form of citizen action involves contentious actions, such as signing a petition, joining a boycott, or participating in protests. For instance, many environmentalists believe that direct actions—hanging an environmental banner from a polluting smokestack, staging

TABLE 4.2

How Are We Active?

People engage in a variety of political activities (percentage).

Type of Participation	United States	Britain	France	Germany	Japan	Russia	Mexico	Brazil	India	China	Iran
Voter turnout in most recent national elections	58	65	77	72	67	62	63	83	62	—	67
Interested in politics	59	44	38	62	64	39	34	49	44	65	46
Belong to environmental group	16	16	15	5	5	5	13	7	—	10	10
Signed a petition	70	68	67	50	60	8	21	56	29	6	—
Joined in a boycott	20	17	14	9	7	3	3	8	15	3	—
Participated in lawful protest demonstration	15	17	38	31	10	16	16	18	19	—	—

Sources: Election turnout data is percent of voting age public for most recent national legislative election from the International Institute for Elections and Democracy, downloaded from www.idea.org; 2005–2008 *World Values Survey* for other statistics. Some of the participation questions were not asked in each survey, and these missing items are noted by a dash in the table.

a mass demonstration outside parliament, or boycotting polluters—effectively generate media attention and public interest in their cause. Political protests arise for quite different reasons. On the one hand, protest and direct action is often used by individuals and groups that feel they lack access to legitimate political channels. The mass demonstrations in Eastern Europe in the late 1980s and the public rallies and marches of black South Africans against apartheid illustrate protests as the last resort of the disadvantaged. On the other hand, peaceful protests are also increasingly used by the young and better-educated citizens in Western democracies. To many democratic citizens, protest is the continuation of "normal" politics by other means.

The majority of the public in most Western democracies say they have signed a petition, although such open disagreement with government policy is more limited in new democracies and autocratic states (see Table 4.2). In addition, about a sixth of Western publics say they have joined in a boycott or participated in a lawful protest. However, we again observe that protest activities are less frequent in developing societies, such as Mexico and Brazil. And the autocratic trends in Russia are suppressing popular dissent. Indeed, there is a general pattern for protest actually to increase with democratization, as governments become more tolerant of dissent and the rights of dissenters are protected.[5]

France is a nation where protests have become part of the tradition of politics. In the late 1960s, the French government nearly collapsed as a result of protests that began when university students stimulated a mass movement against the government. More recently, new policies to raise the retirement age to 62 generated massive protests in 2010, including "Project Escargot" in which truckers intentionally slowed traffic on the highways. In a typical year, Paris might experience protests by students, shopkeepers, farmers, homemakers, government employees, environmentalists, women's groups, and a host of other interest groups. Protest is almost a national political sport in France.

Citizen participation reflects the way that people use the opportunities existing within a political system. In nations with active political parties and competitive elections, many people participate in the electoral process. In nations where such activities are limited, people may turn to group-based activity or protest in order to express their preferences, but it is more likely that they are politically inactive. As we noted in Chapter 3, a participatory political culture is often a by-product of political modernization.

Cross-national research shows that better-educated and higher-social-status individuals are more likely to use the various opportunities for participation. These individuals tend to develop attitudes that encourage participation, such as feelings of efficacy and a sense of civic duty.[6] They also possess the personal resources and skills that are useful in becoming politically active when duty calls or a need arises. Skill and confidence are especially important for demanding activities, such as organizing new groups or becoming a leader in an organization. This inequality in participation is less for easier activities, such as voting. The tendency for the better-off to be politically active is more evident in societies (such as the United States) with weak party organizations, weak working-class groups (such as labor unions), and less party attention to lower-class interests. In nations with stronger working-class parties and labor unions, organizational networks encourage the participation of less affluent citizens.

Participation patterns are important for several reasons. For citizens to influence government policy, they first need to articulate their interests to the government. A wider choice of activities presumably increases the citizens' ability to express their interests and be heard. Moreover, the forms of action differ in their policy content and political pressure (see again Table 4.1). Finally, individuals differ in their level of political activities and the types of activities in which they participate. These differences in voice likely affect policy outputs if the government responds to public pressures. In other words, those who are more active in articulating their interests are more likely to have their interests addressed by policymakers.

INTEREST GROUPS

Interest articulation can also occur through the actions of groups that represent a set of people. In addition, interest groups can participate in the political process, serving on government advisory bodies and testifying at parliamentary hearings. Interest groups vary in structure, style, financing, and support base, and these differences may influence a nation's politics, its economics, and its social life. We begin by defining four types of interest groups: anomic, nonassociational, institutional, and associational.

Anomic Groups

Anomic groups are groups that suddenly form when many individuals react to an event that stimulates frustration, disappointment, or other strong emotions. They are flash affairs, rising and subsiding suddenly. Without previous organization or planning, frustrated people may suddenly take to the streets to vent their anger as news of a government action touches deep emotions or as a rumor of new injustice sweeps the community. Their actions may lead to violence, although not necessarily. Particularly where organized groups are absent or where they have failed to get adequate political representation, smoldering discontent may be sparked by an incident or by the emergence of a leader. It may then suddenly explode in relatively unpredictable and uncontrollable ways.

Some political systems, including both developed and developing nations, report a rather high frequency of violent and spontaneous anomic behavior.[7] Anger over the assassination of a popular political leader or another catastrophic event can also stimulate public outbursts. For instance, one commonly sees relatively spontaneous public demonstrations when one nation makes a hostile action toward another nation. Wildcat strikes (spontaneous strike actions by local workers, not organized actions by national unions), long a feature of the British trade union scene, also occur frequently in other European countries.

Sometimes, anomic groups are a subset of individuals drawn from a larger social grouping, such as a racial or ethnic group. For instance, in 1992, some residents in minority neighborhoods of Los Angeles rioted and looted following the acquittal of police officers accused of excessive violence in the beating of an African-American suspect. Similarly, in 2005 to 2006, protests broke out in many Muslim countries over the depiction of Mohammed in the Western press, producing deaths and mass violence. We treat these as anomic group actions because there is no structure or planning to the event, and the people involved disperse after the protest ends.

We must be cautious, however, about calling something an anomic political behavior when it really is the result of detailed planning by organized groups. For instance, the demonstrations against the World Trade Organization in Seattle in 1999 and Genoa in 2001 owed much to indignation but little to spontaneity (see Box 4.2).

Nonassociational Groups

Like anomic groups, **nonassociational groups** rarely are well-organized, and their activity is episodic. They differ from anomic groups because they are based on common interests and identities of ethnicity, region, religion, occupation, or perhaps kinship. Because of these ties, nonassociational groups have more continuity than anomic groups. Subgroups within a large nonassociational group (such as an ethnic minority or workers) may act as an anomic group, as in the 1992 Los Angeles riots, the 2005 Paris immigrant riots, and the Middle East protests against the Danish cartoons of Mohammed in 2006. Throughout the world, ethnicity and religion, like occupation, are powerful identities that can stimulate collective activity.

BOX 4.2 ATTACKS ON GLOBALIZATION

In July 2001, tens of thousands of protestors arrived in Genoa to demonstrate at the G8 Summit Meeting. Hundreds of different groups came to protest at the meetings, and several of the more radical groups engaged in running battles with the police. Many of the most violent clashes involve the "Black Block." The Block is comprised of several loosely organized anarchist and radical groups, wearing trademark black clothing, black hoods, and gas masks. Confrontations with police often appeared choreographed in advance, coordinated by cell phones, and videotaped by sympathetic activists—and subsequently distributed on the Internet. Many other protest groups in Genoa were worried that the radical anarchist goals of the Block detracted attention from their policy concerns about the economic and social impacts of globalization. Similar violent protests occurred at the G8 summits in Germany in 2007 and Switzerland in 2009. The violence perpetrated by some groups overshadowed both the elected politicians at these summits and the policy goals of the nonviolent groups.

Two kinds of nonassociational groups are especially interesting. One is a large group that is not formally organized, although its members may perceive common interests. Many ethnic, regional, and occupational groups fit into this category. The members share a common interest or need, but there is no formal group to represent their interests.

It can be very difficult to organize such groups because although members share a common problem, none of them will undertake the effort to organize other members because the individual costs outweigh the individual benefits. This is commonly known as the **collective action problem**.[8] If large collective benefits—for example, ending discriminatory legislation or cleaning up water pollution—are achieved, they are shared even by those who did not work, the so-called "free-riders." This pattern of people waiting for the rewards without sharing the cost or risk of action affects other types of groups as well. For instance, students who might benefit from lower tuition fees are typically underrepresented because they lack effective organizations to articulate their interests. Understanding the collective action problem helps us to see why some groups (including governments and revolutionary challengers) become organized and others do not, and under what circumstances the barriers to collective action are overcome.

A second type of nonassociational group is the small community economic group or ethnic subgroup whose members know each other personally. A small, face-to-face group has some important advantages and may be highly effective in some political situations. If its members are well-connected or its goals unpopular or illegal, the group may remain informal or even inconspicuous. Such groups may undertake various actions, such as engaging in work stoppages, circulating student petitions to demand better support and training, requesting that a bureaucrat continue a grain tariff to benefit landowners, or asking a tax collector for favored treatment to benefit relatives. As the last example suggests, personal interest articulation may often have more legitimacy and perpetuate itself by invoking group or personal ties.

Institutional Groups

Institutional groups are formal organizations that have other political or social functions in addition to interest articulation. Political parties, business corporations, legislatures, armies, bureaucracies, and churches often have separate political groups with special responsibility for representing a group's interests. Either as corporate bodies or as smaller groups within these bodies (legislative blocs, officer cliques, groups in the clergy, or ideological cliques in bureaucracies), institutional groups express the interests of their members. The influence of these interest groups is usually drawn from the strength of their primary organizational base—for instance, the size of their membership or their income. A group based on a governmental institution has direct access to policymakers.

In industrial democracies, bureaucratic and corporate interests use their resources and special information to affect policy. In the United States, for instance, the military industrial complex consists of the combination of the U.S. Department of Defense and defense industries that support military expenditures. Similarly, the farm lobby and the U.S. Department of Agriculture together often advocate agricultural policies. Political parties are among the most active institutional participants in the policy process of most democracies. In most societies, government bureaucracies do not simply react to pressures from the outside; they also can act as independent forces of interest representation.

Nonpolitical institutional groups can also participate in the political process. In Italy, for example, the Roman Catholic Church has exerted significant influence on the government. In electoral politics, the Church used to ask Catholics to vote against the communists. Less overtly, the Church has members of the clergy call on officeholders to express opinions on matters of concern to the Church. In Islamic countries, fundamentalist clergy pursue a similar role, prescribing what morals public policy should follow, actively lobbying governmental officials, and sometimes participating in the governing process.

In authoritarian regimes, which prohibit or at least control explicit political groups, institutional groups can still play a large role. Educational officials, party officials, jurists, factory managers, officers in the military services, and government bodies representing other social units had significant roles in interest articulation in communist regimes. In preindustrial societies, which usually have fewer associational groups and with limited popular support, military groups, corporations, party factions, and bureaucrats often play prominent political roles. Even where the military does not seize power directly, the possibility of such action often forces close government attention to military requests.

Associational Groups

Associational groups are formed explicitly to represent the interests of a particular group, such as trade unions, chambers of commerce, manufacturers' associations, and ethnic associations. These organizations have procedures for formulating interests and demands, and they usually employ a full-time professional staff. Associational groups are often very active in representing the interests of their members in the policy process. For instance, in recurring debates about health care in the United States, there is an enormous mobilization of pressure groups and lobbyists—from representatives of doctors and health-insurance organizations to consumer groups and the like—seeking to influence legislation.

Associational interest groups—where they are allowed to flourish—affect the development of other types of groups. Their organizational base gives them an advantage over nonassociational groups, and their tactics and goals are often recognized as legitimate in society. Labor unions, for example, are often central political actors because they represent the mass of the working class; in the same way, business associations often speak for the corporate interests of the nation.

A special subset of associational groups consists of citizens who are united not by a common economic or individual self-interest but by a common belief in a political ideology or a policy goal.[9] The environmental movement, many women's groups, human rights organizations, and other civic groups are examples of this kind of associational group. In some of these issue groups, the members may seldom interact directly and may not even share common social characteristics (such as employment or ethnicity), but are bound together by their support of a political organization, such as Greenpeace or Amnesty International. On the organizational side, many of these new social groups have fluid and dynamic organizations, with frequent turnover in both leadership and membership. On the tactical side, they use a wide range of approaches, often discounting the value of partisan campaigning and conventional lobbying in favor of unconventional protests and direct actions.

Civic associations represent another way for citizens to articulate their policy goals by supporting groups that advocate their preferred policy positions. Such groups have proliferated in most advanced industrial democracies in the past generation, and they are now spreading to the developing world.

In summary, a social interest can manifest itself in many different groups. We can illustrate this point with examples of different groups that might involve members of the working class:

Anomic group: a spontaneous group of working-class individuals living in the same neighborhood
Nonassociational group: the working class as a collective
Institutional group: the labor department within the government
Associational group: a labor union

Distinguishing among the types of groups is important for several reasons. The nature of a group typically reflects the resources it can mobilize to support its political efforts. Perhaps one of the most important resources is an institutional structure that will sustain political efforts until the government responds to the group's interests. The nature of a group also may signify the tactics it uses to gain political access. Finally, since the articulation of interest is the first step in policy influence, the nature of groups suggests which types of interests are more likely to get a hearing in the political system and which interests may be underrepresented.

CIVIL SOCIETY

Political analysts have devoted increasing attention to whether an extensive network of interest groups and public participation in these groups creates a **civil society**—a society in which people are involved in social and political interactions free of state control or regulation. Community groups, voluntary associations, and even religious groups—as well as access to free communication and information through the mass media and the Internet—are important parts of a civil society.[10] Participation in civil society groups can socialize individuals into the political skills and cooperative relations that are part of a well-functioning society. People learn how to organize, express their interests, and work with others to achieve common goals. They also learn that the political process itself is as important as the immediate results. Thus, a system of active associational groups can lessen the development of anomic or nonassociational activity. Group activity can help citizens to develop and clarify their own preferences, provide important information about political events, and articulate the interests of citizens more clearly and precisely than parties and elections.[11] Thus, an active public involved in various interest groups provides a fertile ground for the development of democratic politics.

As political and economic conditions become interdependent across nations, there is also increasing attention directed toward the development of a global civil society. Individuals and groups in one nation are connected to groups with similar concerns in other nations, and jointly reinforce their individual efforts. Environmental groups in the Western democracies, for example, assist environmental groups in developing nations with the expertise and organizational resources to address the issues facing their country. National groups meet at international conferences and policy forums, and the network of social relations, as well as Internet connections, extends across national borders.[12] This is another sign of how the international context of domestic politics is growing worldwide.

One problem facing the nations of Eastern Europe and other newly democratizing nations is building a rich associational group life in societies where the government had suppressed or controlled organized groups.[13] The Communist Party and the government bureaucracy dominated the nations of Eastern Europe for over forty years and prevented autonomous action. The process of building new, independent associational groups to articulate the interests of different citizens is under way and will be important to the democratic process. Similarly, many less economically developed nations need to create a civil society of associational groups to involve citizens in the political process and represent their interests if democratization is to succeed.

INTEREST-GROUP SYSTEMS

The relationship between interest groups and government policymaking institutions is another important feature of the political process. Different types of connections create different interest-group systems. All modern societies have large numbers of interest groups, but their relationships with government can follow different models. Interest-group systems are classified into three major groupings: pluralist, democratic corporatist, and controlled.[14]

Pluralist Interest-Group Systems

Pluralist interest-group systems have several features involving both how interests are organized and how they participate in the political process:

- Multiple groups may represent a single societal interest.
- Group membership is voluntary and limited.
- Groups often have a loose or decentralized organizational structure.
- There is a clear separation between interest groups and the government.

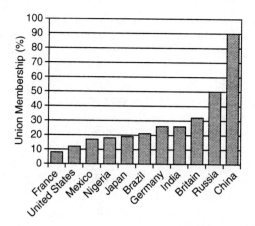

FIGURE 4.1
Union Membership
Labor Union Density Varies Widely across Nations

Source: International Labour Organization, UNION database (www.ilo.org); and International Labour Organization, *World Labour Report 1997–1998,* The Statistical Annex, Table 1.2 (www.ilo.org). The figure plots union membership as a percentage of wage and salary earners.

For instance, not only are there different groups for different social sectors (such as labor, business, and professional interests), but there may be many labor unions or business associations within each sector. These groups compete among themselves for membership and influence, and all simultaneously press their demands on the government. The United States is the best-known example of a strongly pluralist interest-group system; Canada and New Zealand are also cited as examples. Despite its greater labor-union membership (see Figure 4.1) and somewhat greater coordination of economic associations, Britain tends to fall on the pluralist side in most analyses, as do France and Japan.

Democratic Neo-Corporatist Interest-Group Systems

Democratic **neo-corporatist interest-group** systems are characterized by a much more organized representation of interests:

- A single peak association normally represents each societal interest.
- Membership in the peak association is often compulsory and nearly universal.
- Peak associations are centrally organized and direct the actions of their members.
- Groups are often systematically involved in making and implementing policy.

For instance, in a neo-corporatist system, there may be a single peak association that represents all the major industrial interests; a pluralist system may have several different business groups that act autonomously. In addition, in a neo-corporatist system, peak associations are centrally organized, while groups in a pluralist system typically have decentralized organizational structures. The most thoroughly corporatist interest-group systems are in Austria, Finland, the Netherlands, Norway, and Sweden. These nations are characterized by a high level of union membership among the nonagricultural labor force, along with a highly centralized and united labor movement.

Equally important, interest groups such as labor unions in these systems often regularly and legitimately work with the government agencies and/or political parties as partners in negotiating solutions to policy problems. For instance, German labor unions have formal membership on many government commissions, have special access to policy administration, and are very influential through informal channels of influence. Thus, Germany is a close fit to the neo-corporatist model.

Mexico and Brazil are examples of another form of corporatist politics. Union membership is modest in both nations (see again Figure 4.1), although the trade unions and peasant associations are closely tied to political parties or religious interests. Usually, these groups mobilize support for the political parties or social institutions that dominate them, and they are closely tied to the state when their party is in power. This system is changing in both Mexico and Brazil, as democratization encourages the unions to become more politically independent and influential.

The best-studied democratic neo-corporatist arrangements involve economic problems. Democracies with business and labor peak associations that negotiate with each other and the government have had better records than more pluralist countries in sustaining employment, restraining inflation, and increasing social spending.[15] In addition, there is also evidence that neo-corporatist systems are more effective in implementing other public policies, such as environmental protection.[16]

In many advanced industrial societies, however, membership in labor unions has decreased and some bargaining patterns have become less centralized. Thus, some countries that have relied on neo-corporatist patterns have adapted this system to these new consequences and applied corporatism in new ways.[17] In contrast, several nations in Eastern Europe are attempting to develop more corporatist structures to nurture interest-group politics, but the system of autonomous interest groups remains underdeveloped. The experience with neo-corporatist models in developing nations is even more varied.[18] Nigeria and India illustrate a pattern common in other developing democracies. Interest groups, such as unions, are often not well-developed and have a limited mass membership. They are participants in the process, but without the mass membership or formal access that gives labor unions influence in established Western democracies of either the pluralist or corporatist model.

Controlled Interest-Group Systems

Finally, **controlled interest-group systems** follow a different pattern:

- There is a single group for each social sector.
- Membership is often compulsory.

- Each group is normally hierarchically organized.
- Groups are controlled by the government or its agents in order to mobilize support for government policy.

The last point is the most important: Groups exist to facilitate government control of society. The best examples are the traditional communist systems in which the party penetrates all levels of society and controls all the permitted associational groups. For instance, Figure 4.1 shows that 90 percent of wage earners in China belong to a union.[19] Unions and other interest associations are subordinated to the Communist Party, and they are only rarely permitted to articulate the interests of their members. Russia once followed this communist model, and the unions have large memberships as a result of this experience. These unions are struggling to gain autonomy from the state and play an influential role in the postcommunist system. But they have made limited progress.

These nations limit interest articulation to leaders of institutional groups, who can use their positions in political institutions as a base for expressing their demands. Numerous institutional interest groups can also emerge in these societies, especially from parts of the party and bureaucracy, such as the military, as well as informal nonassociational groups.

ACCESS TO THE INFLUENTIAL

To be effective, interest groups must reach key policymakers through **channels of political access**. Otherwise, groups may express their members' interests yet fail to have an impact on policymakers. Political systems vary in the ways they respond to political interests. Interest groups vary in the tactics they use to gain access. Group tactics are partially shaped by the structure of policymaking, as well as by their own values and preferences.

There is a significant distinction between legitimate and constitutional channels of access (such as the mass media, parties, and legislatures) and illegitimate, coercive access channels. These two channels reflect the types of resources that groups can use to influence elites as well as the group's perceptions of which tactics will be most successful. Groups with substantial resources—money, members, or status—typically have an easier time working through legitimate constitutional channels. Groups with limited resources or legitimacy may feel they must act through coercive channels because they are not accepted by the political system. In democracies, groups tend toward legitimate channels because the system expects and allows group activity. In contrast, nondemocratic systems typically limit legitimate access, which might stimulate illegitimate or coercive activities.

Legitimate Access Channels

The legitimate channels of access can take many forms, and these often exist in both democratic and nondemocratic systems. For instance, personal connections are an important means of reaching political elites in all societies—the use of family, school, local, or other social ties. An excellent example is the information network among the British elite based on old school ties originating at Eton, Harrow, or other "public" schools, or at Oxford and Cambridge universities. Similarly, in Japan, many alumni of the University of Tokyo Law School hold top positions among the political and bureaucratic elites who interact because of these personal ties. Although personal connections are commonly used by nonassociational groups representing family or regional interests, they serve other groups as well. In modern nations, personal connections are usually cultivated with special care. In Washington, D.C., the business of advising interest groups and individuals on access to politicians is an increasingly lucrative profession (and increasingly a target of government regulation and potential corruption). These activities are often carried on by former officeholders, who use their personal governmental contacts for their lobbyist clients.

The **mass media**—television, radio, newspapers, and magazines—are another important access channel in democratic societies. The mass media and the Internet can mobilize support for interest-group efforts, leading to donations of time and money, and encouraging sympathizers to support the group. Many interest groups thus hire public-relations specialists, purchase direct advertising, and seek favorable attention in the media. Interest groups encourage media reports on their needs as well as coverage of their policy views. When a cause receives national media attention, the message to policymakers carries added weight if politicians know that millions of voters are interested in the issue. Moreover, groups believe that in an open society, "objective" news coverage has more credibility than sponsored messages.

The potential power of the media could be seen when the communist governments in Eastern Europe loosened control over the media in the late 1980s. This action gave a huge boost to democracy movements. For instance, when asked what caused the democratic revolution in Poland in the 1990s, Lech Walesa pointed to a television and said, "That did." Media reports on the failures in communist government policy and the contrasting lifestyles in the West undermined the legitimacy of the regimes. As democratic protests spread across Eastern Europe, stories of successful protests in other parts of the country, or in other countries, enhanced the confidence of demonstrators. Citizen protests encouraged by mass-media reports helped convince the ruling groups that their support had vanished.

Political parties are another important access point. Democratic political parties often rely on interest groups for financial and voter support, and act as representatives of these interests within government. In a nation like Germany, the various parts of the party organization, particularly parliamentary committees, are important channels for transmitting demands to the cabinet and the party in power. In some cases, other factors limit the role of parties as interest representatives. For instance, highly ideological parties, such as most communist parties, are more likely to control affiliated interest groups than to communicate the interest groups' demands. Decentralized party organizations, like those in the United States, may be less helpful than individual legislators in providing access.

BOX 4.3 LOBBYING BEHIND THE SCENES

British beer companies use a variety of means to support their industry. For example, the industry contributed funds to Labour MPs who recently voted for longer opening hours for British pubs. They also provide travel support for MPs who are favorable to the industry. A group of MPs who support the industry formed the All-Party Parliamentary Beer Group (APBG). The group's announced goal is "to promote the wholesomeness and enjoyment of beer and the unique role of the pub in UK society." The parliamentary group campaigned to have beer taxes reduced, conducted hearings on whether the government overregulates British pubs, and supported the extension of pub hours. The group hosts a series of functions at Westminster, giving industry chiefs the opportunity to meet MPs and showcase their products. The parliamentary group also selects a "beer drinker of the year," who receives an award at their annual dinner. The parliamentary group receives direct financial support from breweries, and the secretary for the group is paid by the alcohol industry.

Visit the APBG Web site: www.publications.parliament.uk/pa/cm/cmallparty/register/memi184.htm.

Legislatures are a common target of interest-group activities (see Box 4.3). Standard lobbying tactics include making appearances before legislative committees and providing information to individual legislators. In the United States, political action committees raise campaign contributions for individual members of Congress and usually receive some political attention in exchange. In Britain and France, the strong party discipline in the legislature lessens the importance of individual members of Parliament (MPs) as access channels. In contrast, in the United States, the combination of loose party discipline and a decentralized legislative system makes the individual members of the Congress major targets of group efforts.

Government bureaucracies are another major access point in most political systems. Contacts with the bureaucratic agencies may be particularly important where the bureaucracy has policymaking authority or where interests are narrow and directly involve few citizens. A bureaucrat sympathetic to a group may try to respond to its demands by exercising administrative discretion without leaving bureaucratic channels. A government official may also give public consideration to an issue or frame an issue in a way that receives a sympathetic hearing by policymakers. The bureaucracy may be an especially important access point in nondemocratic systems because other legitimate channels of citizen access do not exist.

Government officials may consider protest demonstrations, strikes, and other forms of dramatic and direct pressure on government as legitimate or illegitimate tactics, depending on the political system. Protests may be either spontaneous actions of an anomic group or a planned use of unconventional channels by an organized group. In democratic societies, demonstrations often mobilize popular support—or electoral support—or media attention for the group's cause. On a regular basis, the Mall in Washington, D.C., or similar locations in other national capitals host groups protesting a wide variety of policy issues. In nondemocratic societies, such demonstrations are more hazardous and often represent more extreme dissatisfaction that cannot find voice through conventional channels of access.

Lawful demonstrations are another tactic of interest groups, especially those that do not have access or resources to influence policymakers through conventional channels. Protests are also a favored tactic of groups whose ideological commitments focus on challenging the established social and political order. Protests are increasingly used as a means of interest articulation by organized and accepted interests who feel that dramatic actions can heighten support for their cause. Protests can supplement other channels, especially in gaining the attention of the mass media in an age when television comes to every household. Thus, we find doctors in New Delhi, farmers in Japan, and "gray panthers" (the elderly) in Germany using a tactic that once was limited to the poor and minorities.[20]

Coercive Access Channels and Tactics

Most scholars see the level of collective violence as closely associated with the character of a society and the circumstances in the nation. In his studies of civil strife, Ted Robert Gurr argued that feelings of relative deprivation motivate people to act aggressively.[21] These feelings can stimulate frustration, discontent, and anger—which may then lead to violence. People also may turn to violence if they believe it is justified and will lead to success. If they think that their government is illegitimate and that the cause of their discontent is justified, they will more readily turn to political violence. To this end, it is the responsibility of the government and its institutions to provide peaceful alternatives to violence as a means of change.

This general description of political violence should not overlook the differences among the types of violent political activities. A riot, for example, involves the spontaneous expression of collective anger and dissatisfaction by individuals. Though riots have long been dismissed as aberrant and irrational action by social riffraff, modern studies have shown that rioters vary greatly in their motivation, behavior, and social background.[22] Most riots seem to follow some fairly clear-cut patterns, such as confining destruction or violence to particular areas or targets. Relative deprivation appears to be a major cause of riots, but the release of the frustrations is not as aimless as is often supposed.

For instance, the 2005 riots in Paris were triggered by the accidental deaths of two teenagers, but most analysts see their deaths as only a proximate cause, a "spark" that ignited already volatile factors. Gangs of minority youth burned thousands of automobiles, damaged shops, and attacked police who attempted to quell the violence. The French president and then the Parliament declared a state of emergency in reaction to the violent protests, establishing a curfew and limiting civil liberties. Even though much of the mayhem seemed poorly related to effective political action, it was a cry for attention. Youth from immigrant families had high levels of unemployment and felt that social and economic discrimination was limiting their life chances. Even in a democracy, the government sometimes overlooks the needs of its own citizens and allows such frustrations to explode into violence.

While deprivation may help fuel the discontent, strikes and obstructions are typically carried out by well-organized associational or institutional groups. For instance, a long series of violent protests against globalization involve highly organized activities among some of the more radical groups participating in the protests (see again Box 4.2).

Historically, labor unions used the general strike to pressure the government or employers on fundamental issues. The influence of strikes and obstructions has varied, however, depending on the legitimacy of the government and coercive pressure from other groups. A general strike after vote fraud in the 2004 Ukrainian elections produced a transition to a new democratic government, but student-inspired boycotts in Korea in the 1980s had only a modest impact on the government. Most spectacularly, the strikes, obstructions, and demonstrations in Eastern Europe in 1989 and 1990, like the earlier people's power movement in the Philippines, had massive success against regimes that had lost legitimacy.

Finally, radical groups sometimes use **political terror tactics**—including deliberate assassination, armed attacks on other groups or government officials, and mass bloodshed. The tragedies in Northern Ireland; the suicide bombings by Palestinians in Israel; and the attacks of jihadist terrorists in New York City, Madrid, London, Bali, and other cities demonstrate the use of such tactics. The use of terrorism typically reflects the desire of some group to change the rules of the political game or to destroy a political system, rather than to gain political access.

The use of political terror is more often likely to produce negative consequences rather than construct positive policy change. Massive deadly violence may destroy a democratic regime, leading to curtailment of civil rights or even military intervention when many people and leaders feel that any alternative is preferable to more violence. For example, democratically elected governments justified their suppression of democratic institutions in Peru in 1992 and India in 1975 in response to the violent actions of terrorists. An authoritarian, repressive response often promises quick results against terrorists; however, small-group terrorism usually fails when confronted by united democratic leadership.[23] In a democratic society, violence often forfeits the sympathy that a group needs if its cause is to receive a responsive hearing. The current conflict between the West and jihadist terrorists has renewed the debate on how democratic governments should balance the need for security against the preservation of civil liberties.

TABLE 4.3

Examples of Interest Articulation

Interest groups can use either legitimate or coercive channels of action.

Types of Interest Groups	Channel of Action	
	Legitimate Channel	Coercive Channel
Anomic groups	Chinese workers stage impromptu strikes for better pay and working conditions	Iranians attack Danish embassy to protest cartoons depicting Mohammed
Nonassociational groups	Mexican business leaders discuss taxes with president	Minorities in France riot in 2005 over their social conditions
Institutional groups	U.S. Department of Agriculture advocates subsidies for honey production	Indonesian army supports democracy movement to overthrow Suharto regime
Associational groups	Greenpeace lobbies the European Parliament to ban genetically modified foods	Palestinian Hamas launches terror attacks on Israel

Groups and Channels

In order to understand the formation of policies, we need to know which groups articulate interests, their policy preferences, and the channels of influence they use. Table 4.3 gives examples of legitimate and coercive interest articulation for different types of interest groups. Each case provides an example of the differences in legitimate access channels, such as informal meetings by Mexican business leaders lobbying their government to Greenpeace testifying before European Parliament committees. Similarly, coercive acts range from spontaneous outbursts by anomic groups to Hamas using terror tactics in Gaza. This framework also helps us to think about how a single interest group might pursue its goals through multiple channels, including protests, representation by institutional groups, and lobbying by associational groups. For instance, honeybee farmers in the United States have lobbied their representatives in Congress to maintain federal price supports, and they also use their allies in the U.S. Department of Agriculture to support their position (will honeybee protests be next?). This table presents examples from many nations in order to suggest the varied possibilities that exist in each nation.

INTEREST-GROUP DEVELOPMENT

One consequence of modernization is a widespread belief that the conditions of life can be altered through human action. Modernization normally involves education, urbanization, rapid growth in public communication, and improvement in the physical conditions of life. These changes are closely related to

increases in political awareness, participation, and feelings of political competence. Such participant attitudes encourage more diverse and citizen-based
interest articulation.

At the same time, modernization produces an increasing diversity of life
conditions and a specialization of labor as people work in many types of
jobs—a process that leads to the formation of large numbers of special interests. The interdependence of modern life, the exposure provided by mass
communications, and a larger policy role of government further multiply
political interests that are organized into different interest groups. Globalization processes have also increased the interactions between interest groups
across nations, or between domestic groups and international actors.[24] Thus,
the diversity of interest groups and their activities is another by-product of
modernization.

Successful democratic development leads to the emergence of complex
interest-group systems that express the needs of groups and individuals in the
society. Yet this process is by no means automatic. The problems of organizing
large groups for collective action are huge. Societies vary widely in the extent
to which people engage in associational activity. The level of trust shared
among members of a society is one factor influencing social group participation.[25] The resources and societal support available for collective action is
another factor. However, modernization may weaken traditional structures in
some societies and then fail to develop effective associational groups in their
place because of restrictive social attitudes. A nation's ability to achieve either
stability or democracy will be hindered as a result.

In other cases, authoritarian parties and bureaucracies may control associational groups and choke off the channels of political access. For nearly half
a century, the communist governments of Eastern Europe suppressed
autonomous interest groups. Eventually, the processes of economic modernization pressured these systems to allow more open organization and expression
of political interests. In addition, social change expanded interest articulation
activity and a need for associational groups to represent citizens' interests.

The development of organized interest groups should not, however, lead
us to conclude that every group has equal standing. Using the American experience as an example, the articulation of interests is frequently biased toward
the goals of the better-off, who are also often better organized.[26] It is frequently pointed out that the American Association of Retired Persons (AARP)
is a highly effective group that is not counterbalanced by a "Young Taxpayers
Group," and that the traditional labor-management competition leaves consumers underrepresented.

We might test the breadth of citizen representation by evaluating systems
in terms of their inclusiveness: What proportion of the population is represented to what degree in national-level politics? South Africa under apartheid
illustrates the extreme case where the majority was prevented outright from
forming associational groups. In the Third World, competing interests in the
capital rarely involve the interests of rural peasants; peasant organizations are
sometimes brutally suppressed, while urban middle- and upper-class groups
can petition authorities. It is no coincidence that the bias in group inclusion

appears greatest where the gaps in income and education are widest. As noted above, pushed to the extreme, those excluded from the process may engage in anomic activity or resort to violence.[27] Even in less extreme cases, the presence of different levels of political awareness means that every interest-group system is somewhat biased. Democratization involves not only the provision of competitive elections but also the reduction of the bias in interest representation.

Another challenge faces the patterns of interest articulation and representation in advanced industrial democracies. There are claims that participation in associational groups is decreasing in the United States and perhaps in other established democracies.[28] For instance, memberships in labor unions and formal church engagement have steadily trended downward in most Western democracies over the past several decades. Some scholars argue that this trend represents a growing social isolation in developed nations, as people forsake social and political involvement for the comfort of a favorite chair and a favorite television program. However, other researchers argue that we are witnessing a change in how citizens organize and express their interests, such as through public-interest groups, Internet networks, and blogging.[29] Even in nations such as India and China, millions of people are now using the Internet to learn about politics and how they can articulate their interests.

What can be said for certain is that democratic politics rests on a participatory public that uses individual and group methods to express and represent its interests. Thus, developing an active social and political life is an important standard for measuring the political development of a nation.

REVIEW QUESTIONS

1. How do the different forms of citizen action vary in their potential influence on policymakers?
2. What are the main types of interest groups?
3. How does a "civil society" differ from a noncivil society?
4. What are the key differences among pluralist, neo-corporatist, and controlled interest-group systems?
5. What are the consequences when an interest group works through legitimate channels of influence rather than coercive channels?
6. If you studied interest articulation patterns in one of the nations in this book, could you build a table (like Table 4.3) showing examples of the types of groups and the channels they used?

KEY TERMS

anomic groups
associational groups
channels of political
   access
civil society
collective action
   problem

controlled interest-group
   systems
institutional groups
interest articulation
mass media
neo-corporatist interest-
   group systems

nonassociational groups
pluralist interest-group
   systems
political terror tactics
protests

SUGGESTED READINGS

Blais, Andre. *To Vote or Not to Vote: The Merits of Rational Choice Theory.* Pittsburgh, PA: University of Pittsburgh Press, 2000.

Dahl, Robert A. *Polyarchy: Participation and Opposition.* New Haven, CT: Yale University Press, 1971.

———. *Democracy and Its Critics.* New Haven, CT: Yale University Press, 1989.

Dalton, Russell J. *Citizen Politics: Public Opinion and Political Parties in Advanced Industrial Democracies,* 5th ed. Washington, D.C.: CQ Press, 2008.

Hirschman, Albert. *Exit, Voice, and Loyalty.* Cambridge, MA: Harvard University Press, 1970.

Howard, Marc Morjé. *The Weakness of Civil Society in Post-Communist Europe.* New York: Cambridge University Press, 2003.

Maloney, William, and Jan Van Deth. *Civil Society and Activism in Europe: Contextualizing Engagement and Political Orientations.* London: Routledge, 2010.

Norris, Pippa. *Democratic Phoenix: Reinventing Political Activism.* New York: Cambridge University Press, 2003.

Olson, Mancur. *The Logic of Collective Action.* Cambridge, MA: Harvard University Press, 1965.

Paxton, Pamela, and M. Hughes. *Women, Politics and Power: A Global Perspective.* London: Pine Forge Press, 2007.

Putnam, Robert. *Bowling Alone: The Collapse and Revival of American Community.* New York: Simon & Schuster, 2000.

Putnam, Robert D., ed. *Democracies in Flux: The Evolution of Social Capital in Contemporary Society.* Oxford: Oxford University Press, 2002.

Rootes, Christopher. *Environmental Movements: Local, National, and Global.* London: Frank Cass, 1999.

Shi, Tianjian. *Political Participation in Beijing.* Cambridge, MA: Harvard University Press, 1997.

Tarrow, Sidney. *The New Transnational Activism.* New York: Cambridge University Press, 2005.

Thomas, Clive. *Political Parties and Interest Groups: Shaping Democratic Governance.* Boulder, CO: Lynn Rienner, 2001.

Verba, Sidney, Norman H. Nie, and Jae-on Kim. *Participation and Political Equality.* Cambridge: Cambridge University Press, 1978.

Verba, Sidney, Kay Schlozman, and Henry Brady. *Voice and Equality.* Cambridge, MA: Harvard University Press, 1995.

Zurn, Michael, and Gregor Walter, eds. *Globalizing Interests: Pressure Groups and Denationalization.* Albany: State University of New York Press, 2005.

ENDNOTES

1. This framework draws on Sidney Verba, Norman N. Nie, and Jae-on Kim, *Participation and Political Equality* (New York: Cambridge University Press, 1978), Chapter 2.
2. See, for example, the range of activities of Beijing residents described in Tianjin Shi, *Political Participation in Beijing* (Cambridge, MA: Harvard University Press, 1997).
3. Michele Micheletti, Andreas Follesdal, and Dietlind Stolle, *Politics, Products, and Markets: Exploring Political Consumerism Past and Present* (Transaction Publishers, 2003).

4. Pippa Norris, *Democratic Phoenix: Reinventing Political Activism* (New York: Cambridge University Press, 2003); Verba, Nie, and Kim, *Participation and Political Equality*.
5. Russell Dalton, Alix van Sickle, and Steve Weldon, "The Individual-Institutional Nexus of Protest Behavior," *British Journal of Political Science* 40 (2010): 51–73.
6. See Verba, Nie, and Kim, *Participation and Political Equality*; Norris, *Democratic Phoenix*.
7. See the evidence in J. Craig Jenkins and Kurt Schock, "Political Process, International Dependence, and Mass Political Conflict: A Global Analysis of Protest and Rebellion, 1973–1978," *International Journal of Sociology* 33 (2004): 41–63.
8. Studies of these problems were stimulated by the now-classic work of Mancur Olson, *The Logic of Collective Action* (Cambridge, MA: Harvard University Press, 1965). See also Mark Lichbach, *The Rebel's Dilemma* (Ann Arbor: University of Michigan Press, 1994); Todd Sandler, ed., *Collective Action: Theory and Applications* (Ann Arbor: University of Michigan Press, 1992).
9. Christopher Rootes, ed., *Environmental Movements: Local, National, and Global* (London: Frank Cass, 1999); Amrita Basu, ed., *The Challenges of Local Feminism: Women's Movements in Global Perspective* (Boulder, CO: Westview, 1995).
10. Jean Cohen and A. Arato, *Civil Society and Political Theory* (Cambridge: Massachusetts Institute of Technology Press, 1992); M. Walzer, ed., *Toward a Global Civil Society* (Oxford: Berghahn Books, 1995).
11. See Table 4.1; John Pierce et al., *Citizens, Political Communication, and Interest Groups: Environmental Organizations in Canada and the United States* (Westport, CT: Praeger, 1992).
12. Sidney Tarrow, *The New Transnational Activism* (New York: Cambridge University Press, 2005); Margaret Keck and Kathryn Sikkink, *Activists beyond Borders: Advocacy Networks in International Politics* (Ithaca, NY: Cornell University Press, 1998).
13. Marc Morjé Howard, *The Weakness of Civil Society in Post-Communist Europe* (New York: Cambridge University Press, 2003); Russell Dalton, "Civil Society and Democracy," in *Citizens, Democracy, and Markets Around the Pacific Rim*, ed. Russell Dalton and Doh Chull Shin (Oxford: Oxford University Press, 2006).
14. Philippe Schmitter, "Interest Intermediation and Regime Governability," in *Organizing Interests in Western Europe*, ed. Suzanne Berger (New York: Cambridge University Press, 1981), Chapter 12; Arend Lijphart and Markus Crepaz, "Corporatism and Consensus Democracy in 18 Countries," *British Journal of Political Science* 21, no. 2 (April 1991): 235–46.
15. On the relative success of the corporatist systems in economic performance, see Miriam Golden, "The Dynamics of Trade Unionism and National Economic Performance," *American Political Science Review* 87, no. 2 (June 1993): 439–54; Arend Lijphart, Ronald Rogowski, and R. Kent Weaver, "Separation of Powers and Cleavage Management," in R. Kent Weaver and Bert A. Rockman, *Do Institutions Matter? Government Capabilities in the United States and Abroad* (Washington, D.C.: Brookings Institution, 1993), 302–44.
16. Lyle Scruggs, "Institutions and Environmental Performance in Seventeen Western Democracies," *British Journal of Political Science* 29 (1999): 1–31.
17. Oscar Molina and Martin Rhodes, "Corporatism: The Past, Present and Future of a Concept," *Annual Review of Political Science* 2 (2002): 305–31.
18. Howard Wiarda, ed. *Authoritarianism and Corporatism in Latin America—Revisited* (Gainesville: University Press of Florida, 2004); Julius E. Nyang'Oro and Timothy M. Shaw, *Corporatism in Africa: Comparative Analysis and Practice* (Boulder, CO: Westview Press, 1990).

19. We should also note that most Chinese work and live in rural areas and are not wage earners. The figure is based on the share of the labor force that receives a regular salary, which in China means urban workers. But India has a comparable labor structure, and many fewer Indian wage earners are unionized.
20. Norris, *Democratic Phoenix*.
21. T. Robert Gurr, *Why Men Rebel* (Princeton, NJ: Princeton University Press, 1970).
22. See Pippa Norris, Stefaan Walgrave, and Peter van Aelst, "Does Protest Signify Disaffection? Demonstrators in a Postindustrial Democracy," in *Political Disaffection in Contemporary Democracies*, ed. Mariano Torcal and Jose Ramón Montero (London: Routledge, 2006): 279–307.
23. On violence and democratic survival, see G. Bingham Powell, Jr., *Contemporary Democracies: Participation, Stability, and Violence* (Cambridge, MA: Harvard University Press, 1982), Chapter 8; see also the contributions to Juan J. Linz and Alfred Stepan, eds., *The Breakdown of Democratic Regimes* (Baltimore: Johns Hopkins University Press, 1978).
24. Michal Zurn and Gregor Walter, eds., *Globalizing Interests: Pressure Groups and Denationalization* (Albany: State University of New York Press, 2005); Keck and Sikkink, *Activists beyond Borders*.
25. Ronald Inglehart, *Culture Shift in Advanced Industrial Societies* (Princeton, NJ: Princeton University Press, 1990), 34–36.
26. Jeffrey M. Berry, *The Interest Group Society* (New York: Longman, 1997).
27. Many of these studies are reviewed by Mark I. Lichbach, "An Evaluation of 'Does Economic Inequality Breed Political Conflict' Studies," *World Politics* 41 (1989): 431–70. More recent references and analyses appear in T. Y. Wang et al., "Inequality and Political Violence Revisited," *American Political Science Review* 87, no. 4 (Dec. 1993): 979–93.
28. Robert Putnam, *Bowling Alone: The Collapse and Revival of American Community* (New York: Simon & Schuster, 2000); Robert Putnam, ed., *Democracies in Flux: The Evolution of Social Capital in Contemporary Society* (Oxford: Oxford University Press, 2002).
29. Cliff Zukin et al., *A New Engagement? Political Participation, Civic Life, and the Changing American Citizen* (New York: Oxford University Press, 2006); Russell Dalton, *The Good Citizen* (Washington, D.C.: CQ Press, 2007), Chapter 4.

Interest Aggregation and Political Parties

Many voters want their governments to make decisions on the basis of a coherent policy program. For political decisions to be made this way, interests must not only be articulated, but also packaged into alternative visions or programs. **Interest aggregation** is the process by which political demands are combined into policy programs. For example, when politicians make economic policy, they often have to balance farmers' desires for higher crop prices, consumers' preferences for lower prices and taxes, and environmentalists' concerns about water pollution and pesticides. Who prevails in such balancing acts depends in part on political institutions, which is the subject of Chapter 6. But interest aggregation depends also on political skills and resources, such as votes, campaign funds, political offices, media access, or even armed force.

How interests are aggregated is a key feature of politics. The aggregation process determines which interests are heard and who is allowed to participate. Interest aggregation can help create a balanced government program out of competing policy goals, but it can also generate a bundle of compromises that satisfy no one. How stable and effective governments are depends on their success in interest aggregation.

Interest aggregation can occur in many ways. An elected leader or military dictator may have a considerable personal impact. Yet large states usually develop more specialized organizations for aggregating interests. Political parties are just such organizations, and they aggregate interests in democratic, as well as in many nondemocratic, systems. Each party (or its candidates) stands for a set of policies and tries to build a coalition of support for this program. In democracies, two or more parties compete to gain support for their alternative policy programs. In autocracies, the ruling party or institution may try to mobilize citizens' support for its policies, but the process is frequently covert, controlled, and top-down rather than bottom-up. In other words, autocratic (authoritarian) parties mobilize interests to support the government rather than responding to demands by ordinary citizens or social interests.

It is important to remember that political parties may perform many different functions other than interest aggregation and that interests may be aggregated by many different structures. For instance, parties frequently shape the political culture as they strive to build support for their programs and candidates. Parties recruit voters and select candidates for office. They articulate interests of their own and transmit the demands of others. Governing parties are also involved in making public policy and overseeing its implementation and adjudication. Yet parties are particularly important structures of interest aggregation because of their distinctive role in mobilizing support for their policies and candidates. In this chapter, we compare the role of parties in interest aggregation to those of other structures.

PERSONAL INTEREST AGGREGATION

One way to bring political interests together in policymaking is through personal connections. Virtually all societies feature **patron–client networks**—structures in which a central officeholder, authority figure, or group provides benefits (patronage) to supporters in exchange for their loyalty. It was the defining principle of feudalism. The king and his lords, the lord and his knights, the knight and his serfs and tenants—all were bound by ties of personal dependence and loyalty. The American political machines of Boss Tweed of New York or Richard Daley, Sr., of Chicago were similarly bound together by patronage and loyalty. Personal networks are not confined to relationships cemented by patronage only. The president of the United States, for instance, usually has a circle of personal confidants, a "brain trust" or "kitchen cabinet," bound to their chief by ideological and policy propensities as well as by ties of friendship.

The patron–client network is so common in politics that it resembles the cell in biology or the atom in physics—the primitive structure out of which larger and more complicated political structures are composed. Students of politics in all countries report such networks. When interest aggregation is performed mainly within patron–client networks, it is difficult to mobilize political resources behind unified policies of rapid social change. This is because political decisions depend on ever-shifting agreements among many factional leaders (patrons) who all want to benefit. Patron–client politics thus typically means a static political system with little policy innovation.

Contemporary research on patron–client relationships was pioneered in studies of Asian politics, where this structure runs through the political processes of countries such as the Philippines, Japan, and India.[1] But parallels exist in Europe, the Middle East, Latin America, and most regions of the world. Patron–client relationships affect recruitment to political office, interest aggregation, policymaking, and policy implementation. Yet as Table 5.1 shows, patron–client networks are a particularly important means of aggregating political interests in poorer countries.

TABLE 5.1

Structures Performing Interest Aggregation in Selected Contemporary Nations

Parties are not alone.*

	Extensiveness of Interest Aggregation by Actor				
Country	Patron–Client Networks	Associational Groups	Competitive Parties	Authoritarian Parties	Military Forces
Brazil	Moderate	Moderate	Moderate	—	Moderate
Britain	Low	High	High	—	Low
China	Moderate	Low	—	High	High
France	Low	Moderate	High	—	Low
Germany	Low	High	High	—	Low
India	High	Moderate	Moderate	—	Low
Iran	High	Moderate	Low	—	Moderate
Japan	Moderate	High	High	—	Low
Mexico	Moderate	Moderate	Moderate	—	Low
Nigeria	High	Low	Moderate	—	Moderate
Russia	Moderate	Low	Moderate	—	Moderate
United States	Low	Moderate	High	—	Low

*Extensiveness of interest aggregation rated as low, moderate, or high. Rating refers to broad-level performance issue areas at different times. Blank (—) implies that such actors do not exist.

INSTITUTIONAL INTEREST AGGREGATION

In developing societies, as citizens become aware of larger collective interests and have the resources and skills to work for them, personal networks tend to be regulated, limited, and incorporated within broader organizations. Interest groups with powerful resources can easily cross the subtle line between interest articulation and aggregation. Associational groups (see Chapter 4) often support political contenders such as political parties. But they can occasionally wield sufficient resources to become contenders in their own right. For instance, the political power of the labor unions within the British Labour Party historically rested on their ability to develop coherent policy positions and mobilize their members (who were typically also party members) to support those positions. As we discussed in Chapter 4, corporatist interest-group systems empower both labor and business groups to become actively engaged in making economic policies. These arrangements include continuous political bargaining among organized labor, business interests, political parties, and government representatives. Such corporatist systems interconnect organizations that in other political systems play very different, often antagonistic, roles. Table 5.1 illustrates how associational groups tend to play a larger role in democracies that accept interest groups actively attempting to influence government policy, which is often where these groups have close ties with particular political parties.

Institutional groups, such as bureaucratic agencies and military factions, can also be important interest aggregators. Indeed, the bureaucracy performs this function in most societies. Although established primarily to implement public policy, the bureaucracy may negotiate with interest groups to identify their preferences or to mobilize their support. Government agencies may even be "captured" by interest groups and used to press their demands. Bureaucrats often cultivate client-support networks to expand their organizations or to enhance their power. Military organizations, with their special control of physical force, can also be powerful interest aggregators. We shall have more to say about their role later in this chapter.

COMPETITIVE PARTY SYSTEMS AND INTEREST AGGREGATION

In many contemporary political systems, parties are the primary structures of interest aggregation. Political parties are *groups or organizations that seek to place candidates in office under their label.* In any given society, there may be one party, two parties, or as many as ten or twenty. We refer to the number of parties, and the relationships among them, as properties of the **party system.** A major distinction runs between **competitive party systems,** in which parties primarily try to build electoral support, and noncompetitive or **authoritarian party systems,** in which parties seek to direct society. This distinction does not depend on the closeness of electoral victory, or on the number of parties. It depends instead on the ability of political parties to form freely and compete for citizen support, and on whether this competition for citizen support is the key to government control. Thus, a party system can be competitive even if one party wins an election resoundingly or even dominates several consecutive elections, as long as other parties are free to challenge its dominance at the polls.

The role of competitive parties in interest aggregation depends not only on the individual party but also on the structure of parties, electorates, electoral laws, and policymaking institutions. Typically, interest aggregation in a competitive party system occurs at several stages: within the individual parties, as the party chooses candidates and adopts policy proposals; through electoral competition; and after the election through bargaining and coalition-building with other parties in the legislature or executive.

Political parties have been around as long as there have been elections and representative assemblies, but modern democratic parties began developing in Europe and the Americas from about the mid-nineteenth century. They have since emerged in all societies that have adopted free and fair elections and democratic government. Parties differ in their purposes and organization. Some have elaborate policy platforms, whereas others are little more than vehicles for ambitious politicians to get elected (or even to enrich themselves).

BOX 5.1 PERSONALISTIC PARTIES

Political parties are typically formal organizations with officers, members, statutes, and official policy programs. Sometimes, however, parties can be much looser *personalistic* movements built around one political leader, or a small group of leaders. Personalistic parties are particularly common in new democracies. In Russia, for example, President Vladimir Putin (2000–2008) was able to form a party (United Russia) with a strong personal following. Even India and France have highly personalistic parties. In India, the Congress Party has been dominated by the families of its most important founders, Gandhi and Nehru. In France, most presidents have come out of the Gaullist movement, which has had many names but was dominated from the start by President Charles de Gaulle and later by some of his followers. Personalistic parties commonly do not have a very clear policy program. They are often susceptible to clientelistic politics and sometimes become vehicles for purely personal ambitions and rent-seeking.

Shmuel Flatto-Sharon offers an extreme example. Flatto-Sharon was a Polish-born businessman of Jewish background living in France. In 1977, he fled to Israel because the French authorities wanted to prosecute him for embezzling $60 million. To get immunity from prosecution and avoid extradition, he ran for election to the Knesset (the Israeli national assembly). He formed a party, which he ran as a one-man operation—it had no other candidates or officers. Flatto-Sharon refused to identify himself as left, right, or center. He appealed for Jewish solidarity, arguing that Israel should not allow him to be extradited. He also promised a free television set to all Israeli households (this was before television sets became inexpensive and commonplace) and subsidized apartments for young couples. And he promised to pay people who voted for him as "campaign workers." Remarkably, Flatto-Sharon won two parliamentary seats, even though as his party's only candidate he could not fill the second seat. In 1981, however, he lost his bid for reelection. He was later convicted of bribery for his vote-buying scheme and sent to jail in Israel, but never extradited to France.

Some personalistic parties seem to have no other purpose than to make fun of politics and politicians. In Denmark, comedian Jacob Haugaard several times ran for office as a candidate for the Association of Deliberate Work Avoiders. In 1994, he won election to the Danish Parliament. His election platform included demands for disability pensions for people who lack a sense of humor, tailwinds on all Danish bike paths, more generous Christmas presents, more renaissance furniture at IKEA, and more whales in Danish waters. Haugaard also promised his voters free beer, and he used the public funds his party received from the Danish government to fulfill this campaign commitment (he bought beer and hot dogs for his supporters after the election).

Some parties are highly structured mass organizations, whereas others are loose, *personalistic* groups dominated by their leaders (see Box 5.1).

The first parties were typically *internally created*; their founders were politicians who already held seats in the national assembly or other political offices. These parties were often committed to broad constitutional principles (such as republican government, universal suffrage, or separation of church and state), but otherwise they often had only loose policy programs and little organization outside the legislature. They often had colorful names that said little about their policies, such as Whigs and Tories in Britain, Whites ("Blancos") and Reds ("Colorados") in several Latin American countries, Hats and Caps in Sweden, or for that matter, Democrats and Republicans in the United States.

During the late nineteenth and early twentieth centuries, other types of parties emerged as the democratic countries industrialized and urbanized, and as an increasing number of adults gained the right to vote. The growth of the industrial working class led to the formation of socialist, social democratic, communist, and other workers' parties. Farming interests gained representation through agrarian parties, and other parties emerged to represent religious communities (such as Catholics or Hindus) or ethnic or linguistic minorities. In countries that were not independent, parties of national independence often became a dominant force. All of these parties were typically *externally created*—they organized outside parliament before they became a force inside that institution. They often had much stronger mass-membership organizations than their older competitors, and they often had (and continue to have) closer ties to specific interest groups. Thus, social democrats and communists tend to have strong ties to labor unions, agrarian parties to farmers' organizations, and many Christian Democratic parties (at least Catholic ones) to the Vatican and religious organizations.

Most of these parties still exist and continue to play a leading role. They have settled into stable *party families* of Social Democrats, Conservatives, Christian Democrats, Liberals, Nationalists, and others, which often maintain close contacts across national boundaries. The party systems of most established democracies show a great deal of stability, and many of the most important parties today were also the dominant parties a hundred years ago. Yet two important new types of parties have emerged in the past several decades, particularly in advanced industrial countries. "New left" or "Green" parties emerged in many countries in the 1960s and 1970s to champion international peace and disarmament, environmental protection, gender equality, and minority rights. They are often more supportive of alternative lifestyles than traditional working-class parties of the left (such as Social Democrats). The other important type of new party is the "populist right" party, such as the National Front in France. These parties tend to be critical of existing parties and political leaders, whom they see as elitist, corrupt, or out of touch. They are concerned with internal and external security and favor strict law-and-order policies, but criticize what they see as "politically correct" government interventionism in other policy areas. They dislike the distortions that welfare states sometimes create, such as policies that make it unattractive to work and easy to live off welfare benefits (see Chapter 7). And they typically champion national sovereignty and citizenship rights and oppose large-scale immigration and international integration.

The party systems of most democratic countries reflect a mix of these various party families. But no two party systems are exactly alike, and not all party families are represented in all countries. The variations in party systems reflect differences in demographics, economic development, and political histories. They also depend on differences in electoral systems, as we shall discuss below.

Elections

In democracies, political parties live and die by their performance in elections. The act of voting, and thereby giving support to a political candidate, party, or policy proposal, is one of the simplest and most frequently performed political acts. Through voting, citizens can make a collective decision about their future leaders and public policies. Elections are one of the few devices through which diverse interests can be expressed equally and comprehensively.[2]

The simple act of voting can have profound implications for interest aggregation. Electoral outcomes directly or indirectly determine who manages the affairs of government and makes public policy. And parties generally fulfill their electoral promises when they gain control of government.[3] When leftist governments come to power in advanced industrial democracies, they tend to expand the size and ambitions of the government; conservative parties generally slow the growth of government programs and promote private enterprise. Parties that want radical change or have not recently been in office often find it difficult to implement their programs when they eventually come to power. When, for example, the German Greens came to power in 1998 as part of a coalition government, they had to modify their promise to shut down Germany's nuclear power plants immediately. Instead, they negotiated a phase-out over many years. And they had to accept German military involvement in the civil conflict in Kosovo, even though their program was critical of such military interventions. But by and large, parties try hard to implement their programs, and citizens can therefore influence interest aggregation and policymaking through their role in elections.

When they aggregate interests and make policy, party leaders are often caught between the demands of their party activists and the voters. Party activists often want policies that are more radical than those that most voters prefer. And activists typically insist more vigorously that the party program should be implemented, whereas ordinary voters are often happier when governments compromise and listen to opinions outside their own parties. There is a broad and ongoing debate about the extent to which democracy requires political parties to be internally democratic (see Box 5.2). Advocates of participatory democracy strongly support this idea, as do parties such as the European Greens. On the other hand, the famous Austrian economist Joseph A. Schumpeter argued that vigorous competition *between* parties is what matters for a healthy democracy and that democracy *within* parties is irrelevant or even harmful.[4]

Elections often have other functions as well (see also Chapter 4). Autocrats often manipulate elections to legitimize their governments. Until 1990, voters in the Soviet Union were given only one candidate to vote for, and this person was always the nominee of the Communist Party. Voter participation was very high because the government pressured people to participate and express their symbolic support for the regime, not because the elections actually

BOX 5.2 THE IRON LAW OF OLIGARCHY

Can political parties be the main vehicles of democratic representation if they do not govern themselves democratically? This has been a main concern among students of modern political parties. In 1911, young German sociologist Robert Michels published a study of the German Socialist Party in which he formulated the "iron law of oligarchy," which states that all organizations tend toward oligarchy (rule by the few) rather than democracy. "Who says organization says oligarchy," Michels famously observed. He identified several forces that push organizations such as political parties toward oligarchy. One is the need for specialization and differentiation that exists in all large, modern organizations. A second cause of oligarchy lies in the facts that most ordinary members do not have the time or resources to hold their leaders accountable and that they often crave strong leadership. A third reason is that parties foster leaders who live "off" politics rather than "for" politics. They exploit their leadership positions to advance their own ambitions for wealth or power, often to the detriment of their followers. (In contemporary terms, we would refer to such self-interested pursuit of power as *rent-seeking*.) Michels's study was particularly troubling because he found these tendencies even in a party, the German Socialist Party, with which he sympathized and that was considered particularly strongly committed to democratic ideals.

Source: Robert Michels, *Political Parties* (New York: Free Press, 1962).

decided anything. Elections played a role in socializing and shaping citizens' attitudes, but had little to do with interest articulation or aggregation.[5]

In most democracies, citizens can freely choose whether to vote. Yet some countries require citizens to vote and impose penalties on those who do not. Voting choices reflect a mix of motivations.[6] Many citizens try to judge the parties' policy promises. For others, elections are a simple referendum on government performance. They vote to throw the rascals out if times are bad, and to reelect them if times are good. In other cases, elections can be dominated by the charisma of a strong leader or the incompetence of a weak one. In each case, however, elections aggregate these diverse concerns into a collective decision on the composition of the government.

Electoral Systems

The rules by which elections are conducted are among the most important structures that affect political parties. We refer to these rules as the **electoral system**. These rules determine who can vote, how to vote, and how votes are counted. The rules that determine how votes are converted into seats are especially important. The United States, Britain, and many countries influenced by Britain (such as India and Canada) are divided into a large number of election districts. In each district, the candidate who gains more votes than any other—a *plurality*—wins the election. This simple, **single-member district plurality (SMDP) election rule** is often called "first past the post," a horse-racing term, because the winner need only finish ahead of any of the others but need not win a majority of the votes. This system seems obvious and natural to Americans, but it is rarely used in continental Europe or in Latin America. Another version of single-member district elections is the **majority runoff** (or **double-ballot**) system used in France and in presidential elections in Russia. Under this system, voting happens in two stages, normally separated by a couple of weeks. In the first round, it takes a majority of all votes (50 percent + one vote) to win. To win, then, a candidate has to earn not just more votes than any other candidate, but more votes than all other candidates combined. If there is no majority winner in the first round, only a smaller number of candidates (in French and Russian presidential elections, the top two) make it into the second round, in which whoever gets the largest number of votes (a plurality) is elected.

In contrast to the single-member district system, most democracies in Europe and Latin America use some form of **proportional representation (PR)** in multimember districts. In these systems, the country is divided into a few large districts, which may elect as many as twenty or more members. These districts are often the states or provinces that make up the country. In the Netherlands and Israel, the entire country is a single electoral district that elects more than a hundred representatives. The parties offer lists of candidates for the slots in each district. The number of representatives that a party wins depends on the overall proportion of the votes it receives, though no system is perfectly proportional. A party receiving 10 percent of the vote would be awarded approximately 10 percent of the legislative seats. Sometimes, parties must achieve a minimum threshold of votes, usually 3 to 5 percent nationally, to receive any seats at all. If so many parties compete that many of them fall below this threshold, many voters may be left unrepresented, as happened in Russia in 1995.

In order to compete effectively, parties must formulate appealing policy programs and nominate attractive candidates for office. They must anticipate the offerings of their competitors and the preferences of the voters. The procedures that parties use to develop policy positions vary greatly from country to country and from party to party. In the United States, the national party conventions held before each presidential election formalize the party's policy positions, both by adopting a party platform and by selecting a slate of candidates. In other countries, parties have more regular congresses, and centralized party organizations issue party programs (also known as *platforms* or *manifestos*).[7] Whatever the system, a successful program must both spell out policy positions that are popular with the voters and aggregate interests within the party.

Parties must also offer candidates for office. In the United States, voters directly select these candidates through **primary elections**. But primaries are an unusually open form of candidate selection. In most other countries with **single-member district (SMD)** elections, party officials select the candidates, either locally or nationally. In proportional representation elections, the party draws up a list of candidates for each district. In **closed-list PR systems,** the elected representatives are then simply drawn from the top of this list, in declining order, and ordinary voters have no say about their candidates. In **open-list systems**, in contrast, voters can give preference votes to individual candidates, and these votes determine which candidates will represent the party in that district. Besides adopting programs and selecting candidates, parties also attempt to publicize them and mobilize electoral support through rallies, media advertising, door-to-door campaigning, and other activities.

Patterns of Electoral Competition

In democratic party systems, the electoral system is a major determinant of the patterns of electoral competition. Two famous political science theories help us understand this connection: Duverger's Law and Downs's median voter result. **Duverger's Law**, which is named after the French political scientist Maurice Duverger, is one of the best-known theories in political science.[8] It states that there is a systematic relationship between electoral systems and party systems, so that plurality single-member district election systems tend to create **two-party systems** in the legislature, while proportional representation electoral systems generate multiparty systems. Duverger identified two mechanisms behind this regularity. He called them the *mechanical effect* and the *psychological effect*. The **mechanical effect** is to be found in the way that different electoral systems convert votes into seats. In single-member district systems, parties get no representation unless they finish first in at least one district. Therefore, smaller parties that run second, third, or fourth across many districts receive little or no representation. In the 2010 election in Britain, for example, the Liberal Democratic Party (Britain's third-largest party) received 23 percent of the votes, but only 9 percent of the seats in the House of Commons. The **psychological effect** lies in the fact that both voters and candidates anticipate the mechanical effect. Therefore, voters do not throw their support behind "hopeless" parties and candidates. Instead, they may support their second-best (or even third-best) option in order to keep a party that they strongly dislike from winning. And knowing that the voters will not support them, minor party candidates are reluctant to run. Giving your support to a party or candidate that is not your first choice in order to avoid an even worse outcome is known as **strategic voting**. Duverger argued that strategic voting tends to work to the advantage of parties that are already large and to the disadvantage of small ones. In U.S. elections, it has been fairly common for third-party candidates to run well in the polls until close to the election date, when voters realize that these candidates are not going to win. Their support then often declines rapidly.

Anthony Downs examined the effects of the number of parties on their policy positions. He showed that in two-party systems in which the parties are competing along a left–right (or other) policy dimension and are interested only in winning elections, and where all voters choose the party closest to their policy preferences, the parties will moderate their policies so as to try to win the support of the median voter (the voter who is at the midpoint of the policy spectrum, with as many other voters to the right as to the left). Downs's contribution is known as the **median voter result.** According to this theory, two-party systems will exhibit a centrist pull or "convergence." In systems with only two parties, parties have to try to win a majority, so targeting the "center" of the electorate is critical. In PR systems with many political parties, however, no one group has much chance of winning a majority, and parties can survive with much less support. Therefore, there is not the same centrist pull, and parties may instead spread themselves out across the policy spectrum.[9]

Figure 5.1 offers a comparative "snapshot" of parties and voters in several democracies. It shows where party supporters in each country placed their party on a left-to-right scale in recent election surveys, with one identified as Left (or liberal, in the United States) and ten identified as Right (or conservative, in the United States). Note that the meanings of *left*, *right*, and *center* can vary across countries. The height of the columns above the scale shows what percentage of the voters supported each party. The two countries at the top of the figure, the United States and Britain, use SMDP electoral systems, whereas France uses a majority runoff system, Mexico and Japan mixed systems, and Germany and Brazil PR systems. According to Duverger, we should expect the United States and Britain to have only two major parties and the others more. Following Downs, we should expect the two-party systems to be centrist and clustered in policy space and the multiparty systems to be more dispersed.

By and large, Figure 5.1 supports the theories of both Duverger and Downs. In the countries at the top of the figure, especially in the United States, there are only two large parties. Moreover, the parties are fairly close to the center. Democrats are somewhat to the left and Republicans somewhat to the right, with a great deal of overlap. The left–right "gap" between the average party supporters, although larger than it was twenty years ago, is still fairly small. Although the Japanese system is more fluid, it too features two large and fairly similar dominant parties. In France, toward the bottom of the figure, there are many parties and a very large distance between the left-most party (the Communists) and right-most party (the National Front), and even between the two largest parties (Socialists and RPR). Germany falls between these more extreme cases. As Duverger would predict, Britain looks more like the United States, but the parties are farther apart. Mexico has shown that even systems with proportional representation and more than two parties (though only three significant ones) can have convergent and centrist electoral politics. Yet in the most recent years, the Mexican parties have seemed to pull apart and become less centrist. In Brazil, there are many parties and moderate left–right diversity; the largest party, Lula's Worker's Party on the left, won only 15 percent of the vote. Many of the small parties are not shown because the survey did not ask about them.

Table 5.2 presents additional information on the electoral and party systems of the twelve countries in this book. It displays data on the **effective number of parties** in each country. This measure takes into account both the overall number of parties and their relative sizes. For example, if there are two parties and they are exactly the same size, the effective number of parties is 2.0. If, however, one party has 80 percent of the vote and the other 20 percent, the effective

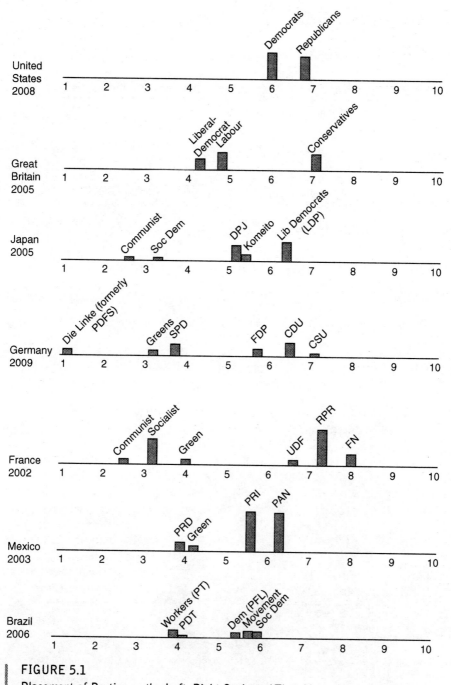

FIGURE 5.1

Placement of Parties on the Left–Right Scale and Their Voter Support in Elections

Source: The Comparative Study of Electoral Systems (www.cses.org), CSES Modules 2, 3; U.S. National Election Study 2008.

TABLE 5.2

Elections and the Effective Number of Parties (Lower House of Legislature)

Rules matter.

Country	Electoral System	Effective Number of Parties— Vote Shares	Effective Number of Parties— Seat Shares	How Are Individual Candidates Selected?
Brazil	PR open list	10.62	9.32	Candidate preference vote
Britain	SMD plurality	3.71*	2.57*	Nominated by local constituency association
China	No contested elections	No contested elections	No contested elections	No contested elections
France	SMD majority runoff	4.32	2.49	Nominated by local constituency association
Germany	Mixed system: SMD plurality + PR closed list	5.58**	4.83**	National party and state party conventions
India	SMD plurality	7.74	5.01	Nominated by local constituency association
Iran	MMD majority runoff	No data	No data	Must be approved by Council of Guardians
Japan	Mixed system: SMD plurality + PR closed list	3.15***	2.10***	National party
Mexico	Mixed system: SMD plurality + PR closed list	3.77	2.75	Nominated by local constituency association and national party
Nigeria	SMD plurality	2.62	2.34	Nominated by local constituency association
Russia	PR closed list	2.22	1.92	National party
United States	SMD plurality	2.09	1.94	Primary elections

Note: Data from the most recent national elections, as of May 10, 2010.
MMD = Multimember district
SMD = Single-member district
PR = Proportional representation
*Calculated on the basis of 649 out of 650 seats due to postponement of the 2010 poll in the constituency of Thirsk and Malton.
**Calculated with CDU and CSU as separate parties.
***Based on total votes and total seats.
Sources: Arend Lijphart, *Patterns of Democracy: Government Forms and Performance in Thirty-Six Countries* (New Haven, CT: Yale University Press, 1999); www.ElectionGuide.org; www.Wikipedia.org.

number of parties is just below 1.5.[10] The effective number of parties can be calculated for either votes or seats, as we have done in Table 5.2. If Duverger's Law is correct, the effective number of parties should be lower in countries that have SMDP electoral systems than in those that have other systems (particularly PR). Table 5.2 shows that this is largely true, as three of the four countries with the lowest effective number of parties do have SMDP elections. At the same time, India is an exception; it has a large number of parties despite an SMDP electoral system. But a closer look at India shows that even though the country has many parties overall, most electoral districts feature only two serious parties.[11] Thus, India helps us understand one limitation of Duverger's Law, which is that while SMDP systems tend to sustain only two parties in each election district, these two parties need not be the same throughout the country.

Table 5.2 also gives us a measure of the mechanical effect in Duverger's Law, the consequences of the counting rules themselves. By comparing the effective number of parties among the voters (vote shares) with the effective number of parties in the national assembly (seat shares), we can see how much the electoral system helps the large parties and disfavors the small ones. This bias exists in all countries and electoral systems, as the numbers in the column for seat shares are always consistently lower than those in the column for vote shares. Duverger's Law suggests that this difference should be greater in "first-past-the-post" (SMDP) systems than elsewhere.

Competitive Parties in Government

If a competitive party wins control of the legislature and the executive branch, it will (if unified) be able to pass and implement its policies. Sometimes, this control emerges directly from the electoral process, as a single party wins a majority of the vote. But in many countries, the election laws help the largest party gain a governing majority even if it does not enjoy majority support among the voters. Thus, less than 50 percent of the vote may be converted into more than 50 percent of the legislative seats. Such "artificial" or "manufactured" legislative majorities have been the rule in countries with SMDP electoral systems, such as Britain.[12]

For example, from 1979 until 2010, either the Conservative Party or the Labour Party consistently won a majority of seats in the British House of Commons, even though neither party was ever supported by a majority of the voters in any of these elections. Margaret Thatcher's Conservative Party won a solid majority in the House of Commons in 1983 and 1987 with only about 42 percent of the vote. With almost exactly the same level of support, Tony Blair and the Labour Party won nearly two-thirds of the seats in 1997 and 2001. In 2005, Labour's share of the vote fell to about 35 percent, but the party still got a clear majority of the seats. In 2010, although they actually received a slightly larger share of the vote than Labour had in 2005, the Conservatives fell just short of a majority in the House of Commons. In all these elections, the 25 to 35 percent of the electorate supporting the smaller British parties received 10 percent or less of the parliamentary seats.

In other countries, multiparty elections do not yield single-party majorities, but party coalitions formed before the election may still offer the voters a direct choice of future governments. Before the election, a group of parties may join forces, agree to coordinate their election campaigns, or agree to govern together if they jointly win a parliamentary majority. When such coalitions form, as they have in many (but not all) elections in France and Germany, it is almost like a two-party system. Voters can clearly identify the potential governments and reward or punish the incumbents if they so choose. They thus have the ability to choose the direction of government policy through their party choice.

When elections do not create a majority party and there is no preelectoral coalition, the political parties and their leaders must negotiate a new government after the election. This is common in many multiparty parliamentary systems, such as the Netherlands and Italy.[13] In these nations, interests are not aggregated through elections because the election does not directly determine who governs. Instead, the aggregation of interests occurs in negotiations between different parties over control of the executive branch, most often after an election but also sometimes when an existing coalition breaks up (see also Chapter 6, specifically Figure 6.2).

The aggregation of interests at the executive rather than electoral level can have both costs and benefits. On the one hand, when elite party coalitions determine government policy, voters may feel that the government is not accountable to them. And because interest aggregation occurs among political elites, different elite coalitions can form on different issues. This can be confusing to citizens (and even informed observers). It may be difficult for voters to assign clear responsibility for government policy, and it may seem unfair that the electoral losers sometimes get to decide. This situation lessens the value of the vote as an instrument to shape future policy or to punish parties responsible for bad policy choices in the past.

On the other hand, there may be benefits for minority interests when all parties, not just the election winners, are represented in policymaking. All citizens hold minority opinions on some issues, and some are in the minority on many issues. If even minority representatives can influence policy between elections, they may feel that they have more political protection. Finally, even governments that win a majority of votes typically do not have majority support for all of their policy proposals. So there may be benefits for the nation as a whole when even the winners have to negotiate the different parts of their programs. Such bargaining may even increase the likelihood that policies reflect different majorities on different issues. The value of elections as instruments of representation may increase when interests are aggregated within a government coalition, though the value of elections as instruments of accountability may diminish.[14]

Cooperation and Conflict in Competitive Party Systems

Competitive party systems can be classified by the number of parties as well as by the patterns of competition or cooperation among them. **Majoritarian two-party systems** either are dominated by just two parties, as in the United States, or have two dominant parties and election laws that usually create legislative majorities for one of them, as in Britain. In **majority-coalition systems**, parties establish preelectoral coalitions so that voters know which parties will attempt to work together to form a government. Germany and France have in most elections been in this category. Pure **multiparty systems** have election laws and party systems that virtually ensure that no single party wins a legislative majority and no tradition of preelection coalitions. Interest aggregation then depends on a coalition of parties bargaining and coming to agreement after the election.

The degree of antagonism or polarization among the parties is another important party system characteristic. In a **consensual party system**, the parties commanding most of the legislative seats are not too far apart on policies and have a reasonable amount of trust in each other and in the political system. These are typically party systems like those shown toward the top of Figure 5.1. Bargaining may be intense and politics exciting, but it seldom threatens the system itself. In a **conflictual party system**, the legislature is dominated by parties that are far apart on issues or are antagonistic toward each other and the political system, such as the Russian party system in the 1990s.

Some party systems have both consensual and conflictual features. The term **consociational** (or **accommodative**) refers to party systems in which political leaders seek to bridge intense social divisions through power-sharing, broad coalition governments, and decentralization of sensitive decisions to the separate social groups.[15] A consociational system can enable a deeply divided nation to find a way to peaceful democratic development. In Austria and Lebanon after World War II, mutually suspicious and hostile groups—the socialists and Catholics in Austria, and the Christians and Muslims in Lebanon—developed consociational arrangements that made stable government possible. Austria's accommodation occurred within a two-party system and Lebanon's among many small, personalistic religious parties. Austria's consociationalism was largely successful. After some twenty years of the consociational "Grand Coalition," in which both major parties held office together, these parties felt much less antagonistic and reverted to "normal" competition for office. The Lebanese experiment was less happy. After 1975, the country fell victim to civil war. South Africa also adopted consociational practices in its transition to democracy in the 1990s. Party leaders representing the white minority as well as different segments of the black majority negotiated power-sharing arrangements for a transitional period. The "Interim Constitution" guaranteed a share of power—cabinet posts—to all parties winning over 5 percent of the vote. Later, as the democratic order became more secure, this feature was abandoned.

Consociational practices thus offer deeply divided democracies hope but no guarantees of long-term stability. As Austria and South Africa show us, consociationalism may be especially suitable as a temporary solution after a period of intense conflict or turmoil. But consociationalism means that small groups of politicians make many important decisions behind closed doors. If these politicians are able to work together more constructively than their respective supporters, consociationalism can be a happy solution. If, however, the politicians are intransigent or self-interested, consociationalism may fail.

The number of parties does not always tell us much about their degree of antagonism. The United States and Britain are relatively consensual majoritarian party systems. They are not perfect two-party systems because minor parties exist in both countries, especially in Britain. In the United States, the degree of consensus changes from election to election because of the shifting programs of presidential candidates. Moreover, the looser cohesion of American parties and the frequency of divided government lead to postelection bargaining that is similar to consensual multiparty systems.

But not all majoritarian party systems are consensual. Austria between 1918 and 1934 was a conflictual majoritarian party system. Antagonism between the Socialist Party and the other parties was so intense that in the mid-1930s, it produced a brief civil war. The Austrian experience also illustrates how party systems can change. As we noted above, after World War II, the two major parties negotiated an elaborate coalition agreement of mutual power-sharing—checks and balances—to contain the country's conflicts. In recent years, Ukraine has been another example of a conflictual majoritarian party system.

Consensual multiparty systems are found in Scandinavia and the Netherlands, among other countries. France (1946–1958), Italy (1945–1992), and Weimar Germany (1919–1933), on the other hand, are historical examples of conflictual multiparty systems, with powerful communist parties on the left and conservative or fascist movements on the right. Cabinets had to form out of centrist movements, which were themselves divided on many issues. This resulted in instability, poor government performance, and loss of citizen confidence in democracy. These factors contributed to the collapse of the French Fourth Republic in 1958, to government instability and citizen alienation from politics in Italy by the 1990s, and to the overthrow of democracy in Weimar Germany.

New democracies, especially those divided by language or ethnicity, sometimes face similar challenges. Some of the emerging party systems in Central and Eastern Europe have fallen into the pattern of conflictual, multiparty competition. For instance, in the 1995 parliamentary elections in Russia, forty-three parties appeared on the ballot, and seven parties won representation in Parliament. But later elections greatly reduced the number of parties.

Thus, although the number of parties affects political stability, the degree of antagonism among parties is more important. Two-party systems are stable and effective, but they may be dangerous if society is too deeply divided. Multiparty systems consisting of relatively moderate parties can often offer stability and fairly effective performance, especially if the parties are willing to commit themselves to preelectoral coalitions. Pure multiparty systems without preelectoral coalitions are more prone to ineffectiveness, but some have worked well over long periods. Where social groups and parties are highly antagonistic, however, collapse and civil war are ever-present possibilities, regardless of the number of parties. When crises develop, the most critical factor is typically how committed party leaders are to working together to defend democracy.[16]

AUTHORITARIAN PARTY SYSTEMS

Authoritarian party systems can also aggregate interests. They develop policy proposals and mobilize support for them, but they do so in a completely different way from competitive party systems. In authoritarian party systems, aggregation takes place within the party or in interactions with business groups, unions, landowners, and institutional groups in the bureaucracy or military. Although there may be sham elections, the citizens have no real opportunity to shape aggregation by choosing between party alternatives.

Authoritarian party systems vary in the degree of top-down control within the party and the party's control over other groups in society. At one extreme is the **exclusive governing party,** which insists on almost total control over political resources. It recognizes no legitimate interest aggregation by groups within the party. Nor does it permit any free activity, much less opposition, from interest groups, citizens, or other government agencies. In its most extreme form, sometimes called *totalitarianism*, it penetrates the entire society and mobilizes support for policies developed at the top. Its policies are legitimated by a political ideology, such as communism or national socialism (Nazism) that claims to identify the true interests of the citizens, regardless of what the citizens themselves believe.[17] At the other extreme is the **inclusive governing party,** which recognizes and accepts at least some other groups and organizations, but may repress those that it sees as serious challenges to its own control.

Exclusive Governing Parties

In a purely totalitarian society, there is only one party with total top-down control of society, and no autonomous opposition parties or interest groups. Totalitarian single-party systems can be impressive vehicles of political mobilization. A clear ideology provides legitimacy and coherence, and the party penetrates and organizes society in the name of that ideology and in accordance with its policies. But totalitarianism is difficult to sustain. Although the ruling communist parties of the Soviet Union before 1985, of Eastern Europe before 1989, and of North Korea, Vietnam, and Cuba today resemble this model, few parties have long maintained such absolute control. China is an interesting mixed case. While the Chinese government has withdrawn from the direct administration of much of the economy, it does not recognize the legitimacy of any opposition groups. The ruling party permits, within bounds, some interest articulation by individuals, but not mass mobilization against government policy.[18]

Not all exclusive governing parties are totalitarian, however. Many leaders committed to massive social change—for example, national independence from colonialism—have used the exclusive governing party as a tool for mass mobilization. Such exclusive governing parties may experience more internal dissent than is commonly recognized. Within the party, groups may unite around such interests as their region or industry, or behind leaders of different policy factions. Beneath the supposedly united front, power struggles may erupt in times of crisis. Succession crises are particularly likely to generate such power struggles, as at the death of Stalin in the Soviet Union and Mao Zedong in China. Several times, the Chinese Communist Party has had to rely on the army, even on coalitions of regional army commanders, to sustain its control.

It is difficult to build an exclusive governing party as an agent for social transformation. The seduction of power regularly leads to rent-seeking or other abuses of power that are not checked by competitive democratic politics and that may distort the original party objectives. The exclusive governing parties in some African states also had limited capacity to control society. Furthermore, the loss of confidence in Marxist–Leninist ideology and in the Soviet model led all eight of the African regimes that had once invoked it to abandon that approach by the early 1990s.

As exclusive governing parties age, many enter a stage in which they maintain control but place less emphasis on mobilization. Some, such as North Korea, may degenerate into vehicles for personal rule and exploitation by the ruler's family and supporters.[19] Finally, as shown by the collapse of communism in the former Soviet Union and Eastern Europe, if and when the party leaders lose faith in the unifying ideology, it is difficult to maintain party coherence.

Inclusive Governing Parties

Among the preindustrial countries, especially those with notable ethnic and tribal divisions, the more successful authoritarian parties have been *inclusive*. These systems recognize the autonomy of social, cultural, and economic groups and try to incorporate them or bargain with them, rather than control and remake them. The more successful African one-party systems, such as in Kenya and Tanzania, have permitted aggregation around personalistic, factional, and ethnic groups within a decentralized party.

Inclusive party systems have sometimes been labeled *authoritarian corporatist systems*. Like the democratic corporatist systems (see Chapter 4), some of these systems encourage the formation of large, organized interest groups that can bargain with each other and the state. Unlike the democratic corporatist systems, however, these authoritarian systems place no power directly in the hands of the people. Authoritarian corporatist systems suppress independent protest and political activity outside of official channels. The party leaders permit only limited autonomous demands within the ranks of the party and by groups associated with it.

The inclusive authoritarian systems may permit substantial amounts of autonomous interest aggregation, which may take many forms. The party typically tries to gather various social groups under the general party umbrella and negotiate with outside groups and institutions. Some inclusive parties have attempted aggressive social change. Others have primarily been arenas for interest aggregation. Many inclusive party governments permit other parties to offer candidates in elections, as long as these opposition candidates have no real chance of winning. Indeed, one interesting feature of politics since about the 1980s, along with the increasing number of liberal democracies, has been the growth of **electoral authoritarianism**. This is where there is a facade of democracy providing "some space for political opposition, independent media, and social organizations that do not seriously criticize or challenge the regime."[20] The Mexican Partido Revolucionario Institucional (PRI) was long a successful example of an inclusive governing party featuring electoral authoritarianism (see Box 5.3).

The fact that some inclusive authoritarian parties have been impressively durable does not necessarily mean that they are strong or successful. In many countries, these parties coexist in uneasy and unstable coalitions with the armed forces and the civilian bureaucracy. In some countries, the party has become window dressing for a military regime or personal tyranny. Seldom have these parties been able to solve the economic or ethnic problems that face their countries.

These political systems were often created in a struggle against colonialism, and as colonialism becomes more distant, they may implode. As memories of

---

BOX 5.3 MEXICO'S PRI

One of the oldest and most inclusive authoritarian parties is the Partido Revolucionario Institucional (PRI) in Mexico. For more than fifty years, the PRI dominated the political process and gave other parties no realistic chances of winning elections. The PRI attained this dominance after President Lázaro Cárdenas turned it into a "big-tent" coalition in the 1930s. It also carefully controlled the counting of the ballots. The PRI incorporated many social groups, with separate sectors for labor, agrarian, and middle-class interests. The party dealt with its opponents in carefully designed ways. While some political dissidents were harassed and suppressed, others were deliberately enticed into the party. The party also gave informal recognition to political factions grouped behind such figures as former presidents. Various Mexican leaders mobilized their factions within the PRI and in other important groups not directly affiliated with it, such as big-business interests. Bargaining was particularly important every six years when the party had to choose a new presidential nominee, since the Mexican Constitution limits presidents to one term. This guaranteed some turnover of elites.

As a consequence of its elaborate schemes of governing, the PRI did not have to fear electoral competition, at least until the 1990s. Yet rising discontent made it increasingly difficult to aggregate interests through a single party. The urban and rural poor who had not shared in Mexico's growth joined with reformers to demand a more fully democratic system. An armed uprising of peasant guerrillas in early 1994 shocked the political establishment and led to promises of genuine democratic competition. Legislative elections in 1997 were more open than earlier contests, and ended the seventy-year rule of the PRI, which then lost the presidency to the National Action Party (PAN) in 2000. After that election, the PRI has quickly diminished as a political force, even though it still controls many state and local governments. In 2006, its candidate ran a distant third in Mexico's presidential election (see Chapter 14).

the independence struggle fade and the leaders die off or retire, the ties of ideology and experience that hold these parties together weaken. These developments, in conjunction with the worldwide expansion of democracy, have led to a general loss of legitimacy for the single-party model. In some cases (as in Tanzania), they have adjusted by permitting real party competition. More frequently, they have resorted to electoral authoritarianism with varying degrees of manipulation to provide a veneer of domestic and international legitimacy. In more than a few cases, they have turned to naked coercion, with the military serving as final arbiter.

THE MILITARY AND INTEREST AGGREGATION

After independence, most Third World nations adopted at least formally democratic governments. But in many countries, these civilian governments lacked effectiveness and authority, which often led to their breakdown and replacement by **military governments**. The military had instruments of force and organizational capacity, and in the absence of a strong constitutional tradition, it was an effective contender for power. Even under civilian rule, the military had substantial political influence and often constituted a significant power contender. In Brazil, for example, the military played a crucial role in interest aggregation even under the civilian government prior to the coup of 1964. After that intervention, it was the dominant actor for the next twenty years. In many other countries, the military has long been a similarly important interest aggregator. Many Latin American countries had military governments on and off for much of the twentieth century, and Africa experienced a wave of military coups after its decolonization in the 1960s.

The military's virtual monopoly on coercive resources gives it great potential power. Thus, when aggregation fails in democratic or authoritarian party systems, the military may emerge by default as the only force able to maintain orderly government. The military may also intervene for more self-interested reasons, such as protecting its autonomy or budgets from civilian interference. And in many countries, military governments have served as a vehicle for ethnic politics.

About two-fifths of the world's nations have confronted military coup attempts at some time, and in about a third of the nations, these coups were at least partially successful in changing leaders or policy (see Box 5.4). Fewer than half of these coup attempts, however, focused on general political issues and public policy. Most coups seemed motivated by the professional interests of the military.

What happens after the military intervenes can vary. The soldiers may support the personal tyranny of a civilian president or a dominant party. Or, the armed forces may use their power to further institutional or ideological objectives. Military rulers may try to create military and/or bureaucratic versions of authoritarian corporatism, linking organized groups and the state bureaucracy with the military as final arbiter. They may undertake "defensive" modernization in alliance with business groups or even more radical modernization. Most

BOX 5.4 TRYING TO MAKE DEMOCRACY WORK

Nigeria is in many ways typical of the rough road to democracy that many developing countries have traveled. After gaining its independence, Nigeria experienced brief periods of democratic government in the 1960s and again in the late 1970s. In both cases, the military quickly intervened and ousted governments that had become oppressive or ineffective. The military government that came to power in 1983 responded to the global democratization wave of the early 1990s by introducing measured reforms leading up to a presidential election in 1993. But the military kept strict control of the electoral process and disqualified politicians who had held office under previous civilian regimes (because they were considered to be tainted by corruption). Voters were left with a choice of only two parties, both created by the government. Voting turnout was low because many voters became cynical about the process. These doubts were confirmed when the military annulled the presidential election even before the results had been announced, apparently because the "wrong" candidate was winning. General Sani Abacha then launched a coup which banned all political activity, dissolved the legislature, dismissed the elected governments in Nigeria's thirty-six states, and thus ended Nigeria's cautious experiment with elections. In 1998, President Abacha suddenly died of a heart attack, and the reform process began anew. In spring 1999, a presidential election was held. The victor was a former army general and president (1976–1979), Olusegun Obasanjo, who went on to implement democratic reforms. He was reelected four years later and stepped down in 2007 after his second term, as the constitution required. The new president that was chosen in the 2007 election later died in office and was replaced by his vice president. Thus, Nigeria has by now experienced its longest period of civilian government ever. But continuing ethnic and religious violence, corruption, and abuses of power have made Nigerian democracy fragile.

Latin American versions of authoritarian corporatism have relied on a strong military component rather than a dominant authoritarian party.

The major limitation of the military in interest aggregation is that it is not designed for that function. The military is primarily organized to have an efficient command structure. It is not set up to aggregate internal differences, to build compromise, to mobilize popular support, or even to communicate with social groups outside the command hierarchy. Nor do military regimes have the legitimacy in the international community that elections provide. Thus, the military lacks many of the advantages held by elected party leaders. These internal limitations may be less serious when the military is dealing with common grievances or responding to abuses of power by unpopular politicians. The same limitations become a major problem, however, when a military government needs to stake out its own course and mobilize support for it. For these reasons, military governments frequently prove unstable and are often forced to share power with other institutions or simply to withdraw from politics.

Recent surveys show little popular support for military government anywhere in the world. Perhaps because most citizens do not consider authoritarian rule legitimate, the military throughout the world is now more likely to dominate from behind the scenes than through direct rule. In such important Latin American countries as Argentina, Brazil, Chile, and Uruguay, military regimes have been replaced by competitive party regimes. The same thing has happened in a number of African countries, including Nigeria.

TRENDS IN INTEREST AGGREGATION

As we have previously noted, the democratic trend in the world gained momentum in the 1980s, when many Latin American countries democratized. This trend began accelerating in 1989 in Eastern Europe, with new pressures for democracy in the developing world also. By the late 1990s, for the first time in world history, there were more free than unfree states. The collapse of communism in Europe and elsewhere was in large part responsible, but the number of military dictatorships also declined. The declining acceptance of authoritarian governments, as well as the withdrawal of Soviet support, contributed to this trend, especially in Africa. Many African nations moved toward a more democratic and free system during the 1990s. Yet a few authoritarian party systems with exclusive governing parties are still around, such as in China and Cuba. Most of the remaining unfree states are in the Middle East, Central Asia, and Africa. Many African nations still feature some variety of the "electoral authoritarianism" discussed earlier, with severe constraints on civil freedom and electoral opposition. A few remain unabashed authoritarian systems (as in Zimbabwe) or are mired in deadly civil war (as in Sudan and Somalia).

We cannot assume that democratization will continue relentlessly. Party politicians who seem unable to cope with economic and social problems often lose their legitimacy. Such is now the challenge facing many developing countries, especially in Africa. In many of these countries, competitive party systems exist, but citizens have very little trust in them and often consider them to be corrupt. And military coups have continued to occur, as in Thailand and Fiji in 2006 and Niger in 2010.

SIGNIFICANCE OF INTEREST AGGREGATION

How interests are aggregated is an important determinant of what a country's government does for and to its citizens. Successful public policy depends on effective interest aggregation. Interest aggregation narrows policy options so that the desires and demands of citizens are converted into a few policy alternatives. Many possible policies are eliminated in the process. Those that remain typically have the backing of significant sectors of society.

In democratic countries, competitive party systems narrow down and combine policy preferences. Through elections, voters throw their support behind some of these parties and thus shape party representation in the legislature.

Even at the legislative stage, further consolidation and coalition-building take place. At some point, however, most policy options have been eliminated from consideration—either no party backed them or the parties supporting them fared badly in the elections.

In noncompetitive party systems, military governments, and monarchies, aggregation works differently, but with the similar effect of narrowing policy options. On some issues, aggregation virtually determines policy, as when a military government or a faction of an authoritarian party can decide the government's program. In other cases, the legislative assembly, military council, or party politburo may contain several factions that must negotiate over policy.

Politics shapes its environment as well as reflecting it. Interest aggregation often alters the political culture. That is one reason why politics is so fascinating. Well-organized and well-led political parties might, at least for a while, be able to dominate politics and limit the strength of extremist groups in the legislature. Conversely, well-organized extremists might be able to appeal to the fears, envies, and prejudices of some groups and get their support at the polls, thus gaining more legislative strength in an otherwise consensual country.

Aggregation ultimately affects the government's adaptability and stability. Authoritarian interest aggregation tends to create political power structures that do not reflect popular opinion. In highly divided and conflict-ridden societies, rulers may portray such lack of representation as a virtue. Leaders of military coups often justify their overthrow of party governments by claiming to depolarize politics and rid the nation of conflict it cannot afford. Similarly, heads of authoritarian parties typically claim that their nation must concentrate all its energies and resources on common purposes and that party competition would be too polarizing.

In contrast, most proponents of democratic interest aggregation argue that the best hope for accommodating conflicting social and political interests lies in free and fair electoral competition, followed by negotiation among those groups that gain the voters' favor. Democracy thus leads policymakers to act as the people wish. In a polarized political culture, the division and uncertainty that interest aggregation implies may be seen as a high price to pay for citizen control. As the frequent instability in authoritarian governments indicates, however, it may be easier to do away with the appearance of polarization than with the reality. Competing demands may find their way to the surface anyway, and the citizens may end up with neither freedom and participation nor stability.

REVIEW QUESTIONS

1. What structures other than political parties aggregate interests?
2. What is Duverger's Law? Which two effects does it imply?
3. What is the median voter result, and why does it pertain only to two-party systems?
4. What are the differences between totalitarian parties and other single-party systems?
5. Why do many countries turn to military governments, and why are military governments often short-lived?

KEY TERMS

accommodative party
    system
authoritarian party system
closed-list PR system
competitive party system
conflictual party system
consensual party system
consociational
double-ballot
Duverger's Law
effective number of parties
electoral
    authoritarianism
electoral system

exclusive governing party
    inclusive governing
    party
institutional groups
interest aggregation
majoritarian two-party
    system
iron law of oligarchy
majority runoff
majority-coalition system
mechanical effect
median voter result
military governments
multiparty system

open-list PR system
party system
patron–client networks
primary elections
proportional
    representation (PR)
psychological effect
single-member district
    (SMD)
single-member district
    plurality (SMDP)
    election rule
strategic voting
two-party system

SUGGESTED READINGS

Bratton, Michael, and Nicolas van de Walle. *Democratic Experiments in Africa*. Cambridge: Cambridge University Press, 1997.

Cox, Gary W. *Making Votes Count: Strategic Coordination in the World's Electoral Systems*. Cambridge: Cambridge University Press, 1997.

Dalton, Russell J., and Martin P. Wattenberg. *Parties without Partisans: Political Change in Advanced Industrial Democracies*. New York: Oxford University Press, 2000.

Decalo, Samuel. *Coups and Army Rule in Africa*, 2nd ed. New Haven, CT: Yale University Press, 1990.

Downs, Anthony. *An Economic Theory of Democracy*. New York: Harper & Row, 1957.

Geddes, Barbara. "What Do We Know about Democratization after Twenty Years?" *Annual Reviews of Political Science* 2 (1999): 115–44.

Jackson, Robert H., and Carl G. Rosberg. *Personal Rule in Black Africa*. Berkeley: University of California Press, 1982.

Kitschelt, Herbert. *The Transformation of European Social Democracy*. New York: Cambridge University Press, 1994.

Laver, Michael, and Norman Schofield. *Multiparty Government*. New York: Oxford University Press, 1990.

Lijphart, Arend. *Electoral Systems and Party Systems*. New York: Oxford University Press, 1994.

———. *Patterns of Democracy: Government Forms and Performance in Thirty-Six Countries*. New Haven, CT: Yale University Press, 1999.

Linz, Juan J. *Totalitarian and Authoritarian Regimes*. Baltimore: Johns Hopkins University Press, 2002.

Michels, Robert. *Political Parties*. New York: Free Press, 1962.

Powell, G. Bingham, Jr. *Contemporary Democracies: Participation, Stability, and Violence*. Cambridge, MA: Harvard University Press, 1982.

———. *Elections as Instruments of Democracy*. New Haven, CT: Yale University Press, 2000.

Riker, William H. *Liberalism Against Populism*. San Francisco: W. H. Freeman, 1982.

Strøm, Kaare, Wolfgang C. Müller, and Torbjörn Bergman, eds. *Cabinets and Coalition Bargaining: The Democratic Life Cycle in Western Europe.* Oxford: Oxford University Press, 2008.

ENDNOTES

1. See, for example, Luis Roniger and Ayse Gunes-Ayata, eds., *Democracy, Clientelism, and Civil Society* (Boulder, CO: Lynne Rienner, 1994); S. Eisenstadt and L. Roniger, *Patrons, Clients, and Friends* (Cambridge: Cambridge University Press, 1984); Lucian W. Pye, *Asian Power and Politics* (Cambridge, MA: Harvard University Press, 1985); and Martin Shefter, "Patronage and Its Opponents," in *Political Parties and the State* (Princeton, NJ: Princeton University Press, 1994).
2. Unfortunately, elections cannot solve all the problems of aggregating interests fairly. For example, giving each citizen one vote does not take into account the varying intensities with which different people may hold their opinions. Moreover, economists and political scientists have found that when there are three or more alternatives in any decision, there is no fair way to aggregate votes to select a single, best outcome (a problem known as "Arrow's Paradox"). See Kenneth Arrow, *Social Choice and Individual Values* (New Haven, CT: Yale University Press, 1951). For an accessible discussion of some political implications, see William H. Riker, *Liberalism Against Populism* (San Francisco: W. H. Freeman, 1982); and Kenneth A. Shepsle, *Analyzing Politics: Rationality, Behavior, and Institutions* (New York: Norton, 2010), Second edition.
3. Hans-Dieter Klingemann, Richard Hofferbert, and Ian Budge, eds., *Parties, Policy, and Democracy* (Boulder, CO: Westview, 1995); Michael Gallagher, Michael Laver, and Peter Mair, *Representative Government in Western Europe*, 4th ed. (New York: McGraw-Hill, 2005); and Richard Rose, *Do Parties Make a Difference?* (Chatham, NJ: Chatham House, 1984), Chapter 5.
4. Joseph A. Schumpeter, *Capitalism, Socialism, and Democracy* (New York: Harper, 1943).
5. However, in China, semicompetitive elections for village leadership positions have in some areas brought the opinions of local leaders and ordinary citizens closer together. See Larry Diamond and Ramon H. Myers, eds., *Elections and Democracy in Greater China* (Oxford: Oxford University Press, 2001).
6. See Russell J. Dalton, *Citizen Politics: Public Opinion and Political Parties in Advanced Industrial Democracies*, 5th ed. (Washington, D.C.: Congressional Quarterly Press, 2008).
7. Ian Budge, David Robertson, and Derek Hearl, eds., *Ideology, Strategy, and Party Change: Spatial Analyses of Post-War Election Programmes in 19 Democracies* (New York: Cambridge University Press, 1987); Richard Katz and Peter Mair, eds., *How Parties Organize: Change and Adaptation in Party Organizations in Western Democracies* (Thousand Oaks, CA: Sage, 1994).
8. Maurice Duverger, *Political Parties: Their Organization and Activity in the Modern State*, trans. Barbara and Robert North (New York: Wiley, 1963). See also Gary W. Cox, *Making Votes Count* (Cambridge: Cambridge University Press, 1997).
9. Anthony Downs, *An Economic Theory of Democracy* (New York: Harper & Row, 1957).
10. The effective number of parties is calculated as follows: First, calculate the proportion of seats (or votes) held by each party. Square each of these proportions and

then add them all up. Finally, divide 1 by the sum of all the squared proportions. See Markku Laakso and Rein Taagepera, "'Effective' Number of Parties: A Measure with Application to West Europe," *Comparative Political Studies* 12 (1979): 3–27.

11. Pradeep Chhibber and Kenneth Kollman, *The Formation of National Party Systems* (Princeton, NJ: Princeton University Press, 2004).

12. Douglas Rae, *The Political Consequences of Election Laws* (New Haven, CT: Yale University Press, 1967); and Arend Lijphart, *Electoral Systems and Party Systems: A Study of Twenty-Seven Democracies, 1945–1990* (Oxford: Oxford University Press, 1994).

13. On government coalitions, see especially Michael Laver and Norman Schofield, *Multiparty Government: The Politics of Coalition in Europe* (New York: Oxford University Press, 1990); and Kaare Strøm, Wolfgang C. Müller, and Torbjörn Bergman, eds., *Cabinets and Coalition Bargaining: The Democratic Life Cycle in Western Europe* (New York: Oxford University Press, 2008).

14. See G. Bingham Powell, Jr., *Elections as Instruments of Democracy* (New Haven, CT: Yale University Press, 2000), Chapters 5–10.

15. Arend Lijphart, *Democracy in Plural Societies* (New Haven, CT: Yale University Press, 1977); and Arend Lijphart, *Patterns of Democracy: Government Forms and Performance in Thirty-Six Countries* (New Haven, CT: Yale University Press, 1999).

16. Lijphart, *Patterns of Democracy*; G. Bingham Powell, Jr., *Contemporary Democracies: Participation, Stability, and Violence* (Cambridge, MA: Harvard University Press, 1982), Chapters 8 and 10; and Juan J. Linz and Alfred Stepan, eds., *The Breakdown of Democratic Regimes* (Baltimore: Johns Hopkins University Press, 1978).

17. Juan Linz, *Totalitarian and Authoritarian Regimes* (Boulder, CO: Lynne Rienner, 2000); Amos Perlmutter, *Modern Authoritarianism: A Comparative Institutional Analysis* (New Haven, CT: Yale University Press, 1981), especially 62–114.

18. Melanie Manion, "Politics in China," Chapter 13, this text; for the earlier period, see, for example, Franz Schurman, *Ideology and Organization in Communist China* (Berkeley: University of California Press, 1966).

19. Juan Linz calls these "sultanistic" regimes; see *Totalitarian and Authoritarian Regimes*, 151–157; Houchang Chehabi and Juan Linz, eds., *Sultanistic Regimes* (Baltimore: Johns Hopkins University Press, 1998); and Robert H. Jackson and Carl G. Rosberg, *Personal Rule in Black Africa* (Berkeley: University of California Press, 1982).

20. Larry Diamond, "Thinking about Hybrid Regimes," *Journal of Democracy* 13 (2002): 26; see also other articles in the same issue.

Government and Policymaking

In a social science class, you might have discussed how to form a government in a new nation. This is a theoretical exercise, but in fact dozens of nations have created new governing systems in the past few decades. Democratization led to new governing systems in postcommunist Europe and in the new democracies of East Asia and Latin America. Other nations have experienced major reforms in the institutions of government.

Policymaking is the pivotal stage in the political process, the point at which bills become law or edicts are issued by rulers. To understand public policy, we must know how decisions are made. Where is power effectively located in different political systems? What does it take to change public policy: a simple majority vote in the legislature or approval also by an independently elected executive? Or is it a decree issued by the military commanders or the party central committee? Or is it merely the whim of the personal dictator?

This chapter focuses on the structures of government—such as legislatures, chief executives, bureaucracies, and courts—and how these agencies enact public policies. While parties, interest groups, and other actors may actively articulate and aggregate interests, government officials do most of the actual initiation and formulation of policy proposals. Interest-group demands for tax relief or for the protection of endangered species cannot succeed unless they are transformed into policy by government officials according to some accepted decision rules. They cannot be effective until these policies are appropriately implemented by other officials.

Yet government action does not flow in one direction only. The interaction between government and citizens is a two-way process. It includes an upward flow of influence and demands from the society, as well as a downward flow of decisions from the government (refer back to Figure 2.2).

CONSTITUTIONS AND DECISION RULES

A constitution establishes the basic rules of decision-making, rights, and the distribution of authority in a political system. We sometimes use the term "constitution" to refer to a specific document laying out such principles—for

133

example, the one adopted by the Founders of the United States in 1787. But a constitution need not be embodied in a single document. In fact, it rarely is. We should therefore think of a constitution as a set of rules and principles, whether it is a specific written document, a set of customs or practices, or, as is usually the case, both. Even a military or party dictatorship typically sets procedures for having decrees proposed, considered, and adopted.

Written constitutions are particularly important in political systems based on the *rule of law*. This means that government should take no action that has not been authorized by law and that citizens can be punished only for actions that violate the law. Under the rule of law, the constitution is the supreme body of laws.

A constitution thus contains a set of **decision rules**—the basic rules governing how decisions are made. Policymaking is the conversion of social interests and demands into authoritative public decisions. Constitutions establish the rules by which this happens. They confer the power to propose policies on specific groups or institutions. They may give others the right to amend, reject, or approve such proposals, or to implement, police, or adjudicate them. They may specify how many resources are needed to make policies, as well as what these resources are.

Decision rules affect political activity because they determine what political resources are valuable in influencing decisions and how to acquire and use these resources. For example, in a federal and decentralized system such as Germany, a pressure group may lobby both the legislative and the executive branches, and it may have to be active both at the state and the federal levels (and also in the European Union). If decisions are made by decree from the commander of the armed forces or the central committee of a single-party state, groups will need to influence these crucial policymakers.

Different decision rules have different attractions. More inclusive rules about policymaking—such as those that require the cooperation of several institutions or the support of over 50 percent of voters—can protect against hasty decisions. They can also prevent decisions that disadvantage large minorities (perhaps close to half) of the voters. At the same time, more inclusive rules can give a minority the power to block proposals favored by a majority. The more inclusive the voting rules are (as the percentage to approve approaches unanimity), the less likely it is that any decision can be made at all. Less inclusive decision rules make it easier to reach a policy, but many interests may be ignored.

Both the government as a whole and its institutions have decision rules. Decision rules may be simple or complex and apply to different circumstances. For example, the U.S. Congress has many different decision rules that apply under different circumstances. Decision rules may be more or less formal and precise. Most legislatures have formal and precise decision rules, whereas cabinets at the head of the executive branch often have informal and flexible rules.

Within each branch of government or other political institution, numerous rules affect the policymaking process. In most modern assemblies, the decision rules about voting are *egalitarian* so that each member has the same voting power—simply speaking, one person, one vote. That is hardly ever true in government departments (ministries), however. Or in dictatorships. There, decision-making is *hierarchical*. Everybody is supposed to defer to his or her superior. In a pure hierarchy, only the vote of the person at the very top counts. Such a decision rule makes it easy to respond quickly in a policymaking emergency, but few interests or ideas may be taken into account.

Even when decisions are made through equal voting, the inclusiveness of the decision rules still shapes the outcomes. Many institutions operate through simple majority voting: In a choice between two options, whichever option gets the larger number of votes wins. For example, the British House of Commons mainly uses the simple majority rule. Alternatively, more inclusive rules—such as "qualified" majorities of three-fifths, two-thirds, or even three-fourths—are sometimes required for particularly consequential decisions. The U.S. Constitution requires two-thirds majorities in both houses of Congress in order to amend the Constitution or override a presidential veto. The most inclusive voting rule is unanimity, which means that any one member can block any decision.

It is important that decision rules in a democracy be transparent and stable. If they are not, citizens will not know what to expect from government. That may erode political legitimacy and make people less willing to accept and support government actions. It may also lead to serious conflicts, and ultimately government may break down and issues be decided by force. Thomas Jefferson suggested the importance of having predictable decision rules in his introduction to the first *Manual of the House of Representatives*: "A bad set of rules is better than no rules at all."

Making Constitutions

Making a constitution is a fundamental political act; it creates or transforms decision rules. Most current constitutions were formed as the result of some break, often violent, with the past—war, revolution, or rebellion against colonial rule. New decision rules were made to accommodate new internal or external powers. Thus, the defeated powers and the successor states of World Wars I and II all adopted new constitutions or had new constitutions imposed on them.

Britain is unusual in having not a formal written constitution but only a long-accepted and highly developed set of customs and conventions, buttressed by important ordinary statutes. This reflects the British record of gradual, incremental, and (on the whole) peaceful political change. Nevertheless, the major changes in British decision rules—such as the shift of power from the Crown to Parliament in the seventeenth century—followed periods of civil war or unrest.

Perhaps the most significant exception to the association between disruptive upheavals and constitution creation is the peaceful development over the last fifty years of the constitution of the European Union, whose growing powers are altering the decision rules affecting about 501 million Europeans in twenty-seven countries. While there has been no violence associated with the formation and growth of the EU, its origins lie in the bitter lessons of World Wars I and II.

The decades since World War II have seen much constitutional experimentation. Not only the defeated powers, but many new states—such as India and Nigeria, which achieved independence with the breakup of colonial empires—introduced new political arrangements. Some developing nations, such as Nigeria, have subsequently changed their form of government several times. In the last two decades, the worldwide trend toward democracy, the end of the Cold War, and the dissolution of the Soviet Union produced a new round of constitutional design. The recent constitutional crafting in Eastern Europe, Russia, East Asia, and Africa has reignited old debates about the virtues and faults of different constitutional arrangements, or about the very wisdom of constitutional engineering.[1]

DEMOCRACY AND AUTHORITARIANISM

The most important distinction in policymaking is between democratic and authoritarian systems. **Democracy** means "government by the people." In small political systems, such as local communities, "the people" may share directly in debating, deciding, and implementing public policy. In large political systems, such as contemporary states, democracy must be achieved largely through indirect participation in policymaking. Policymaking power is delegated to officials chosen by the people.

Elections, competitive political parties, free mass media, and representative assemblies are political structures that make some degree of democracy, some "government by the people," possible in large political systems. Competitive elections give citizens a chance to shape policy through their selection and rejection of key policymakers. Such indirect democracy is not complete or ideal. Moreover, the democratic opportunities in less economically developed societies are often meaningful to educated elites or to those living near the centers of government, but less relevant to the average citizen in the countryside. The more citizens are involved and the more influential their choices, the more democratic the system.

In **authoritarian regimes**, in contrast, the policymakers are chosen by military councils, hereditary families, dominant political parties, and the like. Citizens are either ignored or pressed into symbolic assent to the government's choices.

The basic decision rules of political systems—both democratic and authoritarian—differ along three important dimensions:

1. The separation of powers among different branches of government
2. The geographic distribution of authority between the central (national) government and lower levels, such as states, provinces, or municipalities
3. Limitations on government authority

We shall discuss these dimensions in order, beginning with the separation of authority between executive and legislative institutions.

SEPARATION OF GOVERNMENT POWERS

The theory of **separation of powers** between different institutions of government has a long and venerable history going back at least to the work of Locke and Montesquieu.[2] Separation of powers, they argued, prevents the injustices that might result from an unchecked executive or legislature. Madison and Hamilton elaborated this theory in *The Federalist*,[3] which described and defended the institutional arrangements proposed by the U.S. Constitutional Convention of 1787.

Political theorists often draw upon the two successful historical cases of representative democracy—Britain and the United States—to create the "classic" separation of powers theory. This theory argues that there are essentially two forms of representative democratic government: the presidential and the parliamentary.

The **democratic presidential regime** provides two separate agencies of government—the executive and the legislative—separately elected and authorized by the people (see Table 6.1, column 3). Each branch is elected for a fixed term, neither branch can unseat the other by ordinary means, and each has specific powers under the constitution. Ultimate power to authorize legislation

TABLE 6.1

Distinguishing Features of Parliamentary and Presidential Democracies

Parliamentary and presidential democracies differ in the selection and removal of the chief executive, as well as in the authority to legislate.

Distinguishing Features[a]	Parliamentary Democracies	Presidential Democracies
Title of chief executive	Prime minister (head of government)	President (head of state and government)
Selection of assembly	By citizens in competitive election	By citizens in competitive election
Selection of chief executive	By assembly after election or removal	By citizens in competitive election
Removal of chief executive before fixed term?	By assembly: (No) confidence vote	Fixed terms
Dismissal of assembly before fixed term?	Prime minister may call for early election[b]	Fixed terms
Authority to legislate	Assembly only	Assembly plus president (e.g., veto)
Party relations in assembly and executive	Same parties control both; cohesive party voting	Different party control possible; less cohesive party voting

[a]These define the pure parliamentary and presidential types; as discussed in the text, many constitutional systems, especially in Eastern Europe, "mix" the features of the two types.
[b]Some constitutional systems that are parliamentary in all other ways do not allow for early legislative elections. All parliamentary democracies provide for legislative elections after some maximum time (from three to five years) since the last election.

and approve budgets in these democracies resides with the legislature, whose relationships with the executive are then critical for concentration or dispersal of power. Different presidential regimes provide their presidents with various powers over government appointments and policymaking. For example, some presidents have the authority to veto legislation or to make policy by executive decree under some conditions.[4] In the United States, both the legislature and executive (Congress and the presidency) have large and significant roles in policymaking. In some other democratic presidential systems, such as Brazil, the president may have such a variety of constitutional powers (including the power to make laws through "emergency" decrees) that he or she can reduce the role of the legislature. But coordination between the separate institutions of executive and legislature must somehow be achieved to make policy.

Parliamentary regimes make the executive and legislative branches much more interdependent (see Table 6.1, column 2). First, only the legislative branch is directly elected. The prime minister and the cabinet (the collective leadership of the executive branch) emerge from the legislature. The cabinet is chaired by the prime minister, who is the head of government and selects the other cabinet members.[5] Typically, neither branch has a fixed term of office. The cabinet can be voted out of office at any time, and most often this is true of the legislature (the parliament) as well.

The critical feature that makes this possible is the **confidence relationship** between the prime minister and the parliamentary majority. In a parliamentary system, the prime minister and the cabinet must at all times enjoy the confidence of the parliamentary majority. Whenever the parliamentary majority, for whatever reason, votes a lack of confidence, the prime minister and the cabinet members have to resign. At the same time, the prime minister typically has the power to dissolve parliament and call new elections at any time. The parliamentary majority's dismissal power and the prime minister's dissolution power make the two branches mutually interdependent. This structure induces agreement between them by forcing each branch to be acceptable to the other.

Prime ministers in parliamentary democracies lead precarious political lives. Unlike presidents in presidential systems, prime ministers can be voted out of office at any time, and for any reason, by a parliamentary majority. There are two ways this can happen. First, parliament may pass a motion expressing a lack of confidence in the prime minister—a no-confidence motion. This is typically introduced by the parliamentary opposition in the hope of bringing down the prime minister. Second, parliament may defeat a motion expressing confidence in the prime minister—a confidence motion. Confidence motions are normally introduced by prime ministers themselves.

The confidence vote can be a powerful weapon in the hands of the prime minister. It is typically attached to a bill the prime minister favors but the parliamentary majority does not. By attaching a confidence motion to the bill, the prime minister forces the members of parliament to choose between the bill and the fall of the cabinet. This can be a particularly painful choice for dissident members of the prime minister's own party. If they vote for the bill, they may bring down their own government and perhaps immediately have to face the voters, too (see Box 6.1). Therefore, the possibility of a confidence motion partially explains why party discipline tends to be stronger in parliamentary than in presidential systems.

Thus, parliamentary democracies do not experience the form of divided government that is common under presidentialism when the party that controls the presidency does not control the legislature. Instead, the chief executive (prime minister and cabinet) becomes the agent of the parliamentary majority. In most parliamentary systems, the cabinet consists largely of members of parliament. Conflicts between parliament and the executive are less likely to occur, and decision-making tends to be more efficient than under presidentialism. Since the same party (or parties) controls both branches of government, the cabinet tends to dominate policymaking, and the legislature may be less influential than under a presidential constitution.

Not all democracies fit neatly into the presidential or parliamentary category. Some, such as France, are often characterized as mixed, or "semipresidential." In these types, the president and the legislature are separately elected (as in presidential systems), but the president also has the power to dissolve the legislature (as in parliamentary systems). In these systems, the president may appoint the cabinet (as under presidentialism), but subject to dismissal by the legislature (as under parliamentarism). A variety of arrangements exist for such shared control. Their consequences are often sharply affected by which party or coalition controls the presidency and legislature. Many of the new constitutions of the emergent democracies of Eastern Europe and Asia are of this mixed type.

BOX 6.1 THE CONFIDENCE VOTE IN BRITAIN

British prime ministers can resort to the confidence motion in order to bring rebellious party members into line. Usually, the mere threat of a confidence motion is sufficient. But in 1993, Conservative Prime Minister John Major faced a parliamentary crisis over the ratification of the Maastricht Treaty, which expanded the powers of the European Union. Major had only a slim majority in the House of Commons. Many "Euro-skeptics" in his own party were opposed to the Maastricht Treaty. About twenty of these Conservative dissidents voted with the Opposition and helped defeat the Maastricht Treaty in the House of Commons.

Immediately after this embarrassing defeat, however, Major introduced a confidence motion on his Maastricht policy. He announced that if he lost this vote, he would dissolve the House of Commons and hold new elections. Many of the Conservative dissidents feared that their party would do poorly in such an election and that they might personally lose their seats. Major's confidence motion passed by a vote of 339 to 299, and the House of Commons approved the Maastricht Treaty.

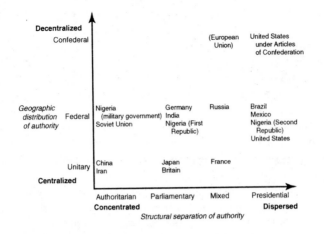

FIGURE 6.1
Division of Governmental Authority
Government authority may be divided along geographic or institutional dimensions, or both.

Reading across Figure 6.1, we see political systems classified by the separation of policymaking powers between executive and legislative institutions, from concentrated to dispersed. The vertical dimension of the table shows geographic division of power, which is discussed in the next section. In authoritarian governments (on the left of the figure), executive, legislative, and judicial power are typically concentrated. Two of the twelve countries discussed in this book—China and Iran—have authoritarian governments not chosen in competitive elections. Britain, Germany, Japan, and India are parliamentary systems in which executive and legislative powers are concentrated in cabinets responsible to the popularly elected lower houses of parliament. At the extreme right of Figure 6.1 are pure presidential systems, such as Brazil, Mexico, and the United States. Nigeria seems to be in transition to a presidential democracy. In between are mixed systems, such as France and Russia, although the latter has become increasingly authoritarian.

In the debate over the best system of representative democracy, many political theorists traditionally favored the British-style parliamentary system. This version of parliamentarism—coupling plurality voting rules that usually create clear single-party majorities in parliament with a cabinet and prime minister responsible to parliament—can result in fairly stable governments responsible to the public will. Parliamentarism coupled with proportional representation—as in Germany and France between the two world wars—seemed more crisis-prone. Such crises occurred because large extremist political parties emerged and produced cabinet instability and even breakdown. However, the Scandinavian countries demonstrate that parliamentary systems with proportional representation can be quite stable when ideological conflict between the political parties remains moderate. Moreover, dominating parliamentary majorities, as in Northern Ireland until 1998, can sometimes threaten minority groups and intensify conflict.[6] In comparison with both versions of parliamentary government, the U.S. presidential system is often criticized for periodically producing divided government, which could result in stalemate or "gridlock."

The third wave of democratization reopened these parliamentary/ presidential debates. Advocates of proportional parliamentarism argue that it provides a consensual framework in which different economic, ethnic, and religious groups can find representation and negotiate their differences. Parliamentary systems also have the flexibility to change governments between elections if the people disapprove of actions of the executive. Since many of the current transitional democracies are deeply divided, a parliamentary, proportional representation system may be particularly suitable. These same experts argue that presidentialism is more susceptible to social conflict and democratic breakdown. Under conditions of divided government, a confrontation between the two legitimately elected institutions representing the people can tear a political system apart. Or, a strong president can use executive powers to repress competition.

Other scholars point out the practical advantages of presidential systems with significant executive power.[7] Even in the domain of the former British empire (such as in Nigeria) and in most of Eastern Europe and the Soviet successor states, the constitutions provide for powerful presidents. Presidential regimes have dominated Latin America for more than a century. A 1993 referendum in Brazil reaffirmed its commitment to presidentialism. Presidentialism also offers the citizens a more direct choice of chief executive, and it puts more effective checks on the power of the majority in the legislature.

GEOGRAPHIC DISTRIBUTION OF GOVERNMENT POWER

Another distinction between governmental structures is the geographic division of power: confederal systems at one extreme, unitary systems at the other extreme, and **federal systems** in the middle (see the vertical dimension of Figure 6.1). The United States under the Articles of Confederation was confederal. Ultimate power rested with the states. The central government had authority over foreign affairs and defense but depended on financial and other support from the states. Under the Constitution of 1787, the U.S. government changed from confederal to federal, which is to say that both central and state governments had separate spheres of authority and the means to implement their power. Today, the United States, Germany, Russia, India, Nigeria, Mexico, and Brazil are federal systems in which central and local units each have autonomy in certain public policy spheres. Britain, France, China, Japan, and Iran are unitary systems with power and authority concentrated in the central government. Regional and local units have only limited powers specifically delegated to them by the central government, which may change or withdraw these powers at will.

Most of the world's states are unitary. In fact, only eighteen states are federal, or fewer than one in ten. Although the federal states are relatively few in number, they tend to be large and politically important. Thus, federal states account for more than one-third of the world's population and 41 percent of its land area. In general, the larger and the more diverse a state is, the more likely it is to be federal.

Analysts attribute several advantages to federalism. In culturally divided societies, it may help protect ethnic, linguistic, or religious minorities, particularly if they are geographically concentrated. It may serve as a check on overly ambitious rulers and thus protect markets and citizen freedoms. Moreover, federalism may allow subunits (such as states) to experiment with different policies. Governments may thus learn from the experiences of others. In addition, citizens may be free to "vote with their feet" and choose the policy environment that best fits their preferences.

While federalism promotes choice and diversity, it does so at the expense of equality. Federalism allows local governments to pursue different policies. One implication is that citizens may get different treatments and benefits from different local governments. Unitary governments may also be in a better position to redistribute resources from richer regions to poorer regions, if that is desirable.

In comparing confederal, federal, and unitary systems, we must distinguish between formal and actual distributions of power. In unitary systems, in spite of the formal concentration of authority at the center, regional and local units may acquire power that the central government rarely challenges. In federal systems, centralized party control may overcome apparent regional autonomy. Thus, the real differences between federal and unitary systems may be considerably less significant than their formal arrangements suggest.

Mexico is an example of the discrepancy between formal and actual federalism. Until recently, the PRI had centralized, authoritarian control in this formally federal system. Recent democratization in Mexico, with formerly opposition parties winning the presidency and many state governments, has produced some "real" federalism to go along with the formalities.

LIMITATIONS ON GOVERNMENT POWER

Unlike authoritarian regimes, democracies are characterized by some legal or customary limitation on the exercise of power. Systems in which the powers of government units are defined and limited by a written constitution, statutes, and custom are called **constitutional regimes**. Civil rights—such as the right to a fair trial and freedom to speak, petition, publish, and assemble—are protected against government interference except under specified circumstances.

The courts are crucial to the limitations on governmental power. As illustrated in Table 6.2, governments may be divided into those at one extreme in which the power to coerce citizens is relatively unlimited by the courts, and those at the other extreme in which the courts protect the rights of citizens and ensure that other parts of the government exercise their powers properly. The United States, Germany, and India are systems in which high courts rule on challenges that other units of government have exceeded the powers allocated by the constitution. This practice of **judicial review** is authorized to various

> **TABLE 6.2**
>
> **Judicial Limitation of Governmental Authority**
>
> The power of judicial review of legislation is found in about half of the world's democracies, but it varies in effectiveness.

Unlimited		Limited
Nonindependent Courts	Independent Courts	Judicial Review
China	Britain	United States
Iran		India
Nigeria		Germany
		France
		Brazil
		Japan
		Russia

degrees in about half of the world's democracies. But judicial review is often weakened by lack of independence of the appointment or tenure of judges or by their ineffectiveness in overcoming executive power.

Some other constitutional regimes have independent courts that protect persons against the improper implementation of laws and regulations, but cannot legally overrule the assembly or the political executive. The citizens' substantive rights in these systems are protected by statute, custom, self-restraint, and political pressure—which are also essential to the effectiveness of courts even where judicial review is authorized. In authoritarian systems, policymakers do not usually allow courts to constrain their use and abuse of power, even where brave judges attempt to rule against them.[8]

Arend Lijphart characterizes only four of the thirty-six democratic systems he examines as having "strong" judicial review: Germany, India, the United States, and Canada after 1982.[9] The Supreme Court of India is most similar to the U.S. Supreme Court, having successfully declared many national laws and ordinances to be unconstitutional. The German Constitutional Court also significantly influences national and state policymaking through its rulings and through government's anticipation of those rulings.[10]

About a quarter of Lijphart's democracies had either strong or medium-strength judicial review. In France, Germany, and Brazil, new legislation may be challenged in court by opposition members of parliament even before it takes effect, a process called "abstract" judicial review. Lijphart classified a little over half of his democracies as having "weak judicial review," with the powers of courts constrained by very limited constitutional authority (as in Sweden) or limited independence of government-appointed judges (as in Japan). In the remaining democracies, courts enjoyed no power of judicial review of legislation, although they may still protect individuals from government abuse not specifically authorized by law (see again Table 6.2).[11]

Many of the new democracies of Eastern Europe proclaimed judicial review in their constitutions, but it has proved harder to implement in practice. There have been striking successes in constraining governments in some countries, but failures in others.

In Nigeria, the courts long retained a striking degree of judicial independence under a succession of otherwise undemocratic military regimes. However, the courts were shown little respect under the Abacha regime of the mid-1990s, which established special military tribunals to prosecute its perceived enemies.

China, in contrast, after explicit rejection of any limits on "mass justice" from the late 1950s to the 1970s, has gradually attempted to introduce a very limited "rule by law." One recent reason is Chinese participation in the global economic system, which requires a legal basis for trade and investment. Chinese rulers see this as a way to encourage stability and economic growth and control corruption. However, the practice falls far short of the promise of limitation on governmental authority.

All written constitutions provide for amending procedures. Most framers of constitutions recognize that basic decision rules must be adaptable, because of potential ambiguities, inefficiencies, changes in citizen values, or unforeseen circumstances. If amendments are too easy to make, they may jeopardize important constitutional protections. Therefore, many constitutions provide that certain arrangements may not be amended (for example, the provision in the U.S. Constitution granting each state equal representation in the Senate).

Amending procedures vary widely, ranging from the complex to the simple. Perhaps the simplest case is that of the United Kingdom, where an ordinary parliamentary statute may alter the constitution. In some cases, constitutional amendments must be approved by a popular vote. The U.S. Constitution has the most difficult formal procedure.

In summary, constitutions may concentrate or disperse government power along several dimensions.[12] There are necessary trade-offs involved in making such constitutional choices. Probably no one who favors democracy and individual liberties would argue for extreme centralization of power in an omnipotent dictator, as in Thomas Hobbes's *Leviathan* (see Chapter 1). However, constitutional democracies that concentrate power to a somewhat lesser degree, such as the British system, have some important advantages. Their governments tend to be effective and efficient, and by relying on majority rule, they tend to treat all citizens equally. No small group can hold up a decision favored by a solid majority. In contrast, constitutions that disperse power, like more inclusive decision rules, have their own advantages. They are more likely to check potential abuses of power, such as the tyranny of a majority, and policies will tend to be stabler over time.

CHECKING THE TOP POLICYMAKERS

One challenge of government is to control the excesses of top political leaders. In many authoritarian systems, there is no legal and institutionalized way to remove the top political leaders if they become unpopular or overstep whatever bounds they may face. Moreover, authoritarian leaders can usually change or simply ignore the formal constitution when it restricts their desires. Democracies have various procedures for keeping the leaders in check, but the procedures vary among the types of systems. In parliamentary systems, chief executives can be removed virtually at any time through a vote of no confidence if they lose the support of a parliamentary majority. In Germany, for example, Social Democratic Party Chancellor Helmut Schmidt was ousted by Helmut Kohl of the Christian Democratic Party in October 1982.

Democratic presidential systems fall somewhere in between. Unlike prime ministers under parliamentary constitutions, presidents have fixed terms of office. Most presidential systems provide for the removal of presidents, but typically only if they are guilty of serious criminal or other wrongdoing. This procedure is called **impeachment.** Impeachment typically involves three components: (1) impeachable offenses are usually identified as presenting unusual danger to the public good or safety; (2) the penalty is removal from office (sometimes with separate criminal penalties); and (3) impeachment cases are decided by the legislature but require more than ordinary majorities and may involve the judiciary in some way. The positive value of impeachment is that it provides a way of legally mobilizing political power against a threat to the constitutional or legal order. At the same time, the danger is that it can be used for mere partisan or personal goals.

In the U.S. system, impeachment procedures can be used against the incumbents in top offices, even the president (as in the cases of Presidents Nixon and Clinton), if their activities stray too far beyond legal bounds. No U.S. president has yet been convicted by the Senate and removed from office, although that fate has befallen other federal officials, such as judges.

Impeachment is associated with constitutions having powerful presidencies with fixed terms of office, such as those in the United States, Brazil, South Korea, and the Philippines (see Box 6.2). Impeachment rules have also been

▶ BOX 6.2 IMPEACHMENT IN LATIN AMERICA

Brazil, Mexico, and many other Latin American nations with strong presidents have impeachment rules and traditions. Many are modeled on the U.S. Constitution. In Mexico, the president, the state governors, and federal judges are subject to impeachment. Brazil has an impeachment process similar to that of the United States, except that it takes a two-thirds vote in the lower house of the assembly to charge the president and other high civil officers with impeachable offenses. A two-thirds vote is also required in the Senate to convict. The clause was invoked in 1992, when Brazil's president, Fernando Collor, was impeached on charges of large-scale corruption. He resigned before trial in the Senate. Impeachment procedures also forced presidents from office in Venezuela in 1993 and Paraguay in 1999. A slightly different procedure was used by the Congress in 1997 to declare the incumbent president of Ecuador mentally unfit.

Source: Anibal Perez-Linan, *Presidential Impeachment and the New Political Instability in Latin America* (New York: Cambridge University Press, 2007).

adopted in the constitutions of semipresidential regimes, such as Russia, and even in purely parliamentary regimes.

In the long run, the ultimate control of democratic order is periodic and competitive elections. This need to achieve and regularly renew their popular mandates is the fundamental device that leads politicians to respond to the needs and demands of citizens. It is deeply imperfect. It may be difficult to tell when elected officials are incompetent, deceitful, or just unlucky. The complexities of policymaking may baffle the attempt of even trained observers to assign responsibility for successes or failures. The multiplicity of political issues may leave citizens torn between their candidate choices. Or, none of the choices may seem very palatable. Yet, deeply imperfect as it is, this remarkable recruitment structure gives every citizen some influence on the policymaking process. For this reason, we consider the competitive election to be the most significant democratic structure.

ASSEMBLIES

Legislative **assemblies** have existed for thousands of years. Ancient Greece and Rome had them, for example. Indeed, the Roman Senate has given its name to modern assemblies in the United States and many other countries.

Almost all contemporary political systems have assemblies, variously called *senates, chambers, diets, houses,* and the like. Assemblies are also known as "legislatures" (regardless of what role they actually play in legislating) or as "parliaments" (mainly in parliamentary systems). Their formal approval is usually required for major public policies. They are generally elected by popular vote, and hence are at least formally accountable to the citizenry. Today, 186 countries have such governmental bodies. The almost universal adoption of legislative assemblies suggests that in the modern world, a legitimate government must formally include a representative popular component.

Assembly Structure

Assemblies vary in their size—from less than 100 to more than 1,000 members—and their organization. They may consist of one chamber (in which case they are called *unicameral*) or two chambers (*bicameral*). Most democracies, and some authoritarian systems, have bicameral (two-chamber) assemblies. Federal systems normally provide simultaneously for two forms of representation; often, representation in one chamber is based on population and representation in the second chamber is based on geographic units. Even in unitary systems (such as France or Japan), **bicameralism** is common, but the purpose of the second chamber is to provide a check on policymaking rather than to represent subnational units. The bicameral German parliament grew out of both federalism and the desire to separate the power of the federal government.

In most bicameral systems, one chamber is dominant, and the second (such as the Russian Council of the Federation or the French Senate) has more limited powers that are often designed to protect regional interests. While representatives in the dominant chamber are popularly elected, those in the second chamber are sometimes chosen by the regional governments (as in Germany) or in other indirect ways. The prime minister in most parliamentary systems is responsible only to the more popularly elected chamber, which therefore has a more important position in policymaking than the second chamber. (See the discussion of the vote-of-confidence procedure earlier in this chapter and in Box 6.1.)

Assemblies also differ in their internal organization in ways that have major consequences for policymaking. There are two kinds of internal legislative organization: party groups and formal assembly subunits (presiding officers, committees, and the like). There is often an inverse relationship between the strength of parties and the strength of other subunits (such as committees): The stronger the parties are, the weaker the committees are, and vice versa. As in most parliamentary systems, British members of Parliament vote strictly along party lines much more consistently than members of the U.S. Congress. Because cabinets generally hold office only as long as they can command a parliamentary majority, deviating from the party line means risking the fall of the government and new elections.

In presidential systems, the president and the legislators are independently elected for fixed terms of office. Thus the fate of the executive is less directly tied up with voting on legislative measures. Moreover, the president and the legislative party leadership may offer conflicting messages to the president's party, leading to party divisions. For both reasons, party voting is less cohesive in presidential systems, depending also on whether the election rules foster competition within the parties.[13]

All assemblies have a committee structure—some organized arrangement that permits legislators to divide their labor and to specialize in particular issue areas. Without such committees, it would be impossible to handle the large flow of legislative business. However, the importance of committees varies.[14] In some legislatures—such as those in the United States, Japan, and Germany—committees are very influential. This is partially because they are highly specialized, have jurisdictions that match those of the executive departments, and have numerous staff resources. Strong committees tend to have a clear legislative division of labor that matches the executive branch, allowing for specialized oversight of executive activity. They are often arenas in which the opposition can be influential. British committees, by comparison, are much weaker since they have small staffs, are dominated by the governing party, and get appointed for one bill at a time. Hence, they cannot accumulate expertise in a particular policy area.

Assembly Functions

Assembly members deliberate, debate, and vote on policies that come before them. Most important policies and rules must be considered and at least formally approved by these bodies before they have the force of law. Assemblies typically also control public-spending decisions; budgeting is one of their major functions. In addition, some assemblies have important appointment powers, and some may serve as a court of appeals. Although laws typically need assembly approval, in most countries, legislation is actually formulated elsewhere, usually by the political executive and the upper levels of the bureaucracy.

When we compare the importance of assemblies as policymaking agencies, the U.S. Congress, which plays a very active role in the formulation and enactment of legislation, is at one extreme. The other extreme is represented by the National People's Congress of the People's Republic of China, which meets infrequently and does little more than listen to statements by party leaders and rubber-stamp decisions made elsewhere. Roughly midway between the two is the House of Commons in Britain. There, legislative proposals are sometimes initiated or modified by ordinary members of Parliament, but public policy is usually initiated and proposed by members of the Cabinet (who are, to be sure, chosen from the members of the parliamentary body). The typical assembly provides a deliberating forum, formally enacts legislation, and sometimes amends it.

Assemblies should not be viewed only as legislative bodies. All assemblies in democratic systems have an important relationship to legislation, but not necessarily a dominant role. Their political importance is based not just on this function but also on the great variety of other political functions they perform. Assemblies can play a major role in elite recruitment, especially in parliamentary systems, where prime ministers and cabinet members typically serve their apprenticeships in parliament. Legislative committee hearings and floor debates may be important sites for interest articulation and interest aggregation, especially if there is no cohesive majority party. Debates in assemblies can be a source of public information about politics and thus contribute to the socialization of citizens generally and elites in particular.

Representation: Mirroring and Representational Biases

Contemporary legislatures, especially in democratic systems, are valued particularly because they represent the citizens in the policymaking process. It is not obvious, however, what the ideal linkage between citizens and government officials should be. Some argue that government officials should mirror the characteristics of the citizens as far as possible. This principle, also known as *descriptive representation*, is held to be particularly important with respect to potentially conflictual divisions (such as race, class, ethnicity, gender, language, and perhaps age).

However, descriptive representation is not the only concern in recruiting public officials. The limits of mirroring were inadvertently expressed by a U.S. senator. In defending a U.S. Supreme Court nominee who was accused of mediocrity, the senator lamely contended, "[E]ven if he were mediocre, there are a lot of mediocre judges and people and lawyers. They are entitled to a little representation, aren't they?"[15] Most people would probably not agree that government officials should mirror the general population in their abilities to do their jobs. Instead, we generally want political elites to be the best possible *agents* for their constituents. In this view, government officials should be selected for their ability to serve the interests of the citizens, whether they share the voters' background characteristics or do not.

For politicians to be good agents, they need to have similar *preferences* to the citizens they represent *and* they need the appropriate *skills* to do their jobs. In democracies, political parties and elections are the most important mechanisms by which the preferences of citizens and the preferences (or at least commitments) of leaders are aligned.[16] As far as skills are concerned, political and governmental leadership—particularly in modern, technologically advanced societies—requires knowledge and skills that are hard to acquire except through education and training. Natural intelligence or experience may, to a limited degree, take the place of formal education.

Hence, it might be a good thing for government officials to be better informed, more intelligent, more experienced, and perhaps better educated than the people who they serve. Just as medical patients tend to look for the most capable physician rather than the one who is most like them, one could argue that citizens should look for the best qualified officeholder. In this view, selecting government officials, including representative policymakers, is like delegating to experts. It may be a hopeful sign that citizens in many modern democracies are increasingly willing to select leaders who do not share their background characteristics.

As in the case of so many other political choices, there is no obvious or perfect way to choose between mirroring and expert delegation. This is an old debate, and in many situations, it is necessary to make a trade-off between the two. Different offices may require different considerations. Most people would, for example, probably put a higher emphasis on mirroring in their local assembly than in a regulatory agency overseeing nuclear technology.

The bad news is that political elites, even democratically elected members of legislatures, hardly ever mirror the citizens they represent on any of the standard social characteristics. Even in democracies such as Britain and France, political leaders tend to be of higher social status, unusually well-educated, or upwardly mobile individuals from the lower classes. There are exceptions. In some countries, trade unions or leftist political parties may serve as channels of political advancement for people with modest economic or educational backgrounds. These representatives acquire political skills and experience by holding offices in working-class organizations. During the long domination of the executive by the Norwegian Labor Party (1935–1981), none of its prime ministers had even completed secondary school. But these are rare and vanishing examples. In most contemporary states, the number of working-class people in high office is small and declining.

Women have traditionally been poorly represented in political leadership positions in most countries. However, the situation has changed significantly in the last thirty years. In 1980, women held about 10 percent of the parliamentary seats around the world. By 2010, that figure had nearly doubled, to 19 percent. Women have also held the chief executive office in a growing number of countries (see Box 6.3). Angela Merkel, for example, became chancellor of Germany in 2005 and was reelected in 2009.

But women's advancement has been uneven.[17] In many Northern European countries, such as Sweden, women by 2010 accounted for 40 percent or more of the legislators and a similar proportion of cabinet members.

BOX 6.3 WOMEN AS CHIEF EXECUTIVES

From about 1970 on, women have gained chief executive office in a growing number of countries. Interestingly, many of the early leaders were from Asian and Middle Eastern countries, where women's roles in public life traditionally have been limited. Sinmavo Bandaranaike of Sri Lanka (1960–1965 and 1970–1977), Indira Gandhi of India (1966–1977 and 1980–1984), and Golda Meir of Israel (1969–1974) were among the pioneers. In the 1980s and 1990s, women also came to power in the Philippines, Pakistan, Bangladesh, and again in Sri Lanka. In Burma, Nobel Peace Prize winner Aung San Suu Kyi won the elections of 1990, but the military prevented her from taking office.

Women have recently made inroads in leadership positions in Europe and the Americas, though they are still few and far between in Africa. The first female leader in a major European country was Prime Minister Margaret Thatcher of Britain (1979–1990). Her strong and decisive leadership made her one of Europe's most influential politicians in the 1980s. Women have come to power in other Western countries as well. Angela Merkel is now chancellor of Germany. In Norway, Gro Harlem Brundtland held the prime ministership for a total of about ten years between 1981 and 1996. In Latin America, female presidents have recently come to office in Argentina, Chile, and Costa Rica.

The career paths of Asian women leaders have tended to differ from those elsewhere. Many of the former have come from prominent political families, such as the Gandhi family in India and the Bhuttos in Pakistan. In several cases, they have been the widows or daughters of important political leaders. In Europe and Latin America, women leaders are more likely to have made independent political careers, and they can rely on stronger women's interest groups.

In Germany, Mexico, Britain, and China, women held over 20 percent of the legislative seats. But in Brazil and Nigeria, women still accounted for fewer than 10 percent. The proportion in Iran was only 3 percent.

Political elites also tend to be unrepresentative with respect to age. In many countries, legislators (much less chief executives) under age 40 are a rarity, whereas a large proportion of leading politicians are past normal retirement age. In many countries, university graduates—and often lawyers and civil servants in particular—are vastly overrepresented, whereas ethnic, linguistic, and religious minorities are often underrepresented. Representational biases are thus numerous and pervasive. And while women's representation is increasing, class biases are getting worse.

POLITICAL EXECUTIVES

In modern states, the executive branch is by far the largest, the most complex, and typically the most powerful branch of government. It is not easy to describe executives in simple ways, but it is sensible to start at the top. Governments typically have one or two **chief executives**, officials who sit at the very top of the often colossal executive branch. Such executives have various names, titles, duties, and powers. They are called *presidents, prime ministers, chancellors, secretaries general*, or even *leader* (in Iran). There are even a few kings who still have genuine power. Titles may mislead us as to what functions these officials perform, but they tend to be the main formulators and executors of public policy.

Structure of the Chief Executive

Democratic governments typically have either a single chief executive (in presidential systems) or a split chief executive of two offices: a largely ceremonial head of state (who represents the nation on formal occasions) and a more powerful head of government (who determines public policies). Table 6.3 distinguishes among executives according to the bases of their power to affect policymaking. In the left column, we see the chief executives in authoritarian systems, whose power ultimately rests on coercion. The middle and right columns show the chief executives in democratic countries. The middle column

TABLE 6.3

Bases of Legislative Power of Chief Executives

Chief executives vary in the effectiveness and in the bases of their legislative powers.

Authoritarian	Democratic: Partisan Influence	Democratic: Constitutional Powers
Effective		
General Secretary, China	British Prime Minister	
	French Prime Minister	
	German Chancellor	
	Indian Prime Minister	
	Japanese Prime Minister	
	(Russian Prime Minister)	
Ceremonial		
Chinese President		British Queen or King
		German President
		Indian President
		Japanese Emperor
Ceremonial and Effective		
Iranian Leader	French President	Brazilian President
		Mexican President
		Nigerian President
		Russian President
		U.S. President

shows executives whose power rests primarily on their partisan influence in the legislature, which is the case of the prime ministers in most parliamentary systems. The right column includes chief executives whose ability to influence legislation resides in powers directly granted them by the constitution, rather than partisan connection alone. Strong presidents may be able to veto legislation, for example, issue legal decrees, or introduce the budget. They usually have the power to appoint and dismiss members of the cabinet.

Reading down the table, we see the distinction between executives with effective power over policy, purely ceremonial roles, or both effective and ceremonial power. Political executives are effective only if they have genuine discretion in the enactment and implementation of laws and regulations, in budgetary matters, or in important government appointments. Where they do not have these powers, they are symbolic or ceremonial. In presidential systems, the ceremonial and effective roles are almost always held by the same person, the president, as we see in both authoritarian and democratic systems at the bottom of Table 6.3. In parliamentary democratic systems, and in some authoritarian systems, the two roles are separated between the "head of state," who is primarily a ceremonial official, and a "head of government," who makes and implements the decisions. The British, German, Indian, and Japanese prime ministers appear in the second column at the top of the table, while their ceremonial counterparts appear at the center right.

These distinctions are not absolute. Some constitutions, such as the German constitution, give substantial formal powers to their prime ministers. At the same time, even largely ceremonial presidents can exert important influence if the parties are divided or by exercising special constitutional powers (or both, as has happened in India in the 1990s). Moreover, partisan influence in the legislature is useful even to the strongest democratic presidents. Still, it is usually easy to determine the primary sources of legislative power, even where the formal names may be misleading.

A few countries have both significant presidents and prime ministers. The balance of power between them depends on the constitutional powers of the president and on the partisan division in the legislature. In Russia, the constitutional powers of veto and decree of the president are very great, and expanded under recent authoritarian trends. Until recently, the prime minister has been mostly just another administrator, with little effective power. In France, however, the president's formal powers are much weaker; when the legislature is unified under opposition parties, it has elected a prime minister who has effectively dominated policymaking, greatly reducing the president's political influence.

In China, the chairman of the Communist Party is the most powerful political figure and the effective chief executive. The Chinese president is the head of state, which is a purely ceremonial role, without associated powers. However, in recent years, the same individual has held both offices, and also a key role as chairman of the party military commission. A separate premier, or head of government, is a largely administrative position.

Monarchies are much rarer at the beginning of the twenty-first century than they were at the beginning of the twentieth. Some monarchs, such as the king of Saudi Arabia and some other Arab monarchs, still exercise real power. Most contemporary monarchs, however, have little or no actual political influence. Monarchs like the British or Scandinavian royal families hold principally ceremonial and symbolic positions with limited political powers. They are living symbols of the state and nation and of their historical continuity. Britain's queen may bestow honors or appointments to the nobility with a stroke of her sword, but these are recommended by the prime minister. The Japanese monarchy has also traditionally been dignified and exalted, and played an important role as a national symbol. In contrast, the Scandinavian monarchies are more humdrum. Because members of these royal families occasionally use humbler means of transportation, these dynasties are sometimes called "bicycle monarchies." In republican democracies with parliamentary systems, presidents perform the functions that fall to kings and queens in parliamentary monarchies. Thus, German presidents give speeches on important anniversaries and designate prime ministers after elections or when a government has resigned.

A system that separates the ceremonial executive from the effective executive has a number of advantages. The ceremonial executive symbolizes unity and continuity and can be above politics. The U.S. presidency, which combines both effective and ceremonial functions, runs the risk that the president will use his ceremonial and symbolic authority to enhance his political power or that his involvement in politics may make him a less effective symbolic or unifying figure.

Recruitment of Chief Executives

Historically, finding effective and legitimate ways to select the individuals to fill the top policymaking roles has been critical to political order and stability. "Recruitment structures" are the means by which nations choose their top policymakers and executives. Table 6.4 shows the recruitment structures in the countries discussed in this book.

A major accomplishment of stable democracies is regulating the potential conflict involved in leadership succession and confining it to the mobilization of votes instead of weapons. The most familiar structures are the presidential and parliamentary forms of competitive party systems. In presidential systems, parties select candidates for nomination, and the electorate chooses among them. Russia and France have directly elected presidents but also give an important role to the prime minister, who is appointed by the president but can be removed by the legislature.

Mexico appears similar to other presidential systems. But for half a century, the PRI had such control over the electoral process that the voters merely ratified the party's presidential nominee. Until the remarkable July 2000 election, many voters remained skeptical that a non-PRI president could really come to power. As the table shows, Mexico now has a democratic presidential system, with parties nominating candidates and voters genuinely choosing among them, as in the very close election of 2006.

In both presidential and parliamentary democracies, the tenure of the chief executive is limited, directly or indirectly. In the presidential system, this is

TABLE 6.4

Recruitment of Chief Executive

Political parties of various kinds are involved in the recruitment of most chief executives.

Country	Chief Executive Structure	Recruitment Structures	How Often Has This Type of Government Survived Succession?[b]
Brazil	President	Party and voters	Often
Britain	Prime minister	Party, House of Commons, voters	Very often
China	Party secretary[a]	Party and military	Often
France	President/Prime minister	Party, (Assembly) voters	Often
Germany	Chancellor	Party, Bundestag, voters	Often
India	Prime minister	Party, Lok Sabha, voters	Often (one interruption)
Iran	Leader	Religious elites	Once
Japan	Prime minister	Party, Diet, voters	Often
Mexico	President	Party and voters	Twice
Nigeria	President	Military, party, voters	Twice
Russia	President	Party, president, voters	Twice
United States	President	Party and voters	Very often

[a]"Party secretary" refers to that position or to a similar one as head of party in a communist regime.
[b]"Often" means that at least three successions have taken place under that type of government.

usually directly, through fixed terms of office for the chief executive. In the parliamentary system, there is a maximum term for the parliament, which then indirectly also limits the life of the cabinet, since the prime minister is accountable to the new parliamentary majority and can be removed by it.

Table 6.4 also illustrates the role of the noncompetitive party and the military organizations in China, the military in Nigeria, and nonelected religious elites in Iran. The important role played by political parties illustrates the great need to mobilize broad political support behind the selection of chief executives. The frequent appearance of parties also reflects, no doubt, the modern legitimacy of popular sovereignty: the promise that the rulers' actions will be in the interest of the ruled.

Authoritarian systems rarely have effective procedures for leadership succession. The more power is concentrated at the top, the riskier it is to transfer it from one person to the next. Very often, authoritarian leaders do not dare to relinquish their power, and leadership succession occurs only when they die or are overthrown. In communist regimes, the Communist Party selects the general secretary (or equivalent), who is the controlling executive force. Individual succession is not a simple matter. These systems do not limit the terms of incumbents, who are difficult to oust once they have consolidated their supporters into key party positions. Nonetheless, they always have to be aware of the possibility of a party coup of the type that ousted Nikita Khrushchev from the Soviet leadership in 1964. As a system, however, the Soviet leadership structure seemed quite stable until the dramatic 1991 coup attempt against Mikhail Gorbachev. Although he was briefly restored to power, the events surrounding the coup stripped the Soviet presidency of power, and legitimacy passed to the presidencies and legislatures of the fifteen constituent republics. Russia managed its first democratic transition surprisingly smoothly, from Boris Yeltsin to his chosen successor, Vladimir Putin, who was elected president in 2000. Putin arranged a less democratic transition in 2008, when Dmitrii Medvedev was elected president in an unfree election.

The poorer nations show substantially less stability, and the regimes usually have had less experience at surviving succession crises.[18] Nigeria experienced a succession of military coups and governments from 1966 until 1979, and then introduced a competitive presidential system, which was overthrown by a military coup shortly after its second election in 1983. The military government again moved toward civilian rule in the early 1990s, but then annulled the 1993 presidential election before the results were announced. The military rulers finally allowed a return to civilian rule in 1999, but the system has seemed fragile.

Military governments, stable or unstable, have also been common in Latin America and the Middle East, although they are now more likely to work with other groups or from behind the scenes (see Chapter 5). The Chinese Communist Party has remained in power for fifty years but has suffered several periods of internal strife, and the army has been involved in recruitment at all levels. India's democracy has been an exception to the rule among poorer nations. It has had a number of democratic successions with a single interruption (authoritarian emergency rule that postponed elections for several years) in the 1970s.

The Cabinet

In many political systems, the **cabinet** is the most important collective decision-making body. Its power can be particularly great in parliamentary systems, where its formation is closely linked to selection of the prime minister. It typically contains the leaders (often called "ministers") of all the major departments (sometimes called "ministries") of the executive branch. The cabinet meets frequently, often several times per week. It is typically led by the head of government: the president in presidential systems and the prime minister in parliamentary ones. In some parliamentary systems, the entire cabinet is collectively responsible to the legislature. The prime minister may be little more than "first among equals," especially under conditions of multiparty coalition governments. In other parliamentary systems, such as Germany, the constitution confers much more authority on the chief executive.[19]

How is the cabinet selected? In presidential systems, selecting cabinet members is typically a presidential prerogative, though sometimes (as with the U.S. Senate), the legislature has approval. The president can typically also dismiss cabinet members at will, whereas the legislature's ability to do so is most often severely limited.

In parliamentary systems, the process is very different, since the prime minister and the cabinet need to maintain the confidence of the parliamentary majority. Therefore, cabinet formation depends on the result of parliamentary elections and on the composition of parliament. If a competitive party wins a parliamentary majority by itself, it will (if unified) be able to form a cabinet of its own members and can then pass and implement its policies. Sometimes the election directly determines who controls the majority. This is always the case in pure two-party systems, where one party always has a parliamentary majority. It can also happen in multiparty systems, whenever one party gets more seats than all its competitors combined. The election laws play an important part in shaping legislative representation of the parties. The more parties there are, the less likely it is that one of them will have a majority on its own. When one party controls a parliamentary majority, the party almost always forms a *majority single-party cabinet* by itself.

In most multiparty countries, the typical election result is that no party has a parliamentary majority by itself. Most commonly under such circumstances, several parties (two, three, or more) join forces and form a *coalition cabinet* in which they are all represented. Sometimes, parties anticipate this need to form coalitions before the election. They may make a formal agreement with one another and inform the voters that they intend to govern together if they collectively get enough votes. The allied parties may thus encourage their voters to support the coalition partners' candidates where their own party's candidates seem weak and often take advantage of special provisions of voting laws. Many German and French governments have come to power in this fashion. In such cases, the voters can have a direct voice in the choice of the future cabinet, much as they do in two-party systems. Voters are thus given a major role in choosing the direction of government policy.

If no party or preelection coalition wins control of the legislature through the election, parties may bargain after the election, or between elections, to form a new cabinet. In the Netherlands, such bargaining took four months after the 2003 election. However, only a few days were needed to form a coalition government of the Conservatives and Liberal Democrats after the British election in 2010.

Whether bargaining takes place before or after the elections, the parties in parliamentary systems typically have many options concerning the composition of the cabinet. In some cases, a single party decides that it can form a minority cabinet alone, often because the other parties disagree too much among themselves to offer any alternative. Figure 6.2 illustrates these various possibilities. With a minority government, the parties in the cabinet must continually bargain

Party System	Election Result	Cabinet Type

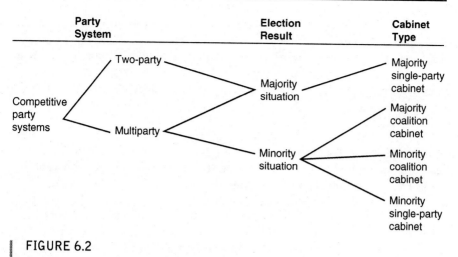

FIGURE 6.2
Cabinet Formation in Parliamentary Democracies
Party system and election results shape cabinet formation processes and outcomes.

with other parties to get policies adopted and even to remain in office. In majority coalitions, bargaining occurs primarily among coalition partners represented in the cabinet. In both of these circumstances, the power of the prime minister may depend on the bargains he or she can strike with leaders of other parties.

These complications illustrate two of the problems of combining parliamentary government with electoral systems of proportional representation. Such systems do not produce a single majority party, which does not give the voters a very clear choice about who will control the executive branch. Instead, the parties may determine this behind closed doors after the election. Sometimes, the results are paradoxical, as when parties that have just lost votes in the elections are able to negotiate their way into a governing coalition. The second problem is that multiparty cabinets are sometimes unstable. Italy, for example, has had on average more than one change of government per year since World War II. Yet such problems need not always emerge. In Germany, cabinets have been quite stable, and the voters have generally been given fairly clear options ahead of elections.

Functions of the Chief Executive

Typically, the chief executive is the most important structure in policymaking. The executive normally initiates new policies. Depending on the division of powers with the legislature and the partisan balance, the executive also has a substantial part in their adoption. In presidential systems, the president very often has veto powers. Thus the chief executive typically has both the first and the last word in policymaking. In parliamentary systems, on the other hand, the chief executive is less likely to be able to exercise a veto.

The political executive also oversees policy implementation and can hold subordinate officials accountable for their performance. The central decisions in a foreign policy crisis are generally made by the chief executive. Political initiatives and new programs typically originate in the executive. A bureaucracy without an effective executive tends to implement past policies rather than initiate new ones. Without politically motivated ministers, bureaucracies tend toward inertia.

The decision of a president, prime minister, cabinet, or central party committee to pursue a new foreign or domestic policy is usually accompanied by structural adaptations—the appointment of a vigorous minister, the establishment of a special cabinet committee, and the like. Where the political executive is weak and divided, as in contemporary Italy (at least until recently), this dynamic force is missing. Initiative then passes to the bureaucracy, legislative committees, and powerful interest groups—and general needs, interests, and problems may be neglected. In a separation-of-powers system, when the presidency and the congress are controlled by different parties, even a strong president may be hampered in carrying out an effective policy. And if the president is hamstrung, the assembly can rarely fill the gap.

Chief executives also perform important system functions. Studies of childhood socialization show that the first political role perceived by children tends to be the chief political executive—the president, prime minister, or king or queen. In early childhood, the tendency is to identify the top political executive as a parent figure. As the child matures, he or she begins to differentiate political from other roles, as well as to differentiate among various political roles (see Chapter 3). The conduct of the chief executive affects the trust and confidence that young people feel in the whole political system, and they carry that with them into adulthood. The role of the chief executive in recruitment is obviously important, appointing the cabinet and other officials. The political executive also plays a central role in communication, in explaining and building support for new policies or in improving performance in various sectors of the society and economy.

THE BUREAUCRACY

Modern societies are dominated by large organizations, and this applies to governments as well. **Bureaucracies**, by which we mean all the members of the executive branch below the top executives, are generally in charge of implementing government policy. The size of government bureaucracies increased over the course of the twentieth century. This is partly due to the expanding policy responsibilities and efforts of governments. It may also be partly due to the tendency for government agencies, once they have been established, to seek growth for its own sake. In reaction to this tendency, and as part of the concern about government inefficiencies, there has been a recent movement in many advanced democracies to reduce government budgets and to downsize the bureaucracy (see Chapter 7).

Structure of the Bureaucracy

The most important officials in bureaucracies are the experienced and expert personnel of the top **civil service**. The British "government" consists of approximately one hundred top executive positions of ministers, junior ministers, and parliamentary secretaries. This relatively small group of political policymakers oversees some 3,000 permanent members of the **higher civil service**. These civil servants spend their lives as an elite corps, moving about from ministry to ministry, watching governments come and go, and becoming increasingly important as policymakers as they rise in rank. Below the higher civil service is a huge body of more than half a million permanent public employees, ordinary civil servants, organized into about twenty government departments and a number of other agencies. The total number of British civil servants rose from 100,000 in 1900 to more than 700,000 in 1979; it declined under Conservative governments of the 1980s to 1990s and numbers about 500,000 today.

The importance of the permanent higher civil service is not unique to Britain. In France, too, the higher civil service is filled with powerful generalists who can bring long tenure, experience, and technical knowledge to their particular tasks. In the United States, many top positions in government agencies go to presidential appointees rather than to permanent civil servants, but there are permanent civil servants in the key positions just below the top appointees in all the cabinet departments. These people tend to be specialists—such as military officers, diplomats, doctors, scientists, economists, and engineers—who exert great influence on policy formulation and execution in their specialties. Below these specialists and administrators are the vast numbers of ordinary government employees—postal workers, teachers, welfare case agents, and so forth—who see that governmental policies are put into practice. In 2009, the United States had 21 million public employees of all kinds (federal, state, and local), or about 17 percent of the total labor force. In many European countries, that proportion is even higher, approaching a third of the labor force in Norway, Denmark, and Sweden.

Functions of the Bureaucracy

Bureaucracies have great significance in most contemporary societies. One reason is that the bureaucracy is almost alone in implementing and enforcing laws and regulations. In so doing, they may have quite a bit of discretion. Most modern legislation is general and can be effectively enforced only if administrative officials work out its detail and implementation. Policy implementation and enforcement usually depend on bureaucrats' interpretations and on the spirit and effectiveness with which they put policies into practice. But the power of bureaucracies is not restricted to their implementation and enforcement of rules made by others. In Chapters 4 and 5, we discussed how bureaucratic agencies may articulate and aggregate interests. Departments such as those for agriculture, labor, defense, welfare, and education may be among the most important voices of interest groups. Moreover, administrative agencies in modern political systems do a great deal of adjudication. Tax authorities, for example, routinely determine whether citizens have faithfully reported their income and paid their taxes, and these authorities assess penalties accordingly. While citizens may in principle be able to appeal such rulings to the courts, relatively few actually do. Finally, political elites, whether executives or legislators, base many of their decisions on the information they obtain from the public administration. Similarly, interest groups, political parties, the business elites, and the public depend on such information.

Bureaucracy and Performance

We commonly use the term "bureaucracy" to refer to all systems of public administration. Strictly speaking, however, *bureaucracy* refers to a particular way of organizing such agencies. According to the classical German sociologist Max Weber, bureaucracies have the following features:

1. Decision-making is based on fixed and official jurisdictions, rules, and regulations.
2. There are formal and specialized educational or training requirements for each position.
3. There is a hierarchical command structure: a firmly ordered system of superordination and subordination, in which information flows upward and decisions downward.
4. Decisions are made on the basis of standard operating procedures, which include extensive written records.
5. Officials hold career positions, are appointed and promoted on the basis of merit, and have protection against political interference, notably in the form of permanent job tenure.[20]

No organization is perfectly bureaucratic in this sense, but professional armies come reasonably close, as do tax revenue departments.

These features of bureaucracies have a number of desirable effects. They promote competence, consistency, fair treatment, and freedom from political manipulation. Imagine what life would be like without bureaucracies. Before the advent of modern bureaucracy, public officials were often a sorry lot. Some of them inherited their jobs; others got them through family or political connections. Yet others bought their posts and used them to enrich themselves, gain social status, or both. They often used their powers arbitrarily, to favor friends and neighbors, and to the disadvantage of others. Many devoted little time to their duties. No wonder, then, that public officials were often incompetent, uninterested in their jobs, corrupt, or all of the above. Given the lack of rules and records, aggrieved citizens typically had few recourses.

The negative connotation associated with the word "bureaucracy" suggests that such organizations have liabilities as well. Bureaucratic organizations can become stodgy, rule-bound, inflexible, and insensitive to the needs of their clients. In many cases, bureaucrats have few incentives to be innovative and efficient or even to work very hard. Although bureaucracies are supposed to be politically and ideologically neutral, they are often influenced by the dominant ideologies of the time, have conservative propensities, and pursue institutional interests of their own.[21] Many citizens are exasperated with bureaucracy and its propensities for inefficiency and lack of responsiveness. This frustration is reflected in popular cynicism as well as in periodic attempts to reform government.

Modern authoritarian systems discovered that the bureaucracy was an essential tool of government control. Thus, recruitment of the bureaucracy was part of a larger pattern of control. Bureaucratic selection in the former Soviet Union, as in China today, was controlled through a device called *nomenklatura*. Under this procedure, important positions were kept under the direct supervision of a party agency that had the final word on recruitment. Moreover, the party offered inducements to control the behavior of the chosen officials. These inducements made it difficult for any but the topmost officials to have much freedom of action. Soviet leaders used normative incentives (such as appeals to party, ideology, and national idealism), financial incentives (such as better salaries, access to finer food and clothing, better housing, and freedom to travel), and coercive control (such as reporting by police, party, and bureaucrats). They used demotion or imprisonment, even execution, as penalties. To avoid a coup by police or military forces, the varied layers of command and inducement structures were interwoven, so that no layer could act independently.

In democracies, assemblies and courts also help control the bureaucracy. Legislative committee hearings or judicial investigations may bring bureaucratic performance into line with political desires. Sweden invented the institution of the **ombudsman** to prevent bureaucrats from doing injury or injustice to individuals.[22] This invention has been copied by other states. In the Scandinavian countries, Britain, Germany, and elsewhere, ombudsmen now investigate citizen claims that they have suffered injury or damage as a result of government action. Ombudsmen typically have no power of their own but report to the legislature for remedial action. Their cases rarely lead to criminal conviction, but government officials often change their policies as a result of embarrassing publicity. Thus, ombudsmen offer a more expeditious and less costly procedure than court action. Among the extragovernmental forces that constrain bureaucracies are public opinion and the mass media, as well as interest groups of various kinds.

Controls on civil servants tend to be less effective outside the advanced industrial democracies. Authoritarian systems lack many potential controls, such as effective elected political executives and legislators, independent courts, free mass media, and interest groups. Therefore, authoritarian regimes are particularly prone to bureaucratic inefficiency and inertia. Moreover, in many developing nations, the mass media are neither independent nor influential, few citizens participate in politics, and lower-level government employees are poorly trained and paid—all conditions that encourage bribery, extortion, and bureaucratic mismanagement.[23]

Successful democracy requires that public policies made by national assemblies and chief executives be implemented fairly and effectively; democracy depends on the rule of law. When ruling parties demand kickbacks of public money from construction firms seeking public-works contracts, the democratic process is subverted by rent-seeking politicians (see Chapter 1, specifically Box 1.2). Similarly, when tax officials and border authorities take bribes to overlook tax deficiencies and customs violations, democratic lawmaking is undermined. Citizens who must bribe teachers to get education for their children or health officials to get immunizations are deprived of the benefits of democratic public policies. Such practices are all too common in the poorer nations of the world.

Failure of the rule of law is difficult to study systematically, but some comparative insight into corruption in public bureaucracies is provided by the surveys of perceptions of corruption on the part of businesspeople, academics, and analysts in different countries. These have been combined into the Corruption Perceptions Index, which rates about one hundred countries each year on a scale from 0 ("highly corrupt") to 10 ("highly clean"). Figure 6.3 shows on the vertical dimension the ratings for 2006 to 2009 of the twelve countries studied in this book. All the countries experience some levels of corruption. However, Figure 6.3 shows that corruption is very strongly associated with poverty and underdevelopment (see also Table 1.3).[24] The affluent democracies in our comparisons—Britain, Germany, the United States, France, and Japan (despite notorious individual corruption cases in each)—rated in the top half of the scale. Developing nations such as Brazil, China, India, and Mexico

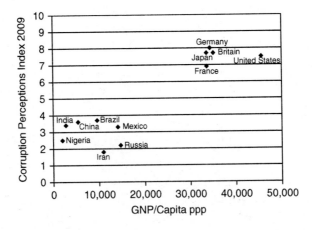

FIGURE 6.3

Perceived Corruption and Economic Development

Economic development encourages higher levels of perceived transparency.

Source: Economic development level from United Nations Development Program, *World Development Report 2009*, downloaded from www.undp.org, July 2010; Corruption Perceptions Index from Transparency International, downloaded from www.transparency. org on June 21, 2010.

are substantially more corrupt, with scores in the lower range of the scale. Nigeria, despite some recent improvement, is still perceived as highly corrupt. Russia, plagued by many problems of its dual economic and political transitions, scores even worse. Russia is also more corrupt than we would expect from its middle-level income. Despite the theocratic nature of its regime, Iran is rated as one of the world's least transparent and most corrupt countries.

The ills of bureaucracy, including inefficiency and inertia, are pandemic. This is truly a dilemma because we are unlikely to invent any schemes for carrying out large-scale social tasks without the organization, division of labor, and professionalism that bureaucracy provides. Its pathologies can only be mitigated. The art of modern political leadership consists of defining and communicating appropriate goals and policies, as well as getting them implemented by a massive and complex bureaucracy—how and when to press and coerce it, reorganize it, reward it, teach it, or be taught by it.

In summary, the structure of government does make a difference in the way the political process functions and in the strengths and weaknesses of the government. Some government structures are better at representing public preferences, while others are more effective in implementing policy. Some government structures allow for more debate and deliberation, while others are more decisive in making policy decisions. There is no perfect form of government, but there are clear differences in the types of interests that get represented, the methods of devising public policy, and the implementation of policy that flow from the organization of the government.

REVIEW QUESTIONS

1. What are the advantages of more inclusive decision rules in making policies? What are the disadvantages?
2. Why is the confidence relationship so important in parliamentary democracies?
3. In what different ways can policymaking power be dispersed and limited by constitutional arrangements?
4. What are the advantages and disadvantages of assembly representation that mirrors the characteristics of citizens?
5. How are cabinets formed after national elections in parliamentary systems?
6. Why are bureaucracies necessary but sometimes liabilities in policymaking?

KEY TERMS

assemblies
authoritarian regimes
bicameralism   000
bureaucracies
cabinet
chief executives
civil service
confidence relationship

constitutional regimes
decision rules
democracy
democratic presidential
   regime
federal systems
higher civil service
impeachment

judicial review
ombudsman
parliamentary regimes
policymaking
semipresidential
separation of powers

SUGGESTED READINGS

Carey, John M. *Legislative Voting and Accountability*. New York: Cambridge University Press, 2009.

Colomer, Josep M. *Political Institutions: Democracy and Social Choice*. New York: Oxford University Press, 2001.

Döring, Herbert, ed. *Parliaments and Majority Rule in Western Europe*. New York: St. Martin's Press, 1995.

Hicken, Allen. *Building Party Systems in Developing Democracies*. New York: Cambridge University Press, 2009.

Huber, John D. *Rationalizing Parliament*. Cambridge: Cambridge University Press, 1996.

Huber, John D., and Charles R. Shipan. *Deliberate Discretion? The Institutional Foundations of Bureaucratic Autonomy*. New York: Cambridge University Press, 2002.

Laver, Michael, and Norman Schofield. *Multiparty Government: The Politics of Coalition in Europe*. Ann Arbor: University of Michigan Press, 1998.

Lijphart, Arend. *Democracy in Plural Societies*. New Haven, CT: Yale University Press, 1977.

———. *Patterns of Democracy: Government Forms and Performance in Thirty-Six Countries*. New Haven, CT: Yale University Press, 1999.

Linz, Juan, and Arturo Valenzuela, eds. *The Failure of Presidential Democracy: Comparative Perspectives*. Baltimore: Johns Hopkins University Press, 1994.

Mainwaring, Scott, and Matthew Shugart, eds. *Presidentialism and Democracy in Latin America*. New York: Cambridge University Press, 1997.

North, Douglass. *Institutions, Institutional Change, and Economic Performance*. Cambridge: Cambridge University Press, 1990.

Perez-Linan, Anibal. *Presidential Impeachment and the New Political Instability in Latin America*. New York: Cambridge University Press, 2007.

Powell, G. Bingham, Jr. *Contemporary Democracies: Participation, Stability, and Violence*. Cambridge, MA: Harvard University Press, 1982.

Secondat, Charles de, Baron de Montesquieu. *The Spirit of the Laws*. London: Hafner, 1960.

Shugart, Matthew, and John Carey. *Presidents and Assemblies: Constitutional Design and Electoral Dynamics*. Cambridge: Cambridge University Press, 1992.

Stone-Sweet, Alec. *Governing with Judges: Constitutional Politics in Europe*. Oxford: Oxford University Press, 2002.

Strøm, Kaare. *Minority Government and Majority Rule*. Cambridge: Cambridge University Press, 1990.

Tsebelis, George. *Veto Players: How Political Institutions Work*. Princeton, NJ: Princeton University Press, 2002.

Weber, Max. "Bureaucracy," in *From Max Weber*, ed. H. H. Gerth and C. Wright Mills. New York: Oxford University Press, 1976, 196–244.

ENDNOTES

1. For a skeptical view of constitutional design, see James G. March and Johan P. Olsen, *Rediscovering Institutions: The Organizational Basis of Politics* (New York: Free Press, 1989), 171–72. For a more sanguine argument, see Giovanni Sartori, *Comparative Constitutional Engineering* (New York: New York University Press, 1995).

2. John Locke, *Two Treatises of Government*, ed. Peter Laslett (Cambridge: Cambridge University Press, 1960); and Charles de Secondat, Baron de Montesquieu, *The Spirit of the Laws* (London: Hafner, 1960).

3. *The Federalist: A Commentary on the Constitution of the United States* (Washington, D.C.: National Home Library Foundation, 1937).

4. On presidential decree powers, see John M. Carey and Matthew S. Shugart, *Executive Decree Authority* (New York: Cambridge University Press, 1998); for more general discussions of presidential powers, see Matthew S. Shugart and John M. Carey, *Presidents and Assemblies: Constitutional Design and Electoral Dynamics* (Cambridge: Cambridge University Press, 1992); and Scott Mainwaring and Matthew S. Shugart, eds., *Presidentialism and Democracy in Latin America* (New York: Cambridge University Press, 1997).

5. It is important to avoid confusion between the formal titles of government officials and the source of their selection and bases of their powers—which determine the type of political system. For example, Germany is a parliamentary system, whose executive is headed by a prime minister, although his official title is *chancellor*. The German head of state is a president, chosen by a federal convention, with little policymaking power. See also Table 6.3.

6. G. Bingham Powell, Jr., *Contemporary Democracies: Participation, Stability, and Violence* (Cambridge, MA: Harvard University Press, 1982); and Arend Lijphart, *Patterns of Democracy: Government Forms and Performance in Thirty-Six Countries* (New Haven, CT: Yale University Press, 1999). On Northern Ireland, see David McKittrick and David McVea, *Making Sense of the Troubles: The Story of the Conflict in Northern Ireland* (Chicago: Ivan R. Dee, 2002).

7. Donald Horowitz, "Comparing Democratic Systems," in *The Global Resurgence of Democracy*, ed. Larry Diamond and Mark F. Plattner (Baltimore: Johns Hopkins University Press, 1993), 127 ff. Also see Shugart and Carey, *Presidents and Assemblies*.

8. Gretchen Helmke and Frances Rosenbluth, "Regimes and the Rule of Law: Judicial Independence in Comparative Perspective,"*Annual Review of Political Science* 12 (June 2009): 345–66.

9. Arend Lijphart, *Patterns of Democracy*, 226.

10. Georg Vanberg, *The Politics of Constitutional Review in Germany* (New York: Cambridge University Press, 2005). Also see Chapter 10.

11. Moreover, in Britain, as in France, Germany, and the twenty-four other members of the EU, the European Court of Justice provides some degree of judicial review to ensure that national laws and government activities are compatible with EU treaties and laws.

12. A major recent trend in the division and limitation of policymaking powers is the growth of independent central banks. Central banks, such as the Federal Reserve in the United States, regulate the supply of money and the interest rates, as well as many financial transactions for government and society. In most countries, such bank policy was long controlled by the chief executive as part of the government bureaucracy. But in the last twenty years, many countries have given their central banks substantial independence and set for them the primary task of using monetary policy to maintain price stability and limit inflation. Such independence reassures investors, domestic and foreign, and seems to constrain inflation, but it limits the economic policy alternatives of the chief executive and cabinet.

13. John Carey, *Legislative Voting and Accountability* (New York: Cambridge University Press, 2009).

14. For a survey of parliamentary committees in Europe, see Ingvar Mattson and Kaare Strøm, "Parliamentary Committees," in *Parliaments and Majority Rule in Western Europe*, ed. Herbert Döring (New York: St. Martin's Press, 1995), 249–307.

15. Senator Roman Houska quoted in *Time* magazine, March 30, 1970.

16. In multiparty systems, the process of building coalitions between executive and legislature also plays a role. See Gary Cox, *Making Votes Count* (New York: Cambridge University Press, 1997), Chapter 12, and G. Bingham Powell, Jr., *Elections as Instruments of Democracy* (New Haven, CT: Yale University Press, 2000). A substantial body of political science research has begun to explore how such congruence between voters, legislatures, and governments is created or disrupted.

17. Data from the Inter-Parliamentary Union. Downloaded from www.ipu.org on June 21, 2010.

18. Adam Przeworski et al., *Democracy and Development: Political Institutions and Well-Being in the World, 1950–1990* (New York: Cambridge University Press, 2000).

19. See the relevant chapters in Michael Laver and Kenneth A. Shepsle, *Cabinet Ministers and Parliamentary Government* (New York: Cambridge University Press, 1994).

20. See the discussion in Julien Freund, *The Sociology of Max Weber* (New York: Random House, 1969), 234–35.

21. See Joel Aberbach, Robert D. Putnam, and Bert A. Rockman, *Bureaucrats and Politicians in Western Democracies* (Cambridge, MA: Harvard University Press, 1981).

22. See Christopher Ansell and Jane Gingrich, "Reforming the Administrative State," in *Democracy Transformed*, ed. Bruce Cain, Russell Dalton, and Susan Scarrow (Oxford: Oxford University Press, 2003).

23. On the difficulties involved in reducing administrative corruption in developing countries, see Robert Klitgard, *Controlling Corruption* (Berkeley: University of California Press, 1989).

24. For a statistical analysis explaining scores on the Corruption Perceptions Index, see Daniel Triesman, "The Causes of Corruption: A Cross-National Study," *Journal of Public Economics* 76 (June 2000): 399–457, who suggests lower levels of economic development, shorter exposure to democracy, and federalism to be among the factors encouraging more perceived corruption. Also see Melanie Manion, *Corruption by Design: Building Clean Government in Mainland China and Hong Kong* (Cambridge, MA: Harvard University Press, 2004).

Public Policy

Public policy consists of all the authoritative public decisions that governments make—the **outputs** of the political system. Policies or outputs are normally chosen for a purpose—they are meant to promote end results that we refer to as political **outcomes**. Different policies may be more or less efficient ways to reach the outcomes that policymakers want. But the values and goals of policymakers and citizens affect their evaluation of the political outcomes they actually reach. Since politicians and citizens often disagree over **political goods** and values, it is important to keep these goals in mind when we study public policy.

GOVERNMENT AND WHAT IT DOES

Governments do many things. Some things they do are timeless. In the days of the Roman Empire, defense against external and internal enemies was a major government responsibility. It continues to be so in most societies today. In other ways, governments today do things that were unthinkable in the past. For example, governments now regulate telecommunications and air traffic, policy areas that were unknown until the twentieth century.

Governments produce many goods and services, though exactly which ones vary a great deal from country to country. In most societies, governments provide law enforcement, roads, and postal services, and in many countries, they do much more. In socialist states and some other authoritarian states, governments own and operate most major industries and produce everything from military equipment to such consumer goods as clothing and shoes. In a capitalist society, such as the United States, most consumer goods are produced in the private sector. In much of Europe, the governments have a larger role than in the United States, but far less than in a socialist system.

The range of government involvement varies not just among countries, but also among different economic sectors within the same country. For example, government agencies in the United States employ few of the people engaged in mining and manufacturing, but a much larger proportion of those working for the utilities that supply gas, water, and electrical power. Yet there is no society in which the government produces no goods or services, and conversely no state in which all industries are run by the government. Even in the former

Soviet Union, part of the agricultural sector was private, as were many simple consumer services, such as babysitting.

Political Goals and Political Goods

To compare and evaluate public policy in different political systems, we need to consider the political goals that motivate different policies. Of course, as we discussed in Chapter 1, the policymakers in any political system may be self-interested, seeking rents rather than development, or exploiting divisions rather than building community. But particularly in democratic societies, politicians also have incentives to pursue political goals that seek to satisfy the values and aspirations of the citizens. We refer to these as "political goods."

We can organize this framework of political goods around each of the three levels of analysis used in this book: system, process, and policy (see Table 7.1).

At the system level, a long tradition in political analysis emphasizes order, predictability, and stability. Citizens are most free and most able to act purposefully when their environment is stable, transparent, and predictable. We call these conditions *system goods*, since they reflect the functioning and effectiveness of the whole political system. While people generally want some measure of change and new opportunities, most prefer stability to abrupt and unforeseeable change. Political instability—constitutional breakdowns, frequent leadership changes, riots, demonstrations, and the like—upsets most people's plans and can cost lives and cause material destruction. Creating and sustaining a compatible political community, whose members share many values and respect differences when they disagree, helps support political stability. System goods address the regularity and predictability with which political systems work, but also their ability to adapt to environmental challenges. Regularity and adaptability are typically somewhat in conflict.

Another category of goods is associated with the political process—citizen participation and free political competition. Democracy is good and authoritarianism is bad, according to this school of thought, because of the way citizens are treated in the process, and not because democracy might produce better economic or security results. Democratic procedures and various rights of due process, then, are *process goods*. Process goods include participation, compliance, and procedural justice. We value participation not merely as a means to responsive government, but for its own sake, since it enhances citizen competence and dignity. Procedural justice (trial by jury, *habeas corpus*, no cruel and unusual punishment, and fair and equal treatment) is another crucial process value, without which citizens would have much greater reasons to fear their governments. Procedural goods also include effectiveness and efficiency. We prefer political processes that actually deliver the desired results, and all else being equal, we especially prefer institutions that give us such outcomes at low cost and relatively quickly.

A third focus is on **policy goods**, such as economic welfare, quality of life, freedom, and personal security. Most people value policies that improve

> **TABLE 7.1**

Political Goods

Difficult trade-offs, as well as constraints, may be involved in obtaining desirable goods.

Levels of Political Goods	Classes of Goods	Content and Examples
System level	System maintenance	The political system features regular, stable, and predictable decision-making processes.
	System adaptation	The political system is able to adapt to environmental change and challenges.
Process level	Participation in political inputs	The political system is open and responsive to many forms of political speech and action.
	Compliance and support	Citizens fulfill their obligations (e.g., military service and tax obligations) to the system and comply with public law and policy.
	Procedural justice	Legal and political procedures are orderly and fair (due process), and there is equality before the law.
	Effectiveness and efficiency	Political processes have their intended effects and are no more cumbersome, expensive, or intrusive than necessary.
Policy level	Welfare	Citizens have access to health care, learning, and economic and environmental goods, which the government seeks to distribute broadly.
	Security	The government provides safety of person and property, public order, and national security.
	Fairness	Government policy is not discriminatory and recognizes individuals from different ethnic, linguistic, or religious groups; both genders are respected; vulnerable or disadvantaged citizens are protected.
	Liberty	Citizens enjoy freedom from excessive regulation, protection of their privacy, and respect for their autonomy.

welfare, reduce inequalities, enhance public safety, enable people to live as they want, and clean up our environment. Yet well-meaning people do not always agree on which of these policy goods are most important. Political philosophers have long debated the content and importance of policies in the public interest. In different cultures and times, these goods have given priority to different needs and aspirations. But over the past two hundred years, a series of public documents from the U.S. Declaration of Independence to the UN Millennium Development Goals have expressed developing public support for expanded human rights. Box 7.1 shows the eight Millennium Development Goals that were officially supported by 189 nations at a summit in 2000. These were not meant to be all-inclusive, but they reflect a consensus on the meaning of improving the lives of citizens around the world. Eradicating extreme poverty, reducing mortality, combating disease, providing primary education, developing environmental sustainability, and promoting gender equality won this support and probably seem unobjectionable to most of us.

Although these eight goals were accepted by leaders of many nations, they conceal sharp differences—not only regarding their relative importance, but on the way they affect other values. For example, at a follow-up summit in 2005, a substantial controversy erupted over their relationship to birth-control policies and to national sovereignty. Yet these goals provide a starting point for

BOX 7.1 MILLENNIUM DEVELOPMENT GOALS

In 2000, the leaders of 147 nations and official representatives of many others attended the Millennium Summit at the United Nations Headquarters in New York City. At the end, 189 nations agreed to support the United Nations Millennium Declaration, which confirmed their intention to help the world's poorest nations improve the lives of their citizens by 2015. The Millennium Development Goals, a concrete series of targets, were derived from this declaration. Many other international organizations have also agreed to these goals. They include eight general goals and suggest specific indicators for monitoring progress in achieving them. The official list of Millennium Development Goals (MDGs) includes:

Goal 1. Eradicate extreme poverty and hunger.
Goal 2. Achieve universal primary education.
Goal 3. Promote gender equality and empower women.
Goal 4. Reduce child mortality.
Goal 5. Improve maternal health.
Goal 6. Combat HIV/AIDS, malaria, and other diseases.
Goal 7. Ensure environmental sustainability.
Goal 8. Develop a global partnership for development.

The Millennium Development Goals represent, at least in principle, a contemporary consensus on policy goals that could be considered policy goods.

Source: http://mdgs.un.org/unsd/mdg/

identification of important policy goals that encompass our discussion in Chapters 1 and 2: the functions and purposes that governments serve and the challenges that confront them.

Even if we were to agree on the Millennium Development Goals, we would not necessarily know what weight to give to one goal when it conflicts with another, or what to do with policies that might help some groups at the expense of others. For example, how do we choose between enhancing one person's health care versus improving another person's educational opportunities? In such difficult cases, one criterion that most of us would agree upon is that government policy should be *fair*. The problem is that people often disagree over what is fair. In some situations, we believe that **fairness** requires all people to be treated equally (as when family members attempt to divide a tempting pie). In other situations, fairness demands that individuals be treated according to performance (as when grades are given in a college course). In yet other situations, fairness means that people are treated according to their needs (for example, in cases of medical treatment). Thus, fairness can imply *equal treatment* in some cases, *just deserts* (reward in proportion to merit or contribution) in others, and *treatment according to need* in yet others. Different value systems, such as ideologies or religious systems, may even define fairness differently. Many **public policies**—for example, pension systems such as social security in the United States—rely on some combination of these criteria. The debate over these various conceptions of fairness is never settled.

A final policy regarded highly in Table 7.1 is *freedom*. As anarchists, libertarians, and other government skeptics would remind us, public policies should promote and protect freedom and basic human and political rights. If two policies are equally efficient and fair, we would prefer the one that better respects the rights and liberties of citizens. But even citizens in democratic societies do not always choose freedom over other political goods. For example, freedom of speech is a constitutional guarantee, but many people want to prohibit speech that is insulting, blasphemous, or offensive.

Liberty is sometimes viewed only as freedom from governmental regulation and harassment. Yet even private individuals and organizations may violate the liberty and privacy of others. In such cases, government intervention may enhance liberty. Much legislation against racial segregation and discrimination generally has been impelled by this purpose. Liberty to act, organize, obtain information, and protest is an indispensable part of effective political participation. Nor is it irrelevant to social, political, and economic fairness. Prior to the breakdown of communism in Eastern Europe and the Soviet Union, it was a common view that these communist countries were trading liberty for equality. In contrast, capitalism was said to trade off equality for liberty. However, the collapse of communism uncovered the extent of corruption and privilege in communist societies. While they had surely traded off liberty for a basic security of employment, it was not clear that the communists had otherwise gained much in the way of equality.

Table 7.1 draws on our three-level analysis of political systems to present a checklist of political goods that are widely valued in contemporary societies. There is no simple way to say which value should prevail when they conflict. In fact, different preferences among such values as freedom, fairness, and efficiency set different cultures, parties, and political philosophies apart. One society or group of citizens may value fairness over liberty; another may make the opposite choice, as in Patrick Henry's famous exclamation, "Give me liberty or give me death!"

This chapter focuses on the third category in Table 7.1—policy goods. We first describe the varieties of activities that governments perform, such as extracting resources to support the government in the various means of providing policy goods. Then we focus on the four policy goods outlined in the table: welfare, security, fairness, and liberty.

PUBLIC POLICY OUTPUTS

One aspect of public policy is the outputs of government activities, or different instruments of policy. We can compare the actions that governments may take to accomplish their policy purposes under four headings:

1. **Extraction** of resources—money, goods, persons, and services—from the domestic and international environments
2. **Distribution**—of money, goods, and services—to citizens, residents, and clients of the state
3. **Regulation** of human behavior—the use of compulsion and inducement to bring about desired behavior
4. **Symbolic outputs**—used to exhort citizens to engage in desired forms of behavior, build community, or celebrate exemplary conduct (see Chapter 1)

Political systems have different policy action profiles. Some governments distribute a great deal of goods and services but regulate little. Elsewhere, the government may be heavily engaged in regulation but may rely on the private sector to produce most goods and services. In the next sections, we discuss these four types of policy outputs, beginning with extraction.

Extraction

Before governments can spend, they must have ways to collect money and other resources. All political systems *extract* resources from their environments and inhabitants. When societies go to war, for example, young people (typically men) may be called on to fight. Anthropologists estimate that in some hunter-gatherer societies, such obligations have been so onerous that about half of all males have died in warfare. (Thomas Hobbes would not have been surprised.) Such direct extraction of services is found in many modern states in the form of compulsory military service, jury duty, or compulsory labor imposed on those convicted of crime.

The most common form of resource extraction is taxation. *Taxation* is the government's extraction of money or goods from members of a political system for which they receive no immediate or direct benefit. A related form of extraction is "social contribution," or "social insurance" revenues, which are typically held as special funds targeted to be spent on social protection benefits, such as old age pensions (social security). Revenue policies are designed to meet many different objectives, which sometimes conflict. On the one hand, governments often want to collect as much revenue as possible to finance various public services. On the other hand, governments do not want to kill the goose that lays the golden egg. The more that governments tax their citizens, the less incentive people and businesses have to increase their income. If the tax burden becomes too great, they may try to evade taxes or even leave the country altogether.

Another common trade-off in extraction policies is between efficiency and equity. *Efficiency* means collecting the most revenue possible at the lowest cost to economic production. *Equity* means taxing so that no one is unfairly burdened, and particularly those who have the least are spared. In most societies, the tax and spending systems redistribute wealth in favor of the less well-off. Therefore, income taxes are generally progressive, which means that citizens with greater incomes pay at higher rates than those who earn less. However, highly progressive taxes can reduce the incentives for high earners to work and invest, and thus lessen the incentives for economic growth. Therefore, such taxes are often inefficient.

Personal and corporate income taxes, property taxes, and taxes on capital gains are called **direct taxes**, since they are directly levied on persons and corporations. If you pay a tax bill at the end of the year, or have taxes withheld in your paycheck, you are paying taxes directly. Payroll taxes tend to hit the middle class and those in the labor force, since the wealthy tend to get a larger share of their income from dividends, interest, and capital gains, and retirees from pensions. High taxes on wages can also hurt employment or drive businesses into the "underground economy," in which they do not report their incomes or expenditures. **Indirect taxes** include sales taxes, value-added taxes, excise taxes, and customs duties. These are commonly included in the prices of goods and services that consumers buy. The redistributive effects of indirect taxes depend on who pays them. Since the poor spend more of their income on food and clothing, sales (or value-added) taxes can be regressive (which means that the poor pay relatively more than the rich), so many nations have a lower tax rate on necessities. In contrast, indirect taxes on luxury goods may be progressive, since the poor rarely purchase luxury items like fine jewelry. Countries with weak administrative capacities often prefer indirect taxes. Particularly where financial record-keeping is imprecise, indirect taxes are easier to collect. In addition, indirect taxes tend to rise with inflation or as the costs of products increase, which provides a natural source of increasing government revenue.

Besides redistribution and efficiency, tax policies often promote such values as charity, energy conservation, or home ownership. For example, many countries stimulate home ownership by making mortgage interest payments tax-deductible. Several European nations have a large gasoline tax to reduce energy consumption and encourage the sale of energy-efficient automobiles. In France, 70 percent of the cost of gasoline is for government taxes, which raises the price to about $7 a gallon.

Given the many difficult issues involving taxation, and the inevitable public resistance to high taxes, it might seem a blessing if a government could receive income windfalls from other sources. Countries with large reserves of oil or other valuable natural resources are often in this situation. Many oil-producing countries, such as Iran, Russia, and Nigeria, can tap their natural resource reserves and sell them at a large profit in the international market. Yet when the riches from easily obtained natural resources are a large share of a government's income, the consequences can be far from an unmitigated blessing. A large political science literature focuses on the problems of so-called "**rentier states**," which derive much of their revenue from the "rents" of selling oil and other natural resources.[1] This literature often refers to a "resource curse" impeding development and democracy when the economy is distorted by oil windfalls.

Why should oil or diamonds or copper constitute a "curse" when they can finance public policies without burdening citizens with taxes?[2] One explanation suggests that windfall resource profits can make governments independent from their citizens. As Samuel Huntington put it, "Oil revenues . . . reduce the need for the government to solicit the acquiescence of its subjects to taxation. The lower the level of taxation, the less reason for the public to demand representation."[3] And if politicians do not feel such demands from their citizens, they may be less likely to behave accountably. Direct resource-based revenues also may enable authoritarian rulers to pay off citizens through patronage (e.g., subsidized goods, services, and loans) without yielding political power to them. Or, the easy money of the rentier state may be a tempting target for predatory authoritarians who use these funds to repress society while taking the profits for themselves. Although the resource curse is common wisdom in studies of less economically developed economies, the windfall income can soften the intensity of redistributive conflict in very unequal societies and have positive consequences for democracy.[4] Nor do such windfalls seem problematic in already economically developed democracies, such as Norway.

Figure 7.1 shows the general government revenues as a percentage of **gross domestic product (GDP)**, the total value of goods and services produced by a country's residents in a year. (In Brazil, India, and Mexico, the figure shows only central government revenue; state and local taxes can increase the total revenue by a third or more.) For the average country, about a quarter of the GDP is extracted by the government, but in some countries, the proportion is much higher. Most of the more developed democracies rely primarily on taxes and social contributions for government revenues. In Germany and France, the social contributions are nearly as large as the taxes.

Figure 7.1, however, shows that some governments also get substantial revenues from nontax and noncontribution sources (the third columns), such as administrative fees, rents, and income from business enterprises that they run. In Iran, a classic "rentier state" (see Chapter 16), nontax income provides over two-thirds of the government's revenues. Russia is also rich in oil and other

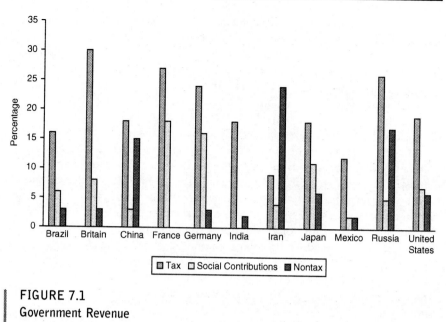

FIGURE 7.1

Government Revenue

In most countries, taxes are the largest source of revenue, especially in democracies.

Source: International Monetary Fund, downloaded from www2.imfstatistics.org/GFS on June 4, 2010, Table W4.

natural resources, and it relies heavily on nontax income. If we had data on Nigeria, it would probably show a similar picture. China also relies on nontax sources from government-owned enterprises, a carryover from its socialist past despite its marketization of much of the economy. Democracy has had a hard time in all these countries, although dependence on nontax revenues is not the only reason.

The tax profiles of different countries vary both in their overall tax burdens and in their reliance on different types of taxes. Sweden has the highest tax rates overall, as it extracts more than 50 percent of its GDP in taxes. France and Russia are in the 45 percent range. Britain and Germany are among the advanced industrial societies that collect about 40 percent of GDP, while the United States and Japan extract about 30 percent. These two countries depend more on direct income taxes than on sales or consumption taxes. Outside the economically developed areas, government revenue rarely exceeds 25 percent of GDP. The central government revenue of India is about 15 percent. For the states that are highly dependent on natural-resource windfalls, these proportions can fluctuate sharply with the price of their export commodities, which can create additional problems for government and for development.

In the long run, governments cannot spend more money than they raise. If governments fail to balance their books and instead run budget deficits, they have to borrow money. This creates debt that future generations of taxpayers have to pay off. Even rich governments are notoriously bad at balancing their books, and many run budget deficits year after year. In 2004, nineteen of the twenty-eight (highly developed) Organization for Economic Co-operation and Development (OECD) countries ran budget deficits, and the average deficit was equal to 3.5 percent of GDP. The United States briefly balanced its budget in the late 1990s, but then slid back into fiscal imbalance. When Germany, France, and many other European countries decided to adopt a common currency, the euro, they also committed themselves to keeping their national deficits smaller than 3 percent of GDP. In practice, however, they have often broken that promise. Since the financial crisis of 2008 and 2009, most of these countries have borrowed massively to finance emergency spending to combat the worldwide recession, greatly increasing their national debts.

Recently, in some European countries, especially Greece, the combination of massive, long-standing deficits and the more recent pressures of the global financial crisis threatened the country's ability to meet its future financial obligations. Despite a large aid package promised by other Euro countries in exchange for Greece's drastically cutting its spending, the debt crisis threatened the financial stability of all the European countries. The 2008 and 2009 economic crisis has produced similar economic strains on the governments of many developing nations. It is a measure of the globalization of trade and financial capital flows that this economic crisis rapidly created difficult budgetary choices in countries throughout the world as economies contracted, unemployment rose, and revenues faltered.

Distributive Policy Profiles

Distributive policies include transfers of money, goods, services, honors, and opportunities to individuals and groups in the society. Distributive policies generally consume more government resources and employ more government officials than anything else that modern governments do. Distributive policies include support for infrastructure, agriculture, and various other industries, but the most common form of distributive policies are social-welfare programs.

The first modern welfare state programs were introduced in Germany in the 1880s. In response to rapid industrialization and urbanization, the German government offered social-insurance programs that protected workers against unemployment, accidents, sickness, and poverty during old age. During the twentieth century, and particularly from the Great Depression of the 1930s until the 1970s, most industrialized states adopted, and greatly expanded, such welfare state policies. Over time, welfare state policies expanded to include broader health-care programs, disability benefits, public education, housing subsidies, child and childcare benefits, pensions, and other distributive policies. As developing countries become wealthier, they also tend to spend more of their resources on welfare programs. In Mexico, for example, the last three presidents have each launched a major social-welfare initiative. In Brazil, the *Bolsa Familia* program is the world's largest conditional cash-transfer program and a flagship of President Lula's administration. The program reaches a quarter of the Brazilian population and is especially targeted at eradicating hunger.

Welfare policies typically combine a social-insurance system and a program of social redistribution. It is partly paternalistic (forcing people to put away money for their old age and potential illnesses) and in part Robin Hood (taking from the rich and giving to the poor). The balance between these two functions depends on which programs a particular country emphasizes and on how it finances them. Thus, not all welfare programs are alike. Even among the advanced industrial countries, some welfare states are larger than others or offer different benefits. All the wealthier nations try to assist the aged, the disabled, and the unemployed. However, differences in expenditures reflect the priorities of citizens and their governments, social and economic conditions (such as a country's age distribution and unemployment levels), and historical experiences.[5] Countries that have more frequently elected social democratic governments, rather than conservative ones, generally have larger welfare states.

Figure 7.2 reports overall governmental expenditures as a percentage of GDP, followed by the percentages spent on health, education, and social protection (such as unemployment benefits and pensions for the elderly). Clearly, both the magnitude and profile of government expenditures depend heavily on a nation's economic development. In the developed world, countries are

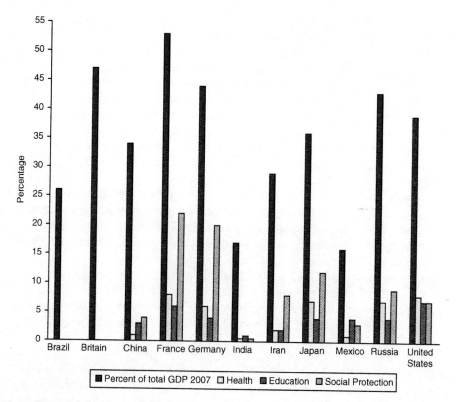

FIGURE 7.2

Government Expenditures

A country's expenditure reflects varying distributive priorities and resources.

Source: International Monetary Fund, downloaded from www2.imfstatistics.org/GFS on June 4, 2010, Table W6.

spending a third to half of their GDP on government. Among the countries shown here, Japan has the smallest government sector in the developed world and France the largest. Government spending in Russia accounts for 43 percent of GDP; in China and Iran, it is about a third. Government spending is a smaller fraction of GDP in most of the other countries, although Brazil, India, and Mexico only provide statistics for the central governments.

Developed countries generally allocate the majority of their government expenditures to health, education, and social protection. France, Germany, and Japan spend more than two-thirds of their budgets in these areas, compared with about one-half in the United States. The U.S. model stresses equality of opportunity through public education, making a greater and earlier effort in this area than did most European nations. Americans began spending on social protection programs later, and, as shown in Figure 7.2, still does less in these areas. This may reflect the U.S. heritage as a nation of immigrants, many of whom arrived poor and have been expected to prosper by their own efforts.

Sadly, as the figure illustrates, the countries that need them most, such as India, have the least to spend on education and health. Public health expenditures in our developed countries, such as the United States, France, Germany, and Japan are $2,000 to $3,000 per capita. In the poorest countries, health spending in absolute dollars is miniscule—$15 per person in Nigeria and $21 per person in India. These spending numbers are generated by varying public policy efforts, as shown in Figure 7.2, and even more by the enormous variations in income created by developed economies (countries also rely on their private sector to varying degrees to finance health spending). Poor nations, with limited budgets and many pressing demands, lack the resources for health and education. Social protection expenditure in poor nations also tends to be low. Resources are scarce, and shorter life expectancies and high birth rates mean that there are comparatively few older people. Also, many people live in the rural areas, where unemployment is less easily observed and where the aged and the infirm typically receive some care through the extended family; these services go unreported in our statistics.

National security spending follows a different pattern. Particularly among less-developed countries, spending varies as much with the international environment as with overall economic means. Some states that are locked in tense international confrontations make extraordinary defense efforts. India, Iran, and the United States spend more than 10 percent of their government outlays (2 to 5 percent of GDP) on defense. Because of its worldwide security commitments and large economy, the United States is by far the heaviest military spender in absolute terms.

Challenges to the Welfare State   Welfare states have many beneficial consequences. The Western European countries that pioneered these programs have virtually eradicated dire poverty, and they have created a much more "level playing field" for their citizens. Crime rates tend to be low in countries with extensive welfare states, and most of the programs are popular with ordinary citizens. Yet the welfare state is also expensive. As total government expenditures have grown to around half of GDP in many industrial democracies, this has created political opposition to high taxes and deficits. One of the most serious problems is the generational deficit that these policies are creating. Welfare programs are committing entitlements that will fall on future generations (your generation) to pay. At the same time that senior citizens qualify for greater pension benefits and health-care costs are rising rapidly, the ranks of the elderly are swelling relative to those in the workforce. Thus, the ratio of those outside the workforce (because they are too young or too old) to those in the working-age population is increasing rapidly in Europe and Japan. A smaller number of working people in future years will have to pay higher taxes just to support existing health and welfare programs.[6]

In addition, some welfare state policies give citizens fewer incentives to work. Norway and Sweden are among the leading countries in the world in life expectancy and public health statistics. Yet workers in these countries are on sick leave about twice as often as workers elsewhere in Europe, and record numbers of these Scandinavians are on permanent disability pensions. This is partly because of generous sick-leave benefits and partly because it is easy to qualify for disability benefits. But these policies are costly and reduce incentives to work.

These problems with the welfare state have stirred efforts to prevent further increases in spending obligations (entitlements) and to contain the costs of those already in effect. Thus, the gradual expansion of welfare benefits that characterized most of the twentieth century in the developed countries can no longer be taken for granted.

Regulation

Regulation is the exercise of political control over the behavior of individuals and groups in the society. Most contemporary governments have a large regulatory role. Our civilization and amenities depend on regulation. As we discussed in Chapter 1, social-contract theorists such as Hobbes and Locke maintain that regulation can facilitate many beneficial activities. Economic production and commerce, for example, rely on government regulation to establish and protect property rights and to enforce contracts. There need to be rules to keep traffic moving smoothly on the freeways, in the air, and on the airwaves. Citizens and consumers often demand protections against fraud, manipulation, and obnoxious externalities, such as toxic waste and pollution. And governments are increasingly involved in setting product standards, particularly for pharmaceuticals and food, to make sure that these products are safe. Governments also regulate to shield their citizens, and often particularly children and women, from physical and other abuse. However, regulation can create an opportunity for government officials to extract bribes from citizens (see Box 7.2).

In the developed democracies, government regulation has proliferated enormously over the last century. Industrialization and urbanization have caused problems in traffic, health, and public order. Industrial growth has also generated concerns about industrial safety, labor exploitation, and pollution. Moreover, the growth of science and the belief that humanity can harness and control nature have led to increased demands for government action. Globalization has created increased pressures to regulate the international flows of capital, trade, and people. Finally, changes in citizen values have led to demands for new kinds

BOX 7.2 REGULATION AND DEVELOPMENT

In the advanced industrial countries of North America, Japan, and Western Europe, regulation has grown enormously along with their industrial and postindustrial economies. It is easy to think, therefore, that there is more regulation in wealthy countries than in poor ones. But this is not always true. In fact, low-income countries sometimes regulate more than rich ones. This is particularly true of regulations of business entry and competition. In many less-developed countries, it is cumbersome and time-consuming, for example, to get the permits necessary to start a new business. Such regulations often mainly serve to create *rents* that government officials can exploit for their own benefit (see Chapter 1). They protect existing businesses by giving them monopolies or other protections. Many politicians expect the businesspeople who benefit from these regulations (often their family members, friends, or business associates) to show their gratitude through kickbacks and other favors. Or, business owners pay off politicians or civil servants to get around onerous regulations or to avoid long delays in handling their applications. Overregulation of this kind tends to hurt economic productivity and keep out foreign investment.

The Peruvian economist Hernando de Soto reports a sobering experience with abusive government regulation. As an experiment, he registered a small clothing factory in Lima, Peru, and decided in advance not to pay bribes. While he was waiting for his business to be registered, government officials asked him for bribes no fewer than ten times. Twice he broke his own rule and paid the bribe so that he would not be forced to give up his experiment. After ten months, his factory was finally registered. In New York, a similar procedure takes four hours.

Source: World Bank, *World Development Report 2005*, Chapter 5; William Easterly, *The Elusive Quest for Growth: The Economists' Adventures and Misadventures in the Tropics* (Cambridge: Massachusetts Institute of Technology Press, 2001), 233.

of regulation. Immigration policy, safety standards for offshore oil drilling, and banking regulation have become major policy disputes. At the same time, however, at least most Western societies have lessened their regulation of birth control, abortion, divorce, blasphemy, obscenity, and sexual conduct.

Governments regulate the lives of their citizens in many ways. Although we often associate regulation with legal means, there are other ways to regulate. Governments may control behavior by offering material or financial inducements or by persuasion or moral exhortation. For example, many governments try to reduce tobacco use by a combination of methods: bans on smoking, tobacco sales, or advertising; sales ("sin") taxes; and information campaigns to convince people of the hazards of smoking.

Even though there are many similarities in regulative policies across the world, states still differ substantially in their policy profiles. Patterns of regulation vary not only with industrialization and urbanization, but also with cultural and ideological values. For example, population-control policies in China and Islamic dress-code policies in Iran illustrate the varieties of ways in which governments

TABLE 7.2

Controlling Markets and the Press

Governments vary in their use of regulatory policy to control the economy and communication.

Country	Regulation of Markets	Regulation of Press
Brazil	42	42
Britain	2	18
China	54	84
France	13	22
Germany	9	16
India	53	35
Iran	97	85
Japan	14	21
Mexico	35	55
Nigeria	70	53
Russia	69	78
United States	7	17

Note: Market regulation is a World Bank measure of "incidence of market-unfriendly policies, such as price controls or inadequate bank supervision, as well as perceptions of the burdens imposed by excessive regulation in areas such as foreign trade and business development" (from www.worldbank.org/governance/wgi/) on a 0-to-100 scale. Press freedom rating also on a 0-to-100 scale, where 100 is least free, downloaded from www.freedomhouse.org on July 9, 2010.

can regulate their societies. Table 7.2 shows the degree to which different countries try to control their economic markets. (This measure is intended to include "market-unfriendly" policies such as price controls or inadequate bank supervision, as well as excessive regulation of foreign trade and business development.) Although the capitalist democracies, such as Britain, the United States, Germany, France, and Japan tend to be the friendliest to market competition, the non-democracies vary greatly in their government regulatory profiles. China is far more open than Iran, and in these policies rather similar to India. Public-policy studies describe regulatory differences among political systems by asking what aspects of human behavior are regulated, what social groups are regulated, and what sanctions are used to pressure people to comply.

Although all modern states use sanctions, they vary in their goals and strategies. Yet one aspect of regulation is particularly important politically: government control over political participation and communication. Table 7.2 also shows freedom of the press, which is heavily shaped by the legal and political environment. Recall from earlier chapters that democracy requires political competition. As we might expect, the authoritarian systems control the press much more severely than their democratic counterparts. China, Iran, and Russia are ranked as "unfree" in their press freedom scores and are shown at the bottom of the table. A recent Freedom House study of Internet regulation in fifteen countries also showed the extensive efforts at controlling access and content of the Internet in China and Iran, while Brazil and Britain allowed their citizens relatively uncontrolled access. Authoritarian governments often suppress political competition by prohibiting party organization, voluntary associations, and political communication. All too often, they repress political opponents through imprisonment, disappearances, and torture. Studies of governmental repression have found that government abuses of physical integrity rights of citizens were best explained by nondemocratic political institutions and conditions of war and social disorder.[7] A lower level of economic development also encourages a weaker human-rights record.

Community Building and Symbolic Outputs

A fourth type of output is symbolic policies. Political leaders often make appeals to the courage, wisdom, and magnanimity embodied in the nation's past; or appeals to values and ideologies, such as equality, liberty, community, democracy, communism, liberalism, or religious tradition; or promises of future accomplishment and rewards. Political leaders appeal to such values for different reasons—for example, to win elections or to push their own pet projects. At the same time, many symbolic appeals and policies are trying to build community, such as by boosting people's national identity, civic pride, or trust in government.

Symbolic outputs also try to enhance other aspects of performance: to make people pay their taxes more readily and honestly; comply with the law more faithfully; or accept sacrifice, danger, and hardship. Such appeals may be especially important in times of crisis. Some of the most magnificent examples are the speeches of Pericles in the Athenian Assembly during the Peloponnesian War, Franklin D. Roosevelt in the depths of the Great Depression, or Winston Churchill during Britain's darkest hours in World War II. Symbolic policies are important even in less extreme circumstances. Public buildings, plazas, monuments, holiday parades, and civic and patriotic indoctrination in schools all attempt to contribute to a popular sense of governmental legitimacy and its willingness to comply with public policy.

DOMESTIC POLICY OUTCOMES

While we can describe different government policy activities in the previous section, their consequences in providing actual policy goods are not always clear. How do extractive, distributive, regulative, and symbolic policies affect the lives of people? Unexpected economic, international, or social events may frustrate the purpose of political leaders. Thus, a tax rebate to stimulate the economy may be nullified by a rise in the price of oil. Increases in health expenditures may have no effect because of unexpected epidemics or rising health costs, or health services may not reach those most in need. Sometimes, policies have unintended and undesirable consequences, as when the introduction of benefits for troubled social groups leads others to simulate the same troubles to get the same favors. Consequently, to estimate the effectiveness of public policy, we have to examine actual policy outcomes as well as governmental policies and their implementation.

Welfare Outcomes

We begin by comparing different measures of public welfare across our set of nations. Welfare can involve the living standards of the average citizen, but also the other social conditions that affect quality of life and life chances.

The first column of Table 7.3 reports a measure of economic well-being or lack thereof: the share of the population living on less than $2 per day. The severe problems of Nigeria and India are particularly notable: the vast majority of those populations live on less than $2 a day. Clearly, this measure of welfare is closely related to the general level of economic development of the society, although inequality of income also plays a role (refer back to Table 1.3). Governments in most poorer countries are trying to encourage economic development with the help of international organizations and donors, but sustained growth is hard to achieve. Eradication of extreme poverty is the number-one goal in the United Nations Millennium Development goals list (see Box 7.1).

The next two columns report the availability of two critical public facilities: safe water in rural areas, and sanitation. While most of the people of the developed world have access to safe water, this is true for less than half of the rural populations of many less-advantaged countries. And often, a majority of those populations live in rural areas. In Nigeria, for example, only 30 percent of the

TABLE 7.3

Welfare Outcomes

Economic development helps sustain basic material and health amenities, but also creates potential for environmental damages.

Country	Population below $2 per Day PPP (%), ca. 2007	Rural Population Access to Safe Water (%), 2006	Access to Sanitation (%) 2006	Carbon Dioxide Emissions, metric tons/capita, 2006
Brazil	12.7	58	77	1.9
Britain	—	100	—	9.4
China	36.3	81	65	4.7
France	—	100	—	6.2
Germany	—	100	100	9.8
India	75.6	86	28	1.4
Iran	8.0	—	—	6.7
Japan	—	100	100	10.0
Mexico	8.2	85	81	4.2
Nigeria	83.9	30	30	0.7
Russia	2.0	88	87	11.0
United States	—	94	100	19.0

Source: World Bank, *World Development Indicators* (downloaded June 6, 2010, from http://data.worldbank.org/indicator/).

large rural population had access to safe water in 2006. Less than a third of the Nigerian and Indian populations overall have access to improved sanitation facilities, which are a major factor in disease prevention. Comparing the performance in China to Nigeria and India, and even rural Brazil, we can see that government policies can to some extent overcome the barriers of low economic development.

The last column in Table 7.3 shows one of the negative outcomes of higher economic development: pollution. Carbon-dioxide emissions per capita, which are a major contributor to air pollution and to global warming, are much higher in developed economies. The worst record is created by the most industrialized country, the United States, followed (distantly) by Russia, Japan, Germany, and Britain. Russia produces many more emissions than we might expect for its development level. These countries have all introduced measures to regulate pollution, but they are lagging far behind need. Carbon-dioxide emissions are not a problem so far in Nigeria, India, or Brazil. But China and Iran are closing in on the more industrialized countries. China's huge population and rapid growth make its pollution a serious threat, both to its own population and the global population. Because of their dual needs for economic growth and pollution control, these countries face hard regulatory policy choices.

Health outcomes also figure largely in the Millennium Development Goals (Box 7.1). Table 7.4 shows that the average developed nation has about

TABLE 7.4

Health Outcomes

Government efforts can help combat the problems of low economic development for citizens' health.

Country	Physicians per 1,000 Citizens, 2009	Life Expectancy at Birth, 2008	Infant Mortality per 1,000 Live Births, 2008	Fertility Rate, 2007
Brazil	1.2	72	18	1.9
Britain	2.3	78	5	1.9
China	1.4	73	18	1.8
France	3.4	82	3	2.0
Germany	3.4	80	4	1.4
India	0.6	64	52	2.7
Iran	0.9	71	27	1.8
Japan	2.1	83	3	1.3
Mexico	2.0	75	15	2.1
Nigeria	0.3	48	96	5.7
Russia	4.3	68	12	1.5
United States	2.6	78	7	2.1

Source: World Health Statistics 2009, downloaded June 7, 2010, from www.who.int/whosis/whostat/2009.

3 physicians per 1,000 people, compared with 1.3 in the developing world. In Nigeria, there are only 0.3 doctors in 1,000 people. The country has a high birth rate, but almost one out of ten infants fails to survive the first year of life. Nigerians have a life expectancy at birth of just forty-eight years (compared with seventy-eight to eighty-three years in advanced industrial countries). Nigeria demonstrates the ills of poverty, as do figures for India, which are also quite grim. But some poorer countries cope more successfully than others. Consider the difference between two low-income nations: China and India. The Chinese average life expectancy is seventy-three years and their infant mortality is 18 per 1,000 live births, while the Indian life expectancy is sixty-four years and their infant mortality is 52 per 1,000. China has nearly three times as many physicians as India relative to its population. Fortunately, health conditions are improving in most of the poor countries, including India.

While the incidence of infant mortality and malnutrition is much lower in advanced economies, these problems are still serious among the poor in advanced industrial countries such as the United States. The United States spends the largest proportion of its GDP on health care (approximately 15 percent, of which about half is from the public sector) of any country. At the same time, however, in 2008, the United States had a somewhat higher infant death rate than Japan and Western Europe due to more widespread poverty, drug abuse, and unequal access to health care (which new policies are attempting to change). As Table 7.4 shows, Japan has an exceptional health record. It has the longest life expectancy and the lowest infant mortality rate among all the study countries in this book. However, its low fertility rate means a declining population. (With no net migration, a fertility rate of approximately 2.1 is needed to produce a steady-state population.)

Education is another vital policy outcome, also stressed in the Millennium Development Goals. It provides individuals with skills and resources that enable them to be engaged in the political process; these skills shape their life chances in establishing a career and improving their personal conditions. Education is also necessary for successful economic development and all that means for many other welfare outcomes. Table 7.5 provides a picture of educational and information attainment. In most industrial democracies, high school education is mandatory and college education is commonplace. At the high end in educational outcomes, France, Germany, Japan, and Britain have virtually all of their primary and secondary school-aged children in schools, and about half of the college-aged population is in some form of advanced education. In the United States, college education is even more common. Nigeria requires only children from ages six to twelve to attend school and has only 10 percent of the appropriate age cohort in tertiary education, by far the poorest record of these countries. India's figure is 14 percent.

The payoff of development and education is clearly reflected in literacy rates: 20 to 23 percent of adult men and 36 to 45 percent of adult women in Nigeria and India are unable to read or write. Yet China has less than 10 percent illiteracy.

Table 7.5 also highlights access to information technologies, such as the Internet and personal computers. As shown, many more people access the

TABLE 7.5

Education, Equality, and Information

Education efforts, gender policies, and development shape information access and inequality.

Country	Gross Percentage of Relevant Age Group Enrolled, Tertiary, 2007	Percentage Fifteen Years and Above Illiterate, Male/Female, 2007	Ratio of Female to Male Earned Income, 2007	Personal Computers per 100 Inhabitants, 2008	Internet Users per 100 Inhabitants, 2008
Brazil	30	10/10	0.60	16	38
Britain	58	–	0.67	80	76
China	22	3/10	0.68	6	22
France	55	–	0.61	65	68
Germany	49	–	0.59	66	75
India	14	23/45	0.32	3	5
Iran	30	13/23	0.32	11	32
Japan	58	–	0.45	–	75
Mexico	26	6/9	0.42	14	22
Nigeria	10	20/36	0.42	1	16
Russia	75	1/1	0.64	13	32
United States	82		0.62	81	76

Source: World Bank, *World Development Indicators* (downloaded June 7, 2010, from http://data.worldbank.org/indicator/); also, for female inequality, United Nations Human Development Report 2009 (downloaded June 7, 2010, from http://hdr.unpd.org/en/reports/global/hdr2009).

Internet in wealthy and well-educated countries, such as Japan, than in the developing world. Yet even in poorer countries, communications have become much easier. Television has become widely available even in countries at modest development levels (e.g., Brazil and Mexico). Internet use is growing very rapidly. Nearly a quarter of the population in China and Mexico report having access to the Internet, as do about a third in Iran and Brazil. Despite the efforts of authoritarian governments in countries such as Iran and China to control Internet use (see the discussion of regulatory policies above), information potential is remarkable. In the developed countries, most adults and many children have cell phones, and even in India and Nigeria, there is already a cell phone for about every three people. The advent of cell phones has made it much easier to connect the rural population in developing countries where there are often very few landlines. Personal computers, however, are much rarer outside the advanced industrial economies. Compared with people in Brazil and Mexico, people in the United States are five times more likely to own a personal computer.

Table 7.5 reveals the sobering difficulties of trying to change societies, even in an area such as literacy, where modern technologies are available. It is hard for a poor country to spend a high percentage of its GDP on education, because it must then make sacrifices elsewhere. And the effects are limited if much of the country's productive effort has to go into feeding a rapidly growing population. No matter how large the educational effort may be, it does not translate into much per child, because the resource base is small and the population is growing rapidly. Moreover, since most older people are illiterate, the net effect on literacy is slow. And in many poorer countries, their best-educated young people often leave the country to take jobs in the big cities of the rich countries.

Fairness Outcomes

Fairness was one of the welfare outcomes discussed in the framework of Table 7.1 on policy goods. Concepts of fairness vary by culture and ideology. Despite these differences, promoting gender equality and empowering women appear on the Millennium Development Goals that were endorsed by so many nations (see again Box 7.1). Column 2 in Table 7.5 shows that women in developing countries often lag behind in literacy. Culture and policy also affect the male/female differences, as we see in comparing gender differences in Brazil and Iran, for example. The discrepancy between male and female literacy rates tells us something of the status of women and the achievement of fairness by gender. Column 3 provides additional insight by showing us the ratio of female to male earned incomes. Differences in the types of jobs in which they are employed and pay discrimination mean that women only earn about two-thirds of the income of men even in the most equal countries—which are China and Britain. Clearly, achievement of gender fairness has far to go everywhere. At the bottom of the scale, in Iran and India, women earn only one-third the income of men.

Faced with poverty, disease, and the absence of a social safety net, parents in poor countries traditionally want to have many children to ensure that some survive and can support them in old age. In large families, mothers usually have few opportunities to educate themselves or hold jobs outside the home (but see Boxes 7.3 and 7.4). Modernizing the status of women generally makes them better informed and more capable of making choices that lead to a stabler and healthier population. As women are educated and/or enter the labor force, they recognize the advantages of smaller families and become more aware of the importance of education and adequate health care. The important place of gender equality and empowering women in the Millennium Development Goals reflects these implications for other aspects of welfare as well as fairness itself (also refer back to Box 1.4).

Fairness in the treatment of minority ethnic, racial, and religious groups is also an issue in many countries. Although democracies are generally less abusive of minorities than are authoritarian systems, democratic majorities can often cruelly ignore their own standards of fairness in treating minority groups. The Minorities at Risk project tracks the status of 282 minority groups using expert informants. The records of our twelve large nations showed that in ten nations, at least one minority group was subject to "significant poverty and underrepresentation due to prevailing social practices by dominant groups" (www.cidcm.umd.edu/mar). Public policies either deliberately contributed to the problem or were inadequate to overcome discriminatory practices. Such minority groups included Afro-Brazilians in Brazil, Corsicans in France, scheduled tribes in India, Mayans in Mexico, Chechens in Russia, and Native Americans in the United States.

Often, unfair treatment of minorities is closely related to the problem of rural poverty. While there are many causes of the inequality between city and countryside in basic health facilities and income, government policy can contribute. In many African states, for example, the rulers tend to favor the urban population because they want the country to modernize and industrialize. Sometimes, politicians also worry that a starving urban population might riot and bring down the government. For these reasons, governments tend to keep food prices artificially low, which hurts farmers. Governments also tend to prefer targeted government agricultural programs (often subsidies), which help particular groups of farmers (often wealthy ones). Such targeted programs help governments gain political supporters but are often wasteful. Even in democratic countries where the majority of voters are poor farmers, government policies often do little for them. Many voters do not trust politicians who promise to deliver broad public goods (such as health care and education), but instead support candidates who promise targeted private goods (such as jobs and subsidies). Thus, even spending on schools becomes a way to create jobs rather than to educate children. In India, teachers' salaries account for 96 percent of recurrent expenditures in primary education. Even so, teacher absenteeism is rampant. When inspectors made unannounced visits to rural schools, about two-thirds of the teachers were absent.[8]

▶ BOX 7.3 **MICROCREDIT**

One of the greatest obstacles to economic growth in many poor areas is the difficulty of obtaining credit. In advanced industrial countries, property owners (for example, farmers or homeowners) typically have a recognized title to their property. If they want to invest to expand their business or start a new one, they can borrow against this collateral. People in poor countries rarely have this opportunity, and it is especially difficult for poor farmers and women to obtain loans. As a result, they often cannot get the funds they need to tide them over during hard times or to take advantage of promising business opportunities.

Muhammad Yunus, a U.S.-educated professor of economics, noticed these problems in his native country of Bangladesh. In 1974, he began extending small loans to poor people to help them out of these circumstances. His first loan amounted to $27 from his own pockets, which he lent to forty-two people, including a woman who made bamboo furniture, which she sold to support herself and her family. In 1976, Yunus founded Grameen Bank to make loans to poor Bangladeshis. The bank has since given out more than $5 billion in loans. To secure its loans, the bank sets up a system of "solidarity groups," which meet on a weekly basis and support each other's efforts. As of May 2006, Grameen Bank had almost 7 million borrowers, 97 percent of whom were women. Their repayment rate is 98 percent. In 2006, Muhammad Yunus and the Grameen Bank received the Nobel Peace Prize for these efforts to help poor people improve their lives.

Of course, great income inequality of all kinds violates most standards of fairness. One of the problems of economic development is that the middle stages of development are often associated with new concentrations of wealth and greater gaps between the newly prosperous, usually urban, middle class and those left behind. Indeed, the hope that new democratic governments would lead to greater equality has historically been one of the driving forces in democratization. Yet even in the wealthiest democracies today, the wealthiest 10 percent of the population earns as much as the poorest 40 percent (refer back to Table 1.4). In the United States, the gap between rich and poor is substantially larger. This gap between rich and poor continues to be a particular problem in middle-level countries like Brazil and Mexico, where the gap is much greater (as we saw in Table 1.4.). On the one hand, social and economic conditions, such as levels of literacy, occupational skills, and land-holding, are derived from historic development experiences and continue to feed income inequality. On the other hand, government policies play an important role through the progressiveness or regressiveness of revenue policies and the redistributiveness of welfare policies. There is a great deal of debate about this gap—how great the injustice it does to the poor, to what extent it is justified by the incentives it provides for individual efforts or by established property rights, and the degree to which it should be eased by the welfare state.

BOX 7.4 WOMEN AND THE INFORMAL ECONOMY

Parmila is an Indian widow in her thirties with two young children. Although she comes from a wealthy family, her husband's death forced her to take various part-time jobs. She collects wood from local forests, dries it, and then twice a week walks five miles to sell it at a local market. In the winter (November to January), she works on farms dehusking rice. She gets to keep some of the rice she produces. Outside of the rainy season, she also works as a laborer on a construction site, where her boss pays her about half of the Indian minimum wage. Parmila's total income is very low by Western standards, but it is enough to allow her to send her two children to school. Parmila does not ask for sympathy or for financial support from her relatives. "Even in times of acute crisis, I held my nerves and did not give in to circumstances," she says. "My God has always stood with me."

Women make up an increasing share of the world's workers. In most non-Islamic countries, they now make up 40 percent or more of the labor force. But in many parts of the world, most women work in the informal economy, where their work is often poorly paid. It commonly also escapes taxation and regulation. In India and in many African countries, for example, more than four out of five women who work outside of agriculture are in the informal economy. Many women choose such jobs voluntarily. They may do childcare for others or produce arts and crafts, often for local consumption. These jobs may be attractive because they can be performed at home while the women also take care of their own children or relatives. But many women also work in the informal sector because they face discrimination elsewhere. And some are enticed or forced into exhausting, dangerous, or degrading work in sweatshops or in the sex industry. While the informal economy can offer job flexibility, it can also be a place where there is little protection against abusive working conditions.

Source: William Easterly, *The Elusive Quest for Growth: The Economists' Adventures and Misadventures in the Tropics* (Cambridge: Massachusetts Institute of Technology Press, 2001), 45.

Liberty and Freedom Outcomes

One of the prime objectives of good government is to provide for the freedom and liberty of its citizens. Even if there is a popular myth that authoritarian governments help make societies more efficient, the goal of government is to empower its citizens so that they can control their own lives. We can measure individual liberty and freedom outcomes in several ways.

Table 7.6 shows political experts' ratings of the political-rights and civil-liberties scores for the countries included in this book. *Political rights* refers to citizen opportunities to participate in the choice of political leaders—voting rights, the right to run for office, and the like. *Civil liberties* refers to protections in such areas as freedom of speech, press, assembly, and religion, as well as to procedural rights, such as trial by a jury of peers and bans on arbitrary or cruel

> ## TABLE 7.6
>
> ### Political and Economic Rights and Liberties, 2009
>
> Political rights, civil liberties, and economic freedom are strongly associated.
>
> | Country | Political Rights | Civil Liberties | Economic Freedom |
> |---|---|---|---|
> | Brazil | 2 | 2 | 5.6 |
> | Britain | 1 | 1 | 7.7 |
> | China | 7 | 6 | 5.1 |
> | France | 1 | 1 | 6.4 |
> | Germany | 1 | 1 | 7.1 |
> | India | 2 | 3 | 5.4 |
> | Iran | 6 | 6 | 4.3 |
> | Japan | 1 | 2 | 7.3 |
> | Mexico | 2 | 3 | 6.8 |
> | Nigeria | 5 | 4 | 5.7 |
> | Russia | 6 | 5 | 5.0 |
> | United States | 1 | 1 | 7.8 |
>
> *Note:* Expert ratings of political rights and civil liberties for each country on 1 (highest) to 7 (lowest) scale. Economic freedom scored on summary scale from 0 (low) to 10 (high).
>
> *Source:* Freedom House Web site, www.freedomhouse.org (downloaded June 10, 2010); 2010 Index of Economic Freedom, product of the Heritage Foundation and the *Wall Street Journal*, www.heritage.org (downloaded June 10, 2010).

treatment. The levels of liberties reflect the outcomes of government policies, especially regulatory policies, but are also affected by social and economic conditions, such as prosperity, inequality, and crime, in the societies. The affluent democratic countries all have positive ratings for both political and civil rights. India, Brazil, and Mexico, which have improved significantly in recent years, follow next. At the other extreme, China, Iran, and most recently Russia substantially suppress both political rights and civil liberties. China in particular has tried to control the media comprehensively (see Table 7.1) and sets few limits on government regulation vis-à-vis the individual. Nigeria is rated in the middle.

These rankings, of course, vary over time. Rights and liberties in the United States have improved since the civil rights movement of the 1960s. Nigeria's military governments of the 1990s were repressive and frequently brutal; political rights and civil liberties have improved there since power was turned over to an elected civilian president in 1999, but remain fragile. Nigeria was downgraded substantially after observers reported massive vote-rigging and fraud in the (disputed) 2007 presidential and gubernatorial elections.

There is a strong correlation between political and civil rights. No country that scores high on participatory rights also scores very low on civil liberties, and no country low on participatory rights is high on civil liberties. This suggests a strong relationship between popular participation and the rule of law and equitable procedure. Studies of governmental repression have also found that limitations on government abuses of physical integrity rights of citizens were best explained by democratic political institutions and conditions of peace and social order. Authoritarian states and those involved in internal or international war were the most frequent violators of personal integrity.

Table 7.6 also reports the level of economic freedom in each country. It is not always true that countries that are politically free also foster economic freedom, or vice versa. For example, Mexico shows substantially more economic freedom than Brazil or India, although its political freedom ratings are similar. And even though Britain and France score the same on political rights and liberties, Britain has a higher level of economic freedom. On the whole, though, political and economic freedoms tend to go together.

Domestic Security Outcomes

As Thomas Hobbes would have reminded us, maintaining domestic law and order and protecting persons and property are among the most basic government responsibilities. Without them, the conduct of personal, economic, and civic life are impossible. It is therefore worrisome that until recently, crime rates were on the increase in many advanced industrial countries as well as in the developing world. For example, in the United States, the crime rate increased by almost 15 percent between 1982 and 1991. In France, the 1990 incidence of crimes against persons and property was almost twice that of 1975. In Russia, the crime rate doubled between 1985 and 1993 as the moral and legal order collapsed.

High crime rates are primarily a problem of the larger urban areas where much of the population of modern countries resides. The causes of urban crime are complex. Rapidly increasing migration into the major cities, from the domestic countryside or from poorer foreign countries, increases diversity and often conflict. The pace of urbanization is particularly explosive in many developing countries, such as Brazil and Nigeria, where there are severe problems of poverty and infrastructure. The newly arrived city-dwellers often find themselves uprooted from their cultures, unwelcome, without a job, and living in squalor far apart from their families and traditional communities. Also, inequality of income and wealth, unemployment, and drug abuse lie behind this general decline in public order and safety. Increased globalization of crime, especially in drugs and human trafficking, has also played its part.

Figure 7.3 presents figures on the number of homicides per 100,000 inhabitants for the nations in this book. Brazil has the most homicides per 100,000 inhabitants. Its murder rate is almost five times as high as that in the United States. Russia and Mexico also have considerably higher murder rates than the United States. Iran and India have rates about half those of the United States, while the other industrialized nations have rates that are a small fraction of the U.S. numbers. China and Nigeria report similarly low murder rates. Yet crime rates have recently come down significantly in the United States and some other countries. The number of murders per 100,000 inhabitants in the United States peaked at 9.4 in 1994 and declined to 5.2 in 2008.

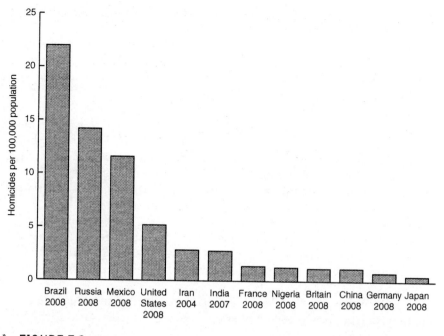

FIGURE 7.3

Homicides per 100,000 Population

Homicide rates vary greatly across countries.

Source: United Nations Office on Drugs and Crime, downloaded from www.unodc.org/unodc/en/data-and-analysis/homicide.html on June 14, 2010.

There are several reasons that crime rates might decrease. One is economic conditions, with crime rates decreasing when the economy is strong. A second reason is stricter law enforcement. This is partially reflected in the number of police officers relative to total population, which ranges from 1 police officer for every 350 persons in the United States to 1 in 820 in India and 1 in 1,140 in Nigeria. In the United States, both federal and state governments have also sought to reduce crime by increasing the length of imprisonment. A third cause of lower crime rates has been a decrease in the number of youth at the age at which most crimes are committed. Yet as the fifteen-to-twenty-five-year-old male population in the United States is now on the rise and youth unemployment has risen sharply with the recession of 2008 and 2009, violent crime may increase once again.

An even greater threat to personal security than private crime can be intense domestic political conflict culminating in civil war. In recent years, much of the world's media focus has been on conflicts in the Middle East, but conflicts in Africa have in fact been more frequent and devastating. Many African countries, newly independent from about 1960, but with borders arbitrarily drawn by colonial powers, have serious problems of national cohesion and have suffered from chronic civil war. Large-scale civil war in Nigeria

(1967 to 1970) cost perhaps a million lives, and more sporadic conflict continues to the present time.

The Uppsala Conflict Data Project reports 128 armed worldwide conflicts (defined as involving at least twenty-five battle deaths) from 1989 through 2008. In 2008, there were thirty-six ongoing conflicts, of which five (in Afghanistan, Iraq, Pakistan, Somalia, and Sri Lanka) involved more than 1,000 deaths.[9] All but one was a civil war occurring within state boundaries, although several were internationalized in that foreign powers were also involved. In every year since the end of World War II in 1945, there have been more civil wars than interstate conflicts (wars between countries), and civil wars have also caused more casualties than interstate wars.

There are many reasons for the high incidence of civil war. Some are related to ethnic or religious conflicts. But others seem mainly due to struggles between warlords over lootable resources, such as diamonds, gold, or oil. External actors—such as the UN, the United States, NATO, or strong regional powers—can sometimes help end civil wars, but in some cases (such as Angola), civil wars have been prolonged because foreign powers have been engaged on both sides of the conflict.

The UN in the post–Cold War world has intervened in some of these conflicts by providing peacekeeping missions when the parties to conflicts are ready to accept these mediations. As of July 2010, there were sixteen peacekeeping missions in various parts of the world. More rarely, the UN intervenes as a peacemaker, as in Bosnia and later in neighboring Kosovo in the 1990s, or when the peacekeeping mission in Sierra Leone (West Africa) was converted into a peacemaking effort. The UN's effectiveness in controlling domestic and international collective violence depends on consensus among the great powers.

INTERNATIONAL OUTCOMES

Most states engage in a great variety of international activities. Such economic, diplomatic, military, and informational activities may result in prosperity or depression, war or peace, secularization or the spread of particular beliefs.[10] The phenomenon known as *globalization* has increasingly demanded more economic, social, and political involvement by ever more states. National economies have become more dependent on international trade and capital flows, creating intense pressures from those advantaged by trade to ease restrictions and those hurt by international competition to increase barriers. These conflicting demands can be a major source of internal conflict.[11] Moreover, a major economic setback in one part of the world, such as the financial credit crisis in the developed nations in 2008 and 2009, ripples though many distant countries. Crippled industrialized economies import fewer goods, hitting the producing countries in turn. Increasingly, countries need coordinated political action to regulate capital flows and encourage trade. The very interdependence that globalization creates can threaten damage to all if key countries break off their involvement, as happened during the 1930s.

Environmental damage, too, flows beyond the boundaries of individual countries, as in the threat that cumulative atmospheric emissions pose to global climate stability. The social side of globalization has also expanded. Personal contacts and information flows, including television and Internet use, have increased, as has the presence of cultural (and economic) symbols such as McDonald's. These have brought pressures to respect international standards of personal integrity and gender equality (see Chapter 3). However, while individuals may benefit greatly from the opportunities that the Internet or McDonald's offer, these exposures may also threaten traditional values. Issues such as controlling immigration loom large in many countries.

Table 7.7 shows the KOF index of globalization, which tracks a wide variety of economic, social, and political measures. Countries with higher globalization scores have more trade and foreign direct investment relative to their GDP and lower import barriers. On the social globalization dimension, they also have more international telephone traffic and letters, more Internet users, and more memberships in international organizations. We see that globalization has increased in most countries during the last thirty-five years, especially since 1990. China, which was once at the lowest levels of globalization, expanded its global exposure—economic, social, and political—into the

TABLE 7.7

Change in the Index of Globalization, 1970–2007

Globalization has been increasing across the world, but government policies can affect the rate and level.

Country	1970	1980	1990	2000	2007
Brazil	37	43	44	58	60
Britain	57	67	73	82	80
China	15	20	35	54	63
France	58	65	75	86	86
Germany	47	58	61	84	84
India	24	25	29	44	51
Iran	25	27	22	35	37
Japan	35	43	48	61	68
Mexico	43	45	52	60	61
Nigeria	27	38	40	49	56
Russia	—	—	39	63	69
United States	60	65	71	78	79

The KOF index of globalization, a 0-to-100 scale, is composed of economic, social, and political elements.

Source: Axel Dreher, "Does Globalization Affect Growth? Evidence from a New Index of Globalization," Applied Economics 38, no. 10 (2006):1091–110, downloaded June 11, 2010, from http:// globalization .kof.ethz.ch/.

TABLE 7.8

Deaths from Collective Civilian–Military Violence, 1900–1995

Citizens in some nations paid a terrible price for the international conflicts of the twentieth century.

Country	Civilian Deaths	Military Deaths	Unspecified Deaths	Total Deaths
Brazil	—	1,000	2,000	3,000
Britain	131,000	1,350,000	—	1,481,000
China	4,047,000	2,671,000	818,000	7,536,000
France	490,000	1,830,000	—	2,320,000
Germany	2,232,000	7,150,000	—	9,382,000
India	889,000	71,000	37,000	997,000
Iran	120,000	468,000	1,000	589,000
Japan	510,000	1,502,000	—	2,012,000
Mexico	125,000	125,000	10,000	260,000
Nigeria	1,005,000	1,000,000	6,000	2,011,000
USSR/ Russia	12,028,000	11,901,000	96,000	24,025,000
United States	—	524,000	—	524,000
TOTALS	21,577,000	28,593,000	970,000	51,140,000

Source: Adapted from Ruth Leger Sivard, "Wars and War Related Deaths, 1900–1995," *World Military and Social Expenditures 1996* (Washington, D.C.: World Priorities, 1996), 18–19. U.S. deaths add Korean and Vietnam war totals, from U.S. Department of State figures, to Sivard report of World War I and II deaths.

middle ranks, from 15 on a 100-point scale in 1970 to 63 in 2007. India and Brazil, too, have exploded onto the global stage, as has Russia since the breakup of the Soviet Union. At the same time, countries like France, Germany, Britain, and the United States, beginning from a much more globalized base, have further expanded their involvement in the global flows of trade, capital, and information, reaching scores in the 70 to 80 range. Of the countries in our set, by far the most resistant to globalization has been Iran, which since the Islamic Revolution in 1979 has tried to maintain its general economic and social isolation. So, while globalization exerts powerful incentives for economic and social integration, government policies can powerfully promote or constrain it.

The most costly outcome of the interaction among nations is warfare. Table 7.8 reports the numbers of deaths from international and internal collective violence for our twelve study countries for almost the entire twentieth century (1900 to 1995). The figures are mostly civilian and military deaths from interstate warfare, but they also include the slaughter of civilians in the efforts to implement communism in the Soviet Union, the holocaust of European Jews under the German Nazis (Hitler's National Socialist Party), many "ethnic cleansing" episodes in Europe and Africa, and civil wars in all parts of the world.

Over the long haul, the deadly costs of international warfare have gradually escalated. Civilian deaths caused by war increased even more rapidly than military ones. In the last decades of the twentieth century, more than three-quarters of the war deaths were civilian.[12]

Table 7.8 shows that the people of USSR/Russia, by a margin of more than two to one, were the most numerous victims of the tormented history of the twentieth century. The enormous Russian casualties during World War I destroyed the czarist regime. Its collapse was followed by the 1917 Bolshevik Revolution, the Civil War (1918 to 1921), and Stalin's Great Terror (particularly in the 1930s), each of which cost the lives of millions. Soviet suffering climaxed in World War II with a total of 17 million civilian and military dead. All told, the USSR/Russia suffered more than 24 million civilian and military deaths in the wars and political horrors of the twentieth century.

Germany suffered the second-largest number of deaths from twentieth-century collective violence. More than 3 million deaths, mostly military, occurred in World War I. In World War II, Germany suffered almost 5 million military and another 1.75 million civilian deaths. Other countries with huge losses include China (7 to 8 million) and Japan, whose more than 2 million deaths include half a million civilians, notably many residents of Hiroshima and Nagasaki. French and British sufferings were of roughly similar magnitude.

After World War II, the most devastating conflicts have occurred in the Third World. The partition of formerly British India into India, Pakistan, and Bangladesh has been associated with numerous deadly conflicts within and among the three countries. Some 2 million lives, mostly civilian, have been lost. The end of the Cold War around 1990 witnessed a wave of instability and conflict in Eastern Europe and Central Asia. The breakup of the Soviet Union and Yugoslavia resulted in bloody border wars and secession conflicts (for example, in Bosnia and Kosovo in the former Yugoslavia, and Chechnya in Russia). These conflicts brought another wave of ethnic slaughter, religious clashes, and struggles for power among different warlords. But since 1992, the number of wars and casualties has gradually declined. And although recent years have seen horrific acts of terrorism, its annual human toll has not changed much. Some students of international conflict see hope in what they call the "democratic peace," the fact that democratic countries hardly ever fight wars against one another. As more countries become democratic, will the world also become more peaceful? International warfare, which would be even more terrible if nuclear powers were involved, is potentially the greatest threat to human security.

THE COMPLEXITY OF POLICY CHOICE

One of the hard facts about political goods is that we cannot always have them simultaneously. A political system often has to trade off one value to obtain another. Spending funds on education is giving up the opportunity to spend them on welfare, or to leave them in the hands of those who earned them. Politicians also have to decide how much to invest for the future rather than spend today (for example, when they determine future retirement benefits). Even more difficult are the trade-offs between security and liberty. Extreme liberty, as Hobbes would tell us, would give us a highly insecure world where the strong might bully the weak and where collective action would be difficult. Yet without liberty, security may be little more than servitude or imprisonment. The trade-offs between political goods are not the same under all circumstances. Sometimes, increasing liberty will also increase security (for example, because riots against censorship will end). And under some conditions, investment in education will be paid back many times in health and welfare, because trained citizens can better care for themselves and work more productively. These are positive trade-offs. But often you "cannot have your cake and eat it too." One of the important tasks of social science is to discover the conditions under which positive and negative trade-offs occur.

Political science has no way of converting units of liberty into units of safety or welfare. And we can never calculate the value of a political outcome gained at the cost of human life. Political decision-makers often have to make such conversions, but as political scientists, we can only point to value judgments that they are willing to make. The weight given to various goods differs across cultures and contexts. A religious faith or a political ideology may tell us how one value should be traded against another and thus offer an orderly basis for choice. Such schemes may be invaluable for those pressed into action in the terrible circumstances of war, revolution, and famine. When people do not share these underlying schemes and values, there may be serious conflicts. Sadly, there is no ideology, just as there is no political science, that can solve all these problems objectively. However, governments should provide a means for the people to decide for themselves, because this may be the only acceptable resolution of complex policy choices.

REVIEW QUESTIONS

1. What explains the growth of the welfare state?
2. What are the advantages and disadvantages of different types of taxes?
3. Why may a "windfall" of natural resources make it more difficult to introduce or sustain democracy?
4. Do some governments tend to promote political rights and others civil rights, or do civil and political rights tend to go together?
5. How is the welfare outcome for women changing in developing countries today?
6. Why does globalization give rise to internal conflict within nations?
7. What sorts of armed conflicts are most common in today's world, and what problems do they cause?

KEY TERMS

direct taxes
distribution
extraction
fairness
gross domestic product
(GDP)

indirect taxes
outcomes
outputs
policy goods
political goods
public policies

regulation
rentier states
symbolic outputs

SUGGESTED READINGS

Bates, Robert H. *When Things Fell Apart: State Failure in Late-Century Africa.* New York: Cambridge University Press, 2008.

Boix, Carles. *Political Parties, Growth, and Equality: Conservative and Social Democratic Economic Strategies in the World Economy.* New York: Cambridge University Press, 1998.

Castles, Francis G., ed. *The Comparative History of Public Policy.* Cambridge: Polity Press, 1989.

Dahl, Robert. *Democracy and Its Critics.* New Haven, CT: Yale University Press, 1989.

Easterly, William. *The Elusive Quest for Growth: The Economists' Adventures and Misadventures in the Tropics.* Cambridge: Massachusetts Institute of Technology Press, 2001.

Flora, Peter, and Arnold Heidenheimer. *The Development of Welfare States in Europe and America.* New Brunswick, NJ: Transaction Books, 1981.

Franzese, Robert. *Macroeconomic Policies of Developed Democracies.* New York: Cambridge University Press, 2002.

Gourevitch, Peter. *Politics in Hard Times.* Ithaca, NY: Cornell University Press, 1986.

Halperin, Morton H., Joseph T. Siegle, and Michael M. Weinstein. *The Democracy Advantage: How Democracies Promote Prosperity and Peace.* New York: Routledge, 2010.

Lijphart, Arend. *Patterns of Democracy: Government Forms and Performance in Thirty-Six Countries.* New Haven, CT: Yale University Press, 1999.

Persson, Torsten, and Guido Tabellini. *The Economic Effects of Constitutions.* Cambridge: Massachusetts Institute of Technology Press, 2003.

Putnam, Robert. *Making Democracy Work: Civic Traditions in Modern Italy.* Princeton, NJ: Princeton University Press, 1993.

Rogowski, Ronald. *Commerce and Coalitions: How Trade Affects Domestic Political Alignments.* Princeton, NJ: Princeton University Press, 1989.

Tsebelis, George. *Veto Players: An Introduction to Institutional Analysis.* Princeton, NJ: Princeton University Press, 2002.

Wilensky, Harold. *Rich Democracies: Political Economy, Public Policy, and Performance.* Berkeley: University of California Press, 2002.

ENDNOTES

1. This literature seems to have originated in studies of the Middle East. See the reviews in Michael L. Ross, "Does Oil Hinder Democracy?" *World Politics* 53 (2001): 325–61 and Thad Dunning, *Crude Democracy: Natural Resource Wealth and Political Regimes* (New York: Cambridge University Press, 2008). Also see Kiren A. Chaudhry, *The Price of Wealth: Economies and Institutions in the Middle East* (Ithaca, NY: Cornell University Press, 1997).

2. See especially Ross, "Does Oil Hinder Democracy?" who sketches multiple causal mechanisms proposed in the literature.

3. Samuel P. Huntington, *The Third Wave: Democratization in the Late Twentieth Century* (Norman: University of Oklahoma, 1991), 65.

4. Dunning, *Crude Democracy*.

5. See, for example, Carles Boix, *Political Parties, Growth, and Equality: Conservative and Social Democratic Economic Strategies in the World Economy* (New York: Cambridge University Press, 1998); Robert Franzese, *Macroeconomic Policies of Developed Democracies* (New York: Cambridge University Press, 2002); Shin-Goo Kang and G. Bingham Powell Jr., "Representation and Policy Responsiveness," *Journal of Politics* 72 (October 2010): 1014–1028; Michael D. McDonald and Ian Budge, *Elections, Parties, Democracy: Conferring the Median Mandate* (New York: Oxford University Press, 2005); Harold Wilensky, *Rich Democracies: Political Economy, Public Policy, and Performance* (Berkeley: University of California Press, 2002).

6. Laurence J. Kotlikoff and Scott Burns, *The Coming Generational Storm: What You Need to Know about America's Economic Future* (Cambridge: Massachusetts Institute of Technology Press, 2004).

7. Steven C. Poe and C. Neal Tate, "Repression of Human Rights to Personal Integrity in the 1980s: A Global Analysis," *American Political Science Review* 88, no. 4 (December 1994): 853–72; also see Christian Davenport, *State Repression and the Democratic Peace* (Cambridge: Cambridge University Press, 2007).

8. Robert H. Bates, *Markets and States in Tropical Africa* (Berkeley: University of California Press, 1981); Philip Keefer and Stuti Khemani, "Why Do the Poor Receive Poor Services?" *Economic and Political Weekly* 28 (February 2004): 935–43; World Bank, *World Development Report, 2002* "Building Institutions for Markets" (A World Bank Publication), 31–32.

9. See Lotta Harbom and Peter Wallensteen, "Armed Conflict, 1946–2008," *Journal of Peace Research* 46, no. 4 (2009): 577–87.

10. Peter Gourevitch, in his book *Politics in Hard Times* (Ithaca, NY: Cornell University Press, 1986), analyzes the policy responses of five Western industrial nations—Britain, France, Germany, Sweden, and the United States—to the three world depressions of 1870–1890, 1930–1940, and 1975–1985. Gourevitch shows how these crises affected business, labor, and agriculture differently in each country; consequences for political structure and policy varied greatly. Thus, the world depression of the 1930s resulted in a conservative reaction in Britain (the formation of a "National" government), a moderate left reaction in the United States (the "New Deal"), a polarization and paralysis of public policy in France ("Immobilisme"), a moderate social democratic reaction in Sweden, and a radical right-and-left polarization in Germany, leading to a breakdown of democracy and the emergence of National Socialism. While the causes of World War II were complex, the pacifism of Britain, the demoralization and defeatism in France, the isolationism of the United States, and the nihilism and aggression of Germany were all fed by the devastating worldwide economic depression of the 1930s.

11. See especially Ronald Rogowski, *Commerce and Coalitions: How Trade Affects Domestic Political Alignments* (Princeton, NJ: Princeton University Press, 1989).

12. Ruth Leger Sivard, *World Military and Social Indicators* (Washington, D.C.: World Priorities, 1993), 20.

INDEX